£1. 00

Desserts To Die For

'I feel the end approaching. Quick, bring me my dessert, coffee and liqueur.'

—BRILLAT-SAVARIN'S GREAT-AUNT PIERETTE

Desserts To Die For

MARCEL DESAULNIERS

PHOTOGRAPHY BY MICHAEL GRAND

RECIPES WITH JON PIERRE PEAVEY

LITTLE, BROWN AND COMPANY
BOSTON NEW YORK TORONTO LONDON

A LITTLE, BROWN BOOK

First published in Great Britain in 1995
by Little, Brown and Company (UK)

Prepared and produced by
Kenan Books, Inc.
15 West 26th Street
New York, New York 10010

A CIP catalogue record for this book is available from the British Library.

ISBN 0-316-91111-9

10 9 8 7 6 5 4 3 2 1

Editor: Nathaniel Marunas
Art Director/Designer: Jeff Batzli
Photography Director: Christopher C. Bain

Colour separations by Ocean Graphic International Company Ltd.
Printed in Singapore by Star Standard Industries (Pte) Ltd.

Little, Brown and Company (UK)
Brettenham House
Lancaster Place
London WC2E 7EN

DEDICATION

For the Desaulniers,
especially my mother, Victoire,
and my sisters, Jeannine, Suzanne, Denise,
Paulette, and Giselle.

Also for my son Marc,
gone but not forgotten.

ACKNOWLEDGEMENTS

As the guru of ganache, I hereby bestow the following honorary titles to all the friends, colleagues and accomplices who made *Desserts To Die For* possible:

Angel of Anglaise—Connie Desaulniers (inamorata)

Bard of Bar-le-Duc—Dan Green (literary agent)

Captain of Caramel—Jon Pierre Peavey (assistant)

Dean of Delectation—John Curtis (partner)

Empress of Ecstasy—Penny Seu (editorial advisor)

Father of Fondant—Andrew O'Connell (chef of the Trellis)

General of Genoise—Tim O'Connor (pastry chef of the Trellis)

High Priest of Hard Sauce—Michael Grand (photographer)

Impresario of Ice Cream—Nathaniel Marunas (editor)

Jester of Jam Rolls—Jeff Batzli (art director)

King of Kirschwasser—Chris Bain (photography editor)

Lady of Linzertorte—Karen Matsu-Greenberg (production director)

Mothers of Meringue—Lisa Ekus and Merrilyn Siciak (publicists)

Nabob of Nesselrode—Simon Green (electronic media agent)

Oracles of Opulence—The kitchen staff at the Trellis

Pooh-bahs of Petit Fours—The front of the house staff at the Trellis

Quarterbacks of Quaff—Ed Digilio and Bill Valois (semper fi)

Raja of Raspberries—Michael Friedman (The Michael Friedman Publishing Group)

Swinging Sultans of Sugar—Everyone at Simon & Schuster

Temptress of Truffles—Rose Levy Beranbaum (advisor)

Usurper of Upside-Down Cakes—Danielle Desaulniers-Shepherd (beautiful daughter and budding culinarian)

Viceroy of Vanilla—Rod Stoner (mentor for more than thirty years)

Warlord of Whipped Cream—John Twichell (former Trellis pastry chef)

Xenophobe of Xylose—Jim Seu (advisor)

Yogis of Yum—Everyone at the Culinary Institute of America

Zombies of Zabaglione—Did I forget anyone?

ALSO BY MARCEL DESAULNIERS

The Trellis Cookbook (1988)

The Trellis Cookbook (expanded edition 1992)

Death by Chocolate (1992)

The Burger Meisters (1994)

CONTENTS

INTRODUCTION

'Excess on occasion is exhilarating; it keeps moderation from becoming a habit.'
—W. SOMERSET MAUGHAM

Wretched excess? Is that what Desserts To Die For *is all about? The answer is an unequivocal, enthusiastic yes. With no apologies from me, this book is not for the faint of heart. Who, then, can benefit from this book?*

Desserts To Die For *is for anyone with a sweet tooth. It is also for anyone who loves the occasional indulgence, or enjoys creating a special dessert with or for a loved one. If you drool over Michael Grand's photographs and think they look so edible you need to loosen your belt, this book is for you. If sharing a piece of buttercream-swathed cake seems like a sensual experience, this book is your next step towards paradise.*

If you have heard the call, follow me into the confectionery arena, where multi-layered and textured cakes flourish, where you will find some startlingly chilling sorbets and uncommon ice creams, where the crispest biscuits await your bite, where comforting favourites are given new vitality and flavour, where refreshing fruit concoctions wait to tantalise your palate, and where the most deadly delectations abound.

Join me if you dare on an outrageous and uncensored excursion. Remember, you only live once, and I can't think of a better way to go.

—MARCEL DESAULNIERS
WILLIAMSBURG, VIRGINIA

NOTES FROM THE TEST KITCHEN

ABOUT THE TEST KITCHEN

In the last eight years, I have tested recipes for several cookery books in the home I share with my wife, Connie, in Williamsburg, Virginia. For me, testing at home is an important process in writing a cookery book, since I feel I should test the recipes myself in a setting that approximates the average home kitchen.

I have spent most of my waking hours over the last thirty years in commercial kitchens, surrounded by stainless steel. So when Connie and I built our home ten years ago, we designed an intimate and cosy kitchen devoid of commercial equipment. The one exception is a large stainless steel table which works well as a space both for food preparation and for eating casual meals.

My favourite aspect of putting together a cookery book is testing the recipes, usually with an assistant manipulating the ingredients while I volley between mixing bowl and word processor. For *Desserts To Die For* I was assisted by the remarkable, enduring, creative and always supportive Jon Pierre Peavey. A testing day began with Jon Pierre gathering the recipe ingredients from local supermarkets. We would meet at my house, which is a little more than half a mile from the Trellis. Typically we would test two to three recipes a day, unless the recipe was more involved, such as Chocolate Caramel Hazelnut Damnation (see page 43).

I should mention that Jon Pierre has worked at the Trellis for the last five years. A graduate of the Culinary Institute of America, Jon Pierre also assisted me with *The Burger Meisters* (Simon & Schuster, 1994). When he works with me on a book, Jon Pierre pre-tests recipes at the Trellis before we test them in my home kitchen. Sometimes this means breaking down a restaurant-quantity recipe from the Trellis' repertoire; at other times he works with an agreed-upon concept and essentially creates a recipe. Jon Pierre has proved invaluable at mastering this very time-consuming and exacting work.

By the time we test a recipe in my home kitchen, Jon Pierre will have prepared it three or four times at the Trellis. Quite often we finalise a recipe, working together in my home kitchen, after just one attempt. Hopefully, all of our testing rewards you with easy-to-follow recipes that enable you to prepare *Desserts To Die For* just like we do at the Trellis—and at my house.

PLEASE READ ME

Oh, horrors, Marcel. You mean I actually have to read your recipes to create these extraordinary desserts?

Yes, you do. But I tried to make the reading fun and informative. It always makes good sense to read a recipe completely before preparation, since it may contain an ingredient you do not like (I hope it's not chocolate) or a necessary piece of equipment that you don't have in the cupboard.

Perhaps around kitchen equipment you are like I am around electronics. That is, I purchase a new video recorder, plug it into the TV set and a convenient socket, and expect it to do everything it was supposed to do with little other attention. Whether fiddling with electronics or baking cakes, ignoring instructions can lead to disappointment. So just read through the recipe at least once to get a feeling for the flavours, textures and techniques—all of which will ultimately help you produce a Dessert To Die For.

AN IMPORTANT NOTE

Spoon measures (1 teaspoon=5ml, 1 tablespoon= 15ml) are always level.

ORGANISING EQUIPMENT AND INGREDIENTS

If it is your passion to explore a world of melted chocolate, crispy meringues, towering cakes, silken ice creams, tantalising sorbets and other confectionery miracles, then read on.

Before you prepare a dessert, first gather all the ingredients in the recipe and organise them as listed. For example, for the Fallen Angel Cake (see page 38), envision that on your kitchen counter you have already arranged in individual, appropriately sized containers:

225g/8oz unsalted butter
225g/8oz bittersweet chocolate, broken
    into 15-g/½-oz pieces
6 size-3 egg yolks
150g/5½oz caster sugar
8 size-3 egg whites
2 tablespoons unsweetened cocoa powder
2 tablespoons icing sugar

With all these ingredients directly in front of you, the process of preparing the cake is more manageable. Additionally, because timing is essential when combining ingredients, you minimise the opportunities for failed desserts.

Regarding equipment, be sure to get your act together. Do you need all the paraphernalia listed in every equipment section of each recipe? For the most part, yes, but certain substitutions can be made. A sharp knife can achieve some of the same results as a food processor, provided you have the extra time and stamina. Although a hand-held mixer can whip whipping cream to the same volume as a table-top model, it will not do the job of a table-top model when incorporating butter into the Buttery Bun Dough (see page 102). So I suggest gathering the listed equipment before beginning your sweet journey.

INGREDIENTS

When a professional chef authors a cookery book for use in the home kitchen, perhaps the most important requirement is to use the same ingredients and equipment available to the non-professional. Many food products are manufactured differently for the catering industry than they are for the supermarket. For instance, a well-known brand of cream cheese has a higher fat content in the catering packet than in the supermarket packet.

In that light, my assistant Jon Pierre Peavey shopped in local Williamsburg, Virginia, supermarkets for all the ingredients we melted, whisked, simmered, baked, cooled, decorated and, yes, eventually consumed right in my home kitchen. A few products were obtained in speciality shops or through mail order (for information on these items, refer to the 'Sources' section, page 142).

The following is additional information on some key components frequently used in *Desserts To Die For*.

BAKING POWDER AND BICARBONATE OF SODA

Without getting into advanced chemistry (especially since I failed chemistry at Mount Saint Charles Academy), anyone who bakes needs an elemental grasp of what happens when using bicarbonate of soda and baking powder (a blend of bicarbonate of soda, cream of tartar and cornflour). Both the soda and the powder are raising agents that are activated by contact with a liquid. In the case of bicarbonate of soda, this liquid must be acidic, such as buttermilk. Baking powder, on the other hand, can be mixed with water, milk or other non-acidic liquids since it already contains acid in the form of cream of tartar.

Be sure to look at the use-by date on the container, since baking powder and bicarbonate of soda do not improve with age. Also, be certain to measure very accurately. Improperly measured, these ingredients can seriously alter the simplest recipe. Lastly, move quickly. Once bicarbonate of soda is added to a batter, the chemical action of creating carbon dioxide gas bubbles begins. Any time lost placing the finished mixture in the oven will almost certainly affect the end result (usually a collapse of the mixture during baking).

BUTTER

There is no substitute for the flavour of real butter. Although margarine and white vegetable fat can be substituted in many recipes that call for butter, the dessert will not have the same smooth, rich flavour. And other aspects, such as moisture and crumb texture, may be adversely affected as well.

For best results, select butter that is specifically labelled 'unsalted'. Without salt, butter can become rancid in a matter of days, especially if your refrigerator is overloaded and not cooling properly. So, if you are not going to use it within a few days, store the butter in the freezer.

When recipes specify softened butter, allow refrigerated or frozen butter to come to room temperature before using. Otherwise, all butter should be at refrigerator temperature (not frozen).

CHOCOLATE

Nothing treats the palate like the sumptuous, sensual and stimulating sensation of chocolate melting in your mouth. That is the exact reason that chocolate is so beloved.

PURCHASING

When it comes to purchasing chocolate, *caveat emptor* ('let the buyer beware'). Read the ingredient label prior to purchasing and be sure to select real chocolate, that is, chocolate that contains cocoa butter, rather than such fat additives as partially hydrogenated palm kernel oil or palm oil, and a high proportion of cocoa solids. The best block chocolate will contain 35-50 percent cocoa butter and at least 50 percent cocoa solids (60 percent and above is even better).

STORING

Chocolate is very susceptible to temperature variances. If improperly stored in a warm environment—above 25°C/78°F—the cocoa butter may separate from the cocoa solids, causing discoloration. If stored in a cold and damp environment, the sugar in the chocolate may crystallise.

Purchase chocolate from a shop that sells a lot of chocolate, and stay away from dusty boxes. You should store the chocolate in a cool, dry place or well wrapped in the refrigerator (allow chocolate to come to cool room temperature—20-25°C/68°-78°F—before using in a recipe). My advice is to purchase chocolate only as you need it.

CHOOSING

I will avoid suggesting specific brands of chocolate. However, I will go on record as saying that many European chocolates have a high content of chocolate liquor or cocoa solids, making them darker and less sweet than British chocolates. Some European chocolate also goes through an extended manufacturing process that creates a smoother, silkier texture when eaten directly out of the box. But remember that the price does not always correspond with the quality. You are better off purchasing a product that is real, is fresh and has been properly stored, rather than an overpriced chocolate that has been gathering dust.

UNSWEETENED CHOCOLATE

Also called chocolate liquor, unsweetened chocolate is the product yielded from the crushing of cocoa nibs (the nibs come from roasted cocoa beans). This is the pure form of chocolate, that is, it contains only cocoa butter and cocoa solids, without sugar or additives. Since unsweetened chocolate contains no sugar, it is too bitter to consume as is. We purchased American-manufactured unsweetened chocolate for testing. Very bitter European chocolate is a good substitute.

BITTERSWEET CHOCOLATE

This chocolate is an amalgam of chocolate liquor (or cocoa mass), cocoa butter, sugar, an emulsifier known as lecithin and sometimes vanilla or vanillin. Take a good look at the label and bypass any chocolate that contains any fat other than cocoa butter. Plain or dark is interchangeable with bittersweet, although the bittersweet (sometimes called dark continental chocolate) has a higher percentage of unsweetened chocolate, giving a more pronounced flavour and darker colour. We purchased both American and European bittersweet chocolate for testing.

WHITE CHOCOLATE

This one gets tricky. In the United States, a product must contain chocolate liquor to be labelled as chocolate. So-called white chocolate contains sugar, cocoa butter, milk and vanilla or vanillin but no chocolate liquor, and therefore, it is not technically chocolate. So, look for white chocolate under such manufacturers' labels as 'white couverture.' Most importantly, check the label to be certain that the only fat listed is cocoa butter, since that is the ingredient that supplies the flavour. We purchased European white chocolate for testing.

COCOA

When unsweetened chocolate is pressed to remove the cocoa butter, the resulting solids are ground into cocoa powder. We tested the recipes in this book using both American and European unsweetened cocoa.

CHOCOLATE CHIPS

Use chips only when specified. Many manufacturers claim that their chocolate chips have the same ingredient formulation as their block chocolate. The fact is that some chips are formulated differently from block chocolate (to keep their shape during baking), and in my opinion are not interchangeable with good plain (dark) or unsweetened chocolate. As with other chocolate, look at the label and choose only those chips that have cocoa butter as the only fat. We used American-manufactured chips for testing.

EGGS

Size-3 eggs, purchased in a supermarket, were used for testing the recipes in *Desserts To Die For*. For best results, I recommend using this size egg only. For more and important information about eggs, refer to 'Handling Eggs' in the 'Techniques and Equipment' section (see page 139).

FLOUR

I recommend purchasing flour in smallish quantities from supermarkets where a rapid turnover will make them less susceptible to problems from improper storage. Both brand names and supermarkets' own brands will do.

CUP OF PLEASURE

To enjoy a dessert completely, you need an appropriate beverage. Your choice may be as prosaic as a steaming cup of coffee or as indulgent as a fine vintage port. However, pairing desserts with a proper drink should not cause angst. You can break away from tradition if you like, but remember, the only rule is don't allow the dessert to overwhelm the beverage or vice versa. For instance, the flavour of a delicate Champagne would be lost if served with a dark and intense chocolate dessert. Likewise, a late harvest Zinfandel would steal the show from a dish of Strawberry and Banana Yin Yang Sorbet (see page 83).

Almost every recipe in this book offers a beverage suggestion. Whether it is a shot of calvados, a tall glass of milk or an effervescent bellini, make sure you enjoy it. After all, enjoyment is the underlying theme of this book.

CHAPTER ONE

LET THEM EAT CAKE

'I am a staunch believer in having one's cake and eating it, a principle I have followed greedily throughout my life.'
—ANNE SCOTT-JAMES

TUXEDO TRUFFLE TORTE

BUTTERSCOTCH WALNUT PUMPKIN CAKE

FOR CHOCOLATE LOVERS ONLY

LEMON BLUEBERRY CHEESECAKE

RED RASPBERRY ALMOND PASSION CAKE

CHOCOLATE VOODOO CAKE

MOCHA ALMOND PRALINE SNAP

CHOCOLATE PECAN BOURBON BASH

GOOEY CHOCOLATE PEANUT BUTTER BROWNIE CAKE

FALLEN ANGEL CAKE WITH GOLDEN HALOS AND SINFUL CREAM

WHITE AND DARK CHOCOLATE PATTY CAKE

CHOCOLATE CARAMEL HAZELNUT DAMNATION

TUXEDO TRUFFLE TORTE

SERVES 16

INGREDIENTS

CHOCOLATE TRUFFLE CAKE

340g/12oz unsalted butter, cut into 12 equal pieces (15g/½oz melted)

675g/1½lb bittersweet chocolate, cut into 15g/½oz pieces

4 size-3 eggs

4 size-3 egg yolks

WHITE CHOCOLATE MOUSSE

170g/6oz white chocolate, cut into 15g/½oz pieces

2 tablespoons water

1 tablespoon Myers's dark rum

125ml/4fl oz whipping cream

WHITE CHOCOLATE GANACHE

185ml/6fl oz whipping cream

15g/½oz unsalted butter

340g/12oz white chocolate, cut into 15g/½oz pieces

DARK CHOCOLATE GANACHE

185ml/6fl oz whipping cream

15g/½oz unsalted butter

250g/9oz bittersweet chocolate, cut into 15g/½oz pieces

EQUIPMENT

Chef's knife, cutting board, measuring jug, measuring spoons, small non-stick pan, pastry brush, 23 × 7.5cm/9 × 3in round springform cake tin, double boiler, heat-resistant cling film, whisk, 5 litre/8 pint stainless steel bowl, rubber spatula, instant-read thermometer, electric mixer with balloon whisk, baking sheet, two 3 litre/5 pint stainless steel bowls, 1.5 litre/2½ pint saucepan, palette knife, 2 piping bags, 2 medium star nozzles, serrated slicer

PREPARE THE CHOCOLATE TRUFFLE CAKE

Preheat the oven to 150°C/300°F/Gas 2.

Lightly coat the inside of a 23 × 7.5cm/9 × 3in springform cake tin with the melted butter. Set aside.

Heat 2.5cm/1in of water in the bottom half of a double boiler over moderate heat. Place the pieces of bittersweet chocolate and the remaining 325g/11½oz butter in the top half of the double boiler. Tightly cover the top with heat-resistant cling film. Allow to heat for 15 minutes. Remove from the heat and stir until smooth. Transfer the chocolate to a 5 litre/8 pint stainless steel bowl, using a rubber spatula to remove all the chocolate from the double boiler. Keep at room temperature until needed.

Heat 2.5cm/1in of water in the bottom half of a double boiler over moderate heat. Place the eggs and egg yolks in the top half of the double boiler. Whisk the eggs for 2 to 3 minutes or until they reach a temperature of 44°C/110°F. Transfer the heated eggs to the bowl of an electric mixer fitted with a balloon whisk. Whisk on high until the eggs become light and pale in colour, about 6 to 7 minutes. Remove the bowl from the mixer. Using a rubber spatula, gently fold one third of the eggs into the melted chocolate. Add the remaining eggs and fold together gently but thoroughly. Pour the mixture into the prepared springform tin. Place the springform tin on a baking sheet on the centre shelf in the preheated oven. Bake for 1 hour 10 minutes to 1 hour 15 minutes or until the internal temperature of the cake reaches 76°C/170°F. Remove the truffle cake from the oven and allow to cool in the tin for 45 minutes. Before releasing the cake from the springform tin, use your fingertips to press down gently on the outside edges of the cake (to create as flat a surface as possible). Remove the sides (but not the bottom) of the springform tin and refrigerate the cake for at least 1 hour or until needed.

PREPARE THE WHITE CHOCOLATE MOUSSE

(This may be done while the truffle cake is baking.) Heat 2.5cm/1in of water in the bottom half of a double boiler over low heat. When the water is hot (do not allow to simmer), place the white chocolate, water and rum in the top half of the double boiler. Using a rubber spatula, constantly stir the white chocolate, water and rum until the chocolate has melted and the mixture is smooth, about 5 to 6 minutes. Remove from the heat and set aside.

Using a hand-held whisk, whip the cream in a well-chilled 3 litre/5 pint stainless steel bowl until stiff. Vigorously whisk one third of the whipped cream into the melted white chocolate (continue to whisk until smooth and thoroughly combined). Add the combined whipped cream and white chocolate to the remaining whipped cream and use a rubber spatula to fold all until smooth. Tightly cover the top of the bowl with cling film and refrigerate for at least 45 minutes or until needed.

MAKE THE WHITE CHOCOLATE GANACHE

Heat the cream and butter in a 1.5 litre/2½ pint saucepan over moderately high heat. Bring to the boil. Place the white chocolate in a 3 litre/5 pint stainless steel bowl. Pour the boiling cream over the chocolate and allow to stand for 5 minutes. Stir until smooth. Set aside until needed.

PREPARE THE DARK CHOCOLATE GANACHE

Heat the cream and butter in a 1.5 litre/2½ pint saucepan over moderately high heat. Bring to the boil. Place the bittersweet chocolate in a 3 litre/ 5 pint stainless steel bowl. Pour the boiling cream over the chocolate and allow to stand for 5 minutes. Stir until smooth. Refrigerate for at least until 30 minutes or until needed.

BEGIN ASSEMBLING THE CAKE

Remove the cake from the refrigerator. Using a palette knife, spread the white chocolate mousse evenly over the top and sides of the cake. Place in the freezer for 1 hour.

Reserve and refrigerate 250ml/8fl oz white chocolate ganache. Pour the remaining white chocolate ganache over the top of the truffle cake. Use a palette knife to spread the ganache evenly over the top and sides of the cake. Refrigerate the cake for 30 minutes.

Fill a piping bag fitted with a medium star nozzle with the reserved white chocolate ganache. Fill another piping bag fitted with a medium star nozzle with the dark chocolate ganache.

Score the top of the cake with two parallel lines 2.5cm/1in from the edge of one side of the cake and 4cm/1½in apart. Score a third line, intersecting the previous two, across the bottom third of the cake. Pipe white chocolate stars (each star touching the other) along the scored lines. Refrigerate the cake for 10 minutes. Pipe dark chocolate stars over the remaining areas on the top of the cake. Refrigerate the cake for at least 1 hour before cutting and serving.

TO SERVE

Heat the blade of the serrated slicer under hot running water and wipe the blade dry before cutting each slice. Allow the slices to stand at room temperature for 15 to 20 minutes before serving.

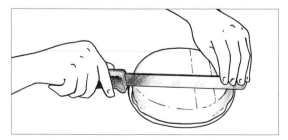

Score the top of the cake with two parallel lines, 4cm/1½ in apart 2.5cm/1in from the edge of one side of the cake. Score a third line, intersecting the previous two, across the bottom third of the cake.

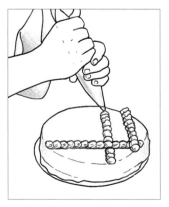

Pipe white chocolate stars (each star touching the other) along the scored lines.

Pipe dark chocolate stars over the remaining areas on the top of the cake.

BUTTERSCOTCH WALNUT PUMPKIN CAKE

SERVES 10 TO 12

INGREDIENTS

WALNUT CAKE

250g/9oz unsalted butter (30g/1oz melted)
210g/7½oz plain flour
2 teaspoons bicarbonate of soda
¼ teaspoon salt
225g/8oz soft light brown sugar
170g/6oz cream cheese, softened
3 size-3 eggs
½ teaspoon pure vanilla essence
115g/4oz toasted walnuts, finely chopped

PUMPKIN CAKE

130g/4½oz unsalted butter (15g/½oz melted)
140g/5oz plain flour
1 teaspoon bicarbonate of soda
½ teaspoon ground cinnamon
½ teaspoon ground cloves
½ teaspoon ground nutmeg
¼ teaspoon salt
185g/6½oz canned pumpkin
125ml/4fl oz buttermilk
115g/4oz soft light brown sugar
100g/3½oz caster sugar
2 size-3 eggs
½ teaspoon pure vanilla essence

BUTTERSCOTCH WALNUT FILLING

185ml/6fl oz whipping cream
150g/5½oz caster sugar
¼ teaspoon fresh lemon juice
115g/4oz unsalted butter, cut into 4 equal pieces
115g/4oz walnuts, chopped into 3mm/⅛in pieces

GLAZED WALNUTS

200g/7oz caster sugar
5 tablespoons water
¼ teaspoon fresh lemon juice
20 walnut halves

BROWN SUGAR ICING

450g/1lb soft light brown sugar
250ml/8fl oz whipping cream
225g/8oz unsalted butter, cut into 8 equal pieces
¼ teaspoon cream of tartar

EQUIPMENT

Measuring jug, measuring spoons, small non-stick pan, baking tray, food processor with metal blade, chef's knife, cutting board, pastry brush, two 23 × 4cm/9 × 1½in round cake tins, baking parchment, sieve, greaseproof paper, electric mixer with flat beater, rubber spatula, wooden cocktail stick, 3 round cake cards, 1 litre/2 pint bowl, two 1.5 litre/2½ pint saucepans, whisk, serrated slicer, palette knife, fork, cooling rack, small plastic container with lid, 3 litre/5 pint saucepan, 3 litre/5 pint stainless steel bowl, piping bag, large star nozzle

MAKE THE WALNUT CAKE

Preheat the oven to 170°C/325°F/Gas 3.

Lightly coat the inside of two 23 × 4cm/9 × 1½in cake tins with melted butter. Line each tin with baking parchment, then lightly coat the parchment with more melted butter. Set aside.

Combine together in a sieve the flour, bicarbonate of soda and salt. Sift on to greaseproof paper and set aside.

Place the remaining 220g/8oz butter, the light brown sugar and cream cheese in the bowl of an electric mixer fitted with a flat beater. Beat on medium for 2 minutes. Increase the speed to high and beat for another 2 minutes. Scrape down the sides of the bowl. Now beat on high for 30 seconds. Scrape down the sides of the bowl. Add the eggs, one at a time, beating on medium for 30 seconds and scraping down the sides of the bowl after each addition. Add the vanilla essence and beat on high for 30 seconds. Operate the mixer on low, while gradually adding the sifted dry ingredients. Once all the dry ingredients have been incorporated, turn off the mixer. Add the finely chopped walnuts and mix on medium for 20 seconds.

Remove the bowl from the mixer and use a rubber spatula to finish mixing until smooth and thoroughly combined.

Immediately divide the cake mixture between the prepared tins, spreading evenly, and bake on the centre shelf in the preheated oven for 28 to 30 minutes or until a wooden cocktail stick inserted in the centre of the cakes comes out clean. Remove the cakes from the oven and cool in the tins for 15 minutes at room temperature. Turn out the cakes on to cake cards. Carefully remove the parchment. Refrigerate the cakes until needed.

MAKE THE PUMPKIN CAKE

Lightly coat the inside of a 23 × 4cm/9 × 1½in cake tin with melted butter. Line the tin with baking parchment, then lightly coat the parchment with more melted butter. Set aside.

Combine together in a sieve the flour, bicarbonate of soda, cinnamon, cloves, nutmeg and salt. Sift on to greaseproof paper and set aside.

Place the canned pumpkin and buttermilk in a small bowl. Mix together thoroughly. Set aside.

Place the remaining 115g/4oz butter, the light brown sugar and caster sugar in the bowl of an electric mixer fitted with a flat beater. Beat on medium for 2 minutes. Scrape down the sides of the bowl. Increase the speed to high and beat for another 2 minutes. Scrape down the sides of the bowl. Add the eggs and beat on medium for 30 seconds. Scrape down the sides of the bowl. Add the vanilla essence and beat on high for 30 seconds. Operate the mixer on low, while gradually adding the sifted dry ingredients. Once all the dry ingredients have been incorporated, turn off the mixer, add the pumpkin and buttermilk mixture and mix on medium for 20 seconds. Remove the bowl from the mixer and use a rubber spatula to finish mixing until smooth and thoroughly combined.

Immediately pour the cake mixture into the prepared tin, spreading evenly. Bake on the centre shelf in the preheated oven for about 45 minutes or until a wooden cocktail stick inserted in the centre of the cake comes out clean. Remove the cake from the oven and cool in the tin for 15 minutes at room temperature. Turn out the cake on to a cake card. Carefully remove the parchment. Turn the cake upright and refrigerate until needed.

MAKE THE BUTTERSCOTCH WALNUT FILLING

Heat the cream in a 1.5 litre/2½ pint saucepan over moderately low heat until warm (do not allow to simmer or boil). Combine the sugar and lemon juice in a separate 1.5 litre/2½ pint saucepan. Stir with a whisk to combine (the sugar will resemble moist sand). Caramelise the sugar for 4 to 5 minutes over moderately high heat, stirring constantly with a whisk to break up any lumps (the sugar will first turn clear as it liquefies, then light brown as it caramelises). Remove the saucepan from the heat. Add the hot cream, one half at a time, stirring vigorously after each addition (the cream will bubble and hiss when added). Add the butter, one piece at a time, stirring to incorporate before adding the next piece. Cool in the refrigerator for 45 minutes before placing in the bowl of an electric mixer fitted with a flat beater. Beat on high for 2 minutes or until light *(but not fluffy)*. Add the walnuts and stir to incorporate. Set aside for a few moments.

BEGIN ASSEMBLING THE CAKE

Remove the cakes from the refrigerator. Use a slicer to trim off just enough of the top of the pumpkin cake to create an even surface. Divide the butterscotch filling in half and use one portion to cover one of the walnut cakes and one portion to cover the pumpkin cake. Evenly spread the filling to the edges. Place the pumpkin cake on top of the butterscotch-coated walnut cake. Now top the pumpkin cake with the remaining walnut cake. Press down gently but firmly to level the layers. Refrigerate the cake while preparing the glazed walnuts and the brown sugar icing.

MAKE THE GLAZED WALNUTS

Heat the sugar, water and lemon juice in a 1.5 litre/2½ pint saucepan over moderately high heat. Bring to the boil. Adjust the heat and allow to simmer gently, stirring frequently with a whisk for about 15 minutes or until the mixture thickens and turns golden. Remove the saucepan from the heat. Using a table fork, dip the walnuts one at a time into the golden sugar. Place the glazed walnuts on a cooling rack, spaced so that they are not touching. Allow the glaze on the walnuts to harden for about 1 minute. Transfer the glazed walnuts to a sealed plastic container and store in the freezer until needed (stored in this fashion, the walnuts will keep for eons).

PREPARE THE BROWN SUGAR ICING

Heat the brown sugar, cream, 2 pieces of butter and the cream of tartar in a 3 litre/5 pint saucepan over moderately high heat for 2 minutes, stirring constantly. Allow the mixture to continue boiling for 7 to 8 minutes, stirring frequently. Transfer the bubbly hot mixture to a 3 litre/5 pint stainless steel bowl and allow to stand at room temperature for 1 hour before proceeding (the mixture needs to be cool enough so that it does not melt the additional butter, yet not so tacky that it will not blend with the butter). Place the cooled mixture in the bowl of an electric mixer fitted with a flat beater. Beat on low for 30 seconds. Then beat on medium for 2 minutes, while adding the remaining 6 pieces of butter, one at a time, until incorporated. Scrape down the sides of the bowl. Increase the speed to high and beat for another 2 minutes. Scrape down the sides of the bowl, then beat on high for 1 more minute or until light and fluffy. Transfer 250ml/8fl oz of icing to a piping bag fitted with a large star nozzle, and place in the refrigerator until needed.

FINISH ASSEMBLING THE CAKE

Remove the cake from the refrigerator and use a palette knife to coat the top and sides of the cake evenly with the brown sugar icing. Pipe a circle of 20 brown sugar icing stars along the outside edge of the top of the cake. Top each star with a glazed walnut. Refrigerate the cake for 30 minutes before cutting and serving.

TO SERVE

Heat the blade of the serrated slicer under hot running water and wipe the blade dry before cutting each slice. Allow the cake to stand at room temperature for 10 minutes before serving.

THE CHEF'S TOUCH

Pumpkin's availability ties it to the autumn season. To encourage you to make this dessert any time, however, I suggest the use of canned pumpkin (look at the ingredient statement on the label—it should list only 100% natural pumpkin). If fresh pumpkins are available, use 450g/1lb of peeled pumpkin flesh, cut into 1cm/½in pieces. Steam the pumpkin in a 3 litre/5 pint saucepan with 125ml/ 4fl oz water for 25 minutes, stirring occasionally to prevent sticking and burning. Cool the cooked pumpkin to room temperature, then purée. This may yield slightly more than the suggested amount, so measure the required 185g/6½oz and snack on the bit that remains.

The walnuts should be toasted before they are chopped. Toasting will both improve flavour and eliminate any moisture the nuts may have acquired in storage. Toast the walnuts on a baking sheet in a 170°C/325°F/ Gas 3 oven for 12 to 14 minutes. Allow the nuts to cool thoroughly before chopping. I suggest using a food processor for finely chopping the walnuts. You can use a chef's knife to chop the nuts into 3mm/⅛in pieces.

You may wish to prepare the butterscotch walnut pumpkin cake over a couple of days or more. The glazed walnuts can be prepared any time and kept frozen indefinitely. Bake the walnut cakes and the pumpkin cake on day 1 (cool and refrigerate until the next day), then make the butterscotch filling and the brown sugar icing on day 2. Assemble the cake as directed in the recipe.

After assembly, you can keep the butterscotch walnut pumpkin cake in the refrigerator for up to two to three days before serving. Allow the slices to stand at room temperature for 10 to 15 minutes before serving.

Although this dessert is delicious year round, it obviously has an autumnal tone. Whether or not you have falling leaves in mind, an excellent seasonally inspired beverage accompaniment would be a glass of hot pressed apple juice, and for those who want a bit of 'enhancement' for their juice, a shot of calvados is a treat.

FOR CHOCOLATE LOVERS ONLY

SERVES 12

INGREDIENTS

CHOCOLATE CAKE

225g/8oz unsalted butter (30g/1oz melted)
225g/8oz bittersweet chocolate, cut into
 15g/½oz pieces
10 size-3 egg yolks
100g/3½oz caster sugar
8 size-3 egg whites

CHOCOLATE MOUSSE

170g/6oz bittersweet chocolate, cut into
 15g/½oz pieces
375ml/12fl oz whipping cream
3 size-3 egg whites
2 tablespoons caster sugar

CHOCOLATE LOVERS' GANACHE

375ml/12fl oz whipping cream
500g/1lb 2oz bittersweet chocolate, cut into
 15g/½oz pieces
280g/10oz toasted hazelnuts, chopped into 5mm/
 ¼in pieces (see page 22 for tips on toasting
 hazelnuts)

EQUIPMENT

Measuring jug, measuring spoons, small non-stick
pan, pastry brush, baking tray, two 100% cotton
tea towels, chef's knife, cutting board, two 23 ×
4cm/9 × 1½in round cake tins, baking parchment,
double boiler, heat-resistant cling film, whisk,
electric mixer with flat beater and balloon whisk,
rubber spatula, 5 litre/8 pint stainless steel bowl,
wooden cocktail stick, two 23cm/9in cake cards,
two 3 litre/5 pint stainless steel bowls, 1 litre/2 pint
container, 1.5 litre/2½ pint saucepan, palette knife,
serrated knife, piping bag, large star nozzle,
serrated slicer

START THE CHOCOLATE LOVE FEAST WITH THE CAKE

Preheat the oven to 170°C/325°F/Gas 3.

Lightly coat the inside of two 23 × 4cm/9 × 1½in cake tins with melted butter. Line each tin with baking parchment, then lightly coat the parchment with more melted butter. Set aside.

Heat 2.5cm/1in of water in the bottom half of a double boiler over moderate heat. Place the remaining 195g/7oz butter and the bittersweet chocolate in the top half of the double boiler. Tightly cover the top with heat-resistant cling film. Allow to heat for 10 to 12 minutes. Remove from heat, stir until smooth and set aside until needed.

Place the egg yolks and sugar in the bowl of an electric mixer fitted with a flat beater. Beat on high for about 4 minutes or until slightly thickened and lemon coloured. Scrape down the sides of the bowl and beat on high for a further 2 minutes.

While the egg yolks are beating, whisk the egg whites in a 5 litre/8 pint stainless steel bowl until stiff but not dry, about 5 to 6 minutes (use a handy cordless beater and this task will take about 3 minutes).

Using a rubber spatula, fold the melted chocolate mixture into the beaten egg yolk mixture. Add one quarter of the whisked egg whites and stir to incorporate, then gently fold in the remaining egg whites.

Divide the mixture between the prepared tins, spreading evenly, and bake on the centre shelf in the preheated oven for 32 to 35 minutes or until a wooden cocktail stick inserted in the centre of the cake comes out clean. Remove the cakes from the oven and allow to cool in the tins for 15 minutes. (During baking, the surface of the cakes will form a crust; this crust will normally collapse when the cakes are removed from the oven.) Turn out the cakes on to cake cards. Remove the parchment and refrigerate the cakes for 1 hour.

PREPARE THE CHOCOLATE MOUSSE

Heat 2.5cm/1in of water in the bottom half of a double boiler over moderate heat. Place the bittersweet chocolate in the top half of the double boiler. Tightly cover the top with heat-resistant cling film. Allow to heat for 10 to 12 minutes. Remove from the heat and stir until smooth. Transfer the melted chocolate to a 5 litre/8 pint stainless steel bowl and set aside until needed.

Place the cream in the well-chilled bowl of an electric mixer fitted with a well-chilled balloon whisk. Whip on high for 1 minute or until peaks form. Set aside for a few moments until needed.

Whisk the egg whites in a 3 litre/5 pint stainless steel bowl until soft peaks form, about 2½ to 3 minutes. Add the sugar and continue to whisk until stiff peaks form, 1 to 1½ minutes more. Add one quarter of the whipped cream to the chocolate and whisk quickly and vigorously, then add the chocolate and cream mixture to the egg whites, followed by the remaining whipped cream. Fold all together gently but thoroughly. Refrigerate the chocolate mousse until needed.

PREPARE THE GANACHE

Heat the cream in a 1.5 litre/2½ pint saucepan over moderately high heat. Bring to the boil. Place the bittersweet chocolate in a 3 litre/5 pint stainless steel bowl. Pour the boiling cream over the chocolate. Tightly cover the top with cling film and allow to stand for 5 minutes, then stir until smooth.

Combine 375ml/12fl oz chocolate ganache with 140g/5oz of the chopped hazelnuts, and hold this mixture at room temperature to use for the filling. Keep the remaining chocolate ganache at room temperature until needed.

ASSEMBLE AND DECORATE THE CAKE

Remove the cakes from the refrigerator. Using a palette knife, spread the chocolate and hazelnut ganache mixture over the top of one cake. Spread evenly to the edges. Invert the other cake on top of the ganache-covered cake. Gently press the cakes together. Using a very sharp serrated knife, trim the outside edges of the top layer to create a more uniform shape. At this point the cake must be refrigerated for 30 minutes.

Evenly spread 185ml/6fl oz of the chocolate mousse over the sides of the cake. Chill the cake in the freezer for 30 minutes, or refrigerate for 1 hour.

Remove the cake from the freezer and pour the room-temperature chocolate ganache over the cake, spreading with a palette knife to create an even coating of ganache on both the top and the sides of the cake. Refrigerate the cake for 20 to 25 minutes to set the ganache.

Remove the cake from the refrigerator. Press the remaining 140g/5oz chopped hazelnuts into the ganache on the sides of the cake, distributing them evenly. Transfer the remaining chocolate mousse to a piping bag fitted with a large star nozzle. Pipe mousse stars over the entire top of the cake. Refrigerate the cake for at least 1 hour before cutting and serving.

PREPARE FOR LOVE AT FIRST BITE

Heat the blade of the serrated slicer under hot running water and wipe the blade dry before cutting each slice. Allow the slices of For Chocolate Lovers Only to stand at room temperature for 15 to 20 minutes before serving.

THE CHEF'S TOUCH

For Chocolate Lovers Only seems to have entered the confectioner's vernacular in much the same way as Death by Chocolate. Although our version is different from others, I would wager that all versions share a measure of tender loving care.

This cake is risen with egg whites. To ensure that your cakes attain the appropriate volume (and reach the same heights as ours do at the Trellis), be sure the whites are whisked in an immaculately clean bowl and that the whites are incorporated into the mixture exactly as stated in the recipe. (One quarter of the whites is stirred into the mixture to lighten it so it will easily accept the remaining whites.) The crust on the surface of the cakes will usually be smooth upon their removal from the oven, though sometimes slight cracks will be obvious. Do not be appalled by what happens next: the cake will collapse and the surface will resemble that of an earthquake-torn landscape (a bit hyperbolic perhaps, but when you see it happen you will get my point). It is supposed to look like that.

At the Trellis, we are fond of serving For Chocolate Lovers Only with Double Chocolate Sauce (see page 130) or with two scoops of Blackberry Chocolate Praline Ice Cream (see page 80).

After assembly, you can keep this cake in the refrigerator for one to two days before serving. Allow the slices to stand at room temperature for 15 to 20 minutes before serving.

If the hazelnuts purchased have not been skinned, you can skin them yourself. First, toast the nuts on a baking tray at 170°C/325°F/Gas 3 for 18 to 20 minutes (be careful not to over-toast the nuts as they have a tendency to become bitter). Remove the toasted nuts from the oven and immediately cover with a damp 100% cotton tea towel. Invert another baking tray over the first one to hold in the steam (this makes the nuts easier to skin). After 5 minutes, remove the skins from the nuts by placing them, a few at a time, inside a folded dry tea towel and rubbing vigorously between your hands. If skinned hazelnuts are purchased, toast at 170°C/325°F/Gas 3 for 10 to 12 minutes, then allow the nuts to cool before using. Chop the cooled hazelnuts, by hand using a chef's knife or in a food processor fitted with a metal blade, into 5mm/¹⁄₄in pieces.

To complete the loving experience, I suggest accompanying each slice of For Chocolate Lovers Only with a 1977 Fonseca vintage port.

LEMON BLUEBERRY CHEESECAKE
SERVES 10 TO 12

INGREDIENTS

CITRUS SHORTBREAD CRUST

45g/1½oz unsalted butter, melted

12 Citrus Shortbread Biscuits (see page 133)

LEMON BLUEBERRY CHEESECAKE

675g/1½lb cream cheese, softened

400g/14oz caster sugar

2 teaspoons finely chopped lemon zest

35g/1¼oz plain flour

2 tablespoons cornflour

1 teaspoon pure vanilla essence

½ teaspoon salt

6 size-3 eggs

125ml/4fl oz fresh lemon juice

170g/6oz fresh blueberries, stemmed and washed

SOURED CREAM AND BLUEBERRY TOPPING

4 tablespoons soured cream

2 teaspoons caster sugar

340g/12oz fresh blueberries, stemmed and washed

EQUIPMENT

Measuring jug, measuring spoons, small non-stick pan, vegetable peeler, chef's knife, cutting board, 23 × 4cm/9 × 1½in round cake tin, pastry brush, 23 × 7.5cm/9 × 3in round springform cake tin, food processor with metal blade, 2 litre/3 pint bowl, electric mixer with flat beater, rubber spatula, baking tray, instant-read thermometer, whisk, serrated knife, palette knife, serrated slicer

PREPARE THE CITRUS SHORTBREAD CRUST

Preheat the oven to 130°C/250°F/Gas ½. Place a 23 × 4cm/9 × 1½in cake tin partially filled with 1 litre/1⅔ pints of hot water on the bottom shelf of the oven (the bottom shelf should be at least 7.5cm/3in below the centre shelf).

Coat the inside of a 23 × 7.5cm/9 × 3in springform cake tin with 15g/½oz melted butter. Set aside.

In a food processor fitted with a metal blade, chop the shortbread biscuits in two batches. Pulse each batch until all the biscuits are in crumbs. Transfer the crumbs to a 2 litre/3 pint bowl. Combine the shortbread crumbs with the remaining 30g/1oz melted butter. Mix by hand until the crumbs bind together. Press the crumbs around the buttered sides of the springform tin, then on to the buttered bottom of the tin. Place the tin in the freezer until needed.

MAKE THE LEMON BLUEBERRY CHEESECAKE

Place the cream cheese, sugar and finely chopped lemon zest in the bowl of an electric mixer fitted with a flat beater. Beat on low until smooth, about 3 minutes. Scrape down the sides of the bowl. Add the flour, cornflour, vanilla essence and salt. Beat on medium for 2 minutes. Scrape down the sides of the bowl. Add 2 of the eggs and beat on low for 2 minutes. Scrape down the sides of the bowl. Add the remaining 4 eggs and beat on medium for 2 minutes. Once again, scrape down the sides of the bowl (all this mixing and scraping creates a beautifully smooth cheesecake). Add the lemon juice and mix on low for 1 minute. Remove the bowl from the mixer. Use a rubber spatula to finish mixing until smooth and thoroughly combined. Pour the cheesecake mixture into the prepared springform tin, spreading evenly. Place the springform tin on a baking tray (the tin will remain on the baking tray throughout baking and cooling).

Sprinkle the blueberries over the top of the mixture. The weight of the blueberries should cause them to sink to various depths in the mixture (if the berries do not sink, distribute them with a little more force—somewhere between a sprinkle and a pitch).

Place the baking tray with the springform tin on the centre shelf of the preheated oven and bake for 1 hour. Lower the oven temperature to 120°C/225°F/Gas ¼ and bake for another 1 hour. Reduce the temperature to 100°C/200°F/Gas very low and bake the cheesecake for a futher 1½ hours or until the internal temperature of the filling reaches 79°C/175°F. (The timing depends on how frequently you peek at the cheesecake. If you open the oven door more often than necessary, it may take an additional 30 minutes or more for the filling to reach the desired temperature.) Remove the cheesecake from the oven and cool on the baking tray at room temperature for 1 hour. Refrigerate the cheesecake for 12 hours (do not remove the cake from the tin) before proceeding.

PREPARE THE SOURED CREAM AND BLUEBERRY TOPPING

Combine the soured cream and caster sugar in a small bowl and whisk until smooth.

Release the cheesecake from the sides of the springform tin. (If the cake does not immediately separate, wrap a damp, hot tea towel around the sides of the tin. Make sure the towel covers the sides completely. Hold the towel around the tin for about 1 minute, then carefully release and remove the springform tin.) If the top crust of the cake is not level, trim with a serrated knife.

Use a palette knife to spread the soured cream mixture over the top of the cake, spreading evenly to the edges. Neatly arrange the blueberries on top of the soured cream. Refrigerate for 30 minutes before cutting and serving.

TO SERVE

Heat the blade of the serrated slicer under hot running water and wipe the blade dry before cutting each slice. Serve immediately.

THE CHEF'S TOUCH

A cheesecake dessert is an indulgence that even the most health-conscious people seem to justify. My theory is that cheesecake lovers are a bit like chocolate lovers—they are easily seduced. And this Lemon Blueberry Cheesecake is worth falling for. The balance of sweetness and acidity combined with the textural contrast between the velvety filling and the sprightly berry produces extraordinary sensations in your mouth.

One whole medium-size lemon should yield 2 to 2½ teaspoons of finely chopped lemon zest. Use a sharp vegetable peeler to zest the lemon. Be careful to remove only the coloured zest and not the bitter white pith, which lies directly beneath. After removing the coloured zest with a vegetable peeler, cut it into thin strips and then chop the strips finely with a very sharp chef's knife.

Preparation of the cheesecake can be spread out over two days or more. The shortbread can be baked and kept in the freezer for several days before using. For an even quicker start out of the gate, set up the springform tin with the shortbread crumbs, cover the tin with cling film, and keep it in the freezer for one to two days before using.

After assembly, the cheesecake can be kept in the refrigerator for two to three days.

If you love fresh blueberries as much as I do, you may want to sprinkle additional berries on to each dessert plate before serving. Otherwise I suggest no other accompaniment.

Once you have tasted this dessert you will understand why it needs no embellishment, although with a little coaxing, I could enjoy a rich and lively Château Rieussec Sauternes.

RED RASPBERRY ALMOND PASSION CAKE

SERVES 10 TO 12

INGREDIENTS

RASPBERRY ALMOND CAKE

370g/13oz unsalted butter (30g/1oz melted)

340g/12oz plain flour

2 teaspoons bicarbonate of soda

½ teaspoon salt

400g/14oz caster sugar

140g/5oz toasted flaked almonds, finely chopped

5 size-3 eggs

2 teaspoons almond essence

1 teaspoon pure vanilla essence

250ml/8fl oz soured cream

250ml/8fl oz hot water

RED RASPBERRY COULIS

450g/1lb frozen whole red raspberries, thawed

2 tablespoons caster sugar

1 teaspoon fresh lemon juice

BITTER CHOCOLATE ALMOND BUTTERCREAM

170g/6oz bittersweet chocolate, cut into
    15g/½oz pieces

115g/4oz unsweetened chocolate, cut into
    15g/½oz pieces

450g/1lb unsalted butter, cut into 16 equal pieces

2 teaspoons almond essence

4 size-3 egg whites

200g/7oz caster sugar

EQUIPMENT

Measuring jug, measuring spoons, small non-stick pan, baking sheet, food processor with metal blade, chef's knife, cutting board, pastry brush, two 23 × 4cm/9 × 1½in round cake tins, baking parchment, fine sieve, greaseproof paper, electric mixer with flat beater and balloon whisk, rubber spatula, wooden cocktail stick, 4 round cake cards, serrated slicer, medium sieve, two 3 litre/5 pint stainless steel bowls, double boiler, heat-resistant cling film, whisk, 5 litre/8 pint stainless steel bowl, instant-read thermometer, palette knife, piping bag, medium star nozzle

PREPARE THE RASPBERRY ALMOND CAKE

Preheat the oven to 170°C/325°F/Gas 3.

Lightly coat the inside of two 23 × 4cm/9 × 1½in cake tins with melted butter. Line each tin with baking parchment, then lightly coat the parchment with more melted butter. Set aside.

Combine together in a fine sieve the flour, bicarbonate of soda and salt. Sift on to greaseproof paper and set aside.

Place the remaining 340g/12oz butter and the caster sugar in the bowl of an electric mixer fitted with a flat beater. Beat on low for 3 minutes. Scrape down the sides of the bowl and beat on medium for 3 minutes. Scrape down the sides of the bowl, add the chopped almonds, and beat on medium for an additional 30 seconds. Add the eggs, one at a time, beating on medium for 30 seconds and scraping down the bowl after each addition. Add the almond essence and vanilla essence and beat on high for 2 more minutes. While operating the mixer on low, add half of the sifted dry ingredients and allow to mix for 15 seconds. Add half of the soured cream followed by the remaining dry ingredients, then add the remaining soured cream and mix for another 30 seconds.

Add the hot water and mix for 15 seconds. Increase the mixer speed to medium and beat for an additional 20 seconds before removing the bowl from the mixer. Use a rubber spatula to finish mixing until smooth and thoroughly combined.

Immediately divide the mixture between the prepared tins, spreading evenly. Bake on the centre shelf in the preheated oven for 35 to 40 minutes or until a wooden cocktail stick inserted in the centre of the cake comes out clean. Remove the cakes from the oven and cool in the tins for 15 minutes at room temperature. Turn out on to the cake cards. Carefully remove the parchment, then allow to cool at room temperature for an additional 30 minutes. Turn the cakes over. Using a slicer, trim off just enough of the top of each cake to make an even surface. Slice each cake horizontally into 2 equal layers. Place each layer on a cake card. Refrigerate uncovered while preparing the red raspberry coulis.

MAKE THE RED RASPBERRY COULIS

In the bowl of a food processor fitted with a metal blade, process the raspberries, caster sugar and lemon juice until smooth, about 15 to 20 seconds. Pass the purée through a medium sieve, using a rubber spatula to press down on the seeds and pulp (discard the seeds and pulp). This should yield about 250ml/8fl oz of red raspberry coulis.

Remove the cake layers from the refrigerator. Drizzle 3 to 4 tablespoons red raspberry coulis over each cake layer (even if you have extracted more than 250ml/8fl oz of purée, do not drizzle more than 4 tablespoons on each cake; otherwise the cake will become soggy. Use a rubber spatula to spread evenly to the edges. Refrigerate the raspberry-soaked cake layers.

PREPARE THE BITTER CHOCOLATE ALMOND BUTTERCREAM

Heat 2.5cm/1in of water in the bottom half of a double boiler over moderate heat. Place the bitter-sweet chocolate and unsweetened chocolate in the top half of the double boiler. Tightly cover the top with heat-resistant cling film. Allow to heat for 8 to 10 minutes. Remove from the heat and stir until smooth. Transfer to a small bowl and set aside until needed.

Place the butter pieces in the bowl of an electric mixer fitted with a flat beater. Beat the butter on low for 2 minutes, then on medium for 3 minutes. Scrape down the sides of the bowl. Beat on high until light and fluffy, about 4 to 5 minutes. Add the almond essence and beat on high for 1 minute. Remove about ¼ of the butter mixture and whisk it into the melted chocolate (this makes it easier to incorporate the chocolate into the remaining butter; if you do not first introduce a little butter in the chocolate you may end up with a marbleised icing). Place the chocolate and butter mixture in the mixing bowl with the remaining butter and beat on medium until the chocolate and butter are thoroughly combined, about 1 minute. Scrape down the sides of the bowl. Now one last time: beat on high for 2 minutes or until light and fluffy. Transfer the mixture to a 5 litre/8 pint stainless steel bowl and set aside until needed.

Heat 2.5cm/1in of water in the bottom half of a double boiler over moderate heat. Place the egg whites and caster sugar in the top half of the double boiler. Gently whisk the egg whites until they reach a temperature of 50°C/120°F, about 2 to 3 minutes. Transfer the heated egg whites to the bowl of an electric mixer fitted with a balloon whisk. Whisk on high until stiff peaks form, about 6 minutes. Remove the bowl from the mixer. Use a rubber spatula to fold the whisked egg whites gently but thoroughly into the chocolate and butter mixture. Hold at room temperature until needed.

ASSEMBLE THE PASSION CAKE

Remove the cake layers from the refrigerator. Use a palette knife to spread 185ml/6fl oz of Bitter Chocolate Almond Buttercream evenly over 3 of the cake layers. Stack these 3 layers one on top of the other. Invert the last cake layer on to the stacked layers, pressing down gently but firmly to level the layers. Smoothly spread 500ml/16fl oz of buttercream on the top and sides of the cake (half on top and half on the sides). Refrigerate the cake for 15 minutes.

Fill a piping bag fitted with a medium star nozzle with the remaining buttercream. Remove the cake from the refrigerator. Pipe a circle of stars (each touching the other) along the outside edge of the top of the cake. Continue to pipe out the stars until the top is covered. Refrigerate the cake for 30 minutes before cutting and serving.

TO SERVE

Heat the blade of the serrated slicer under hot running water and wipe the blade dry before making each slice. Allow the cake to stand at room temperature 10 to 15 minutes before serving.

THE CHEF'S TOUCH

As soon as you cut into this confection you will come to understand why it was named Red Raspberry Almond Passion Cake; the author assumes no responsibility for what happens after the first bite.

Toast the almonds for 10 minutes in a 170°C/325°F/Gas 3 oven before using them. This will improve the flavour as well as eliminate any moisture the nuts may have acquired in storage.

The red raspberry coulis can also be prepared using fresh red raspberries.

Be sure to remove the melted chocolate from the top half of the double boiler after melting so that the chocolate can cool to room temperature before it is added to the whipped butter. If the chocolate is too warm (more than 27°C/80°F), it may melt the butter.

I strongly urge using a table-top electric mixer with a balloon whisk to prepare the buttercream. Using a hand-held whisk (be it manual or electric) will not create the desired texture.

One additional caveat about the buttercream: be sure that the mixing bowl is impeccably clean before whisking the egg whites. Any grease or soap residue will reduce the volume of the egg whites, spoil the taste and—alas—cool the flames of passion.

The final touches: garnish the outside ring of buttercream stars with fresh red raspberries, then gently and evenly press 100g/3½oz of toasted flaked almonds into the sides of the cake.

As we all know, well-chilled Champagne certainly can induce passion. Choose a 1985 Veuve Clicquot La Grande Dame and discover how far this pairing of sweet and bubbly can take you.

CHOCOLATE VOODOO CAKE

SERVES 10 TO 12

INGREDIENTS

DRUNKEN ZOMBIE CAKE

140g/5oz raisins

125ml/4fl oz Myers's dark rum

250g/9oz unsalted butter (30g/1oz melted)

140g/5oz plain flour

20g/²⁄₃oz unsweetened cocoa powder

2 teaspoons baking powder

½ teaspoon ground cinnamon

½ teaspoon ground allspice

pinch of salt

280g/10oz bittersweet chocolate, cut into
  15g/½oz pieces

225g/8oz soft light brown sugar

4 size-3 eggs

1 teaspoon pure vanilla essence

MOCHA RUM MOUSSE

225g/8oz bittersweet chocolate, cut into
  15g/½oz pieces

4 tablespoons strong black coffee

2 tablespoons Myers's dark rum

250ml/8fl oz whipping cream

3 size-3 egg whites

2 tablespoons caster sugar

BLACKENED MOLASSES GLAZE

185ml/6fl oz whipping cream

45g/1½oz unsalted butter

2 tablespoons blackstrap molasses

170g/6oz bittersweet chocolate, cut into
  15g/½oz pieces

CHOCOLATE CARAMEL
VOODOO NEEDLES

200g/7oz caster sugar

¼ teaspoon lemon juice

15g/½oz bittersweet chocolate

EQUIPMENT

Measuring jug, measuring spoons, small non-stick pan, 1 litre/2 pint plastic container with tight-fitting lid, pastry brush, two 23 × 4cm/9 × 1½in round cake tins, baking parchment, sieve, grease-proof paper, double boiler, heat-resistant cling film, whisk, electric mixer with flat beater and balloon whisk, rubber spatula, wooden cocktail stick, 2 round cake cards, 5 litre/8 pint stainless steel bowl, 1.5 litre/2½ pint saucepan, palette knife, 3 litre/5 pint stainless steel bowl, 4 non-stick baking sheets, plastic container with lid, serrated slicer

WHY WE CALL IT DRUNKEN

Combine the raisins and dark rum in a plastic container with a tight-fitting lid. Allow to stand at room temperature for 6 hours or overnight.

MAKE THE DRUNKEN
ZOMBIE CAKE

Preheat the oven to 170°C/325°F/Gas 3.

Lightly coat the inside of two 23 × 4cm/9 × 1½in cake tins with melted butter. Line each tin with baking parchment, then lightly coat the parchment with more melted butter. Set aside.

Combine together in a sieve the flour, cocoa powder, baking powder, ground cinnamon, ground allspice and salt. Sift on to greaseproof paper and set aside.

Heat 2.5cm/1in of water in the bottom half of a double boiler over moderate heat. Place the bittersweet chocolate in the top half of the double boiler. Tightly cover the top with heat-resistant cling film. Allow to heat for 8 minutes. Remove from the heat and stir until smooth. Keep at room temperature until ready to use.

Place the remaining 225g/8oz butter and the brown sugar in the bowl of an electric mixer fitted with a flat beater. Beat on medium for 2 minutes. Use a rubber spatula to scrape down the sides of the bowl. Beat on high for 2 minutes. Scrape down the sides of the bowl. Add the eggs, one at a time, beating on medium for 30 seconds and scraping

down the sides of the bowl after each addition. Add the vanilla essence and beat on high for 30 seconds. Add the melted chocolate and beat on medium for 30 seconds. Operate the mixer on low while gradually adding the sifted dry ingredients. Once all the dry ingredients have been incorporated, turn off the mixer and add the rum-infused raisins. Mix on medium for 30 seconds (at this point, the aromas wafting up from the mixing bowl are quite extraordinary). Remove the bowl from the mixer and use a rubber spatula to finish mixing until smooth and thoroughly combined.

Immediately divide the cake mixture between the prepared tins, spreading evenly. Bake on the centre shelf in the preheated oven for 32 to 35 minutes or until a wooden cocktail stick inserted in the centre of the cakes comes out clean. Remove the cakes from the oven and cool in the tins for 15 minutes at room temperature. Turn out the cakes on to cake cards. Carefully remove the parchment. Place the cakes in the freezer for 1 hour or in the refrigerator for at least 2 hours (the cakes must be thoroughly cooled before adding the mousse, as described later).

MAKE THE MOCHA
RUM MOUSSE

Heat 2.5cm/1in of water in the bottom half of a double boiler over moderate heat. Place the bittersweet chocolate, coffee and dark rum in the top half of the double boiler. Tightly cover the top with heat-resistant cling film. Allow to heat for 5 to 6 minutes. Remove from the heat and stir until smooth. Transfer the chocolate mixture to a 5 litre/8 pint stainless steel bowl and keep at room temperature until ready to use.

Place the cream in the well-chilled bowl of an electric mixer fitted with a well-chilled balloon whisk. Whip on high for 1 minute or until peaks form. Set aside for a few moments.

Whisk the egg whites in a 3 litre/5 pint stainless steel bowl until soft peaks form, about 2½ to 3 minutes. Add the caster sugar and continue to

whisk until stiff peaks form, a further 1 to 1½ minutes. Use a rubber spatula to quickly fold one third of the whisked egg whites into the melted chocolate. Then place the whipped cream and the remaining egg whites on top of the chocolate and use a rubber spatula to fold all together until smooth and completely combined. Refrigerate the mocha rum mousse for 30 to 45 minutes (the mousse must be refrigerated until slightly firm before beginning to assemble the cake).

BEGIN ASSEMBLING THE CAKE

Remove the cake layers from the freezer or refrigerator and the mousse from the refrigerator. Reserve 250ml/8fl oz of mousse and set aside in the refrigerator for a few moments. Spoon the remaining mousse on to one of the inverted cake layers, using a palette knife to spread evenly to the edges. Place the other inverted cake layer on top of the mousse and press gently into place. Use a palette knife to coat the top and sides of the cake with the reserved mousse. Place the cake in the freezer while preparing the blackened molasses glaze and the voodoo needles.

PREPARE THE BLACKENED MOLASSES GLAZE

Heat the cream, butter and molasses in a 1.5 litre/2½ pint saucepan. Stir to dissolve the molasses, then bring to the boil. Place the bittersweet chocolate in a 3 litre/5 pint stainless steel bowl. Pour the boiling cream mixture over the chocolate and allow to stand for 5 minutes. Stir until smooth. Keep the glaze at room temperature for 1 hour before using (the glaze will thicken to the desired texture during that time period).

PREPARE THE CHOCOLATE CARAMEL VOODOO NEEDLES

Combine the sugar and lemon juice in a 1.5 litre/2½ pint saucepan. Stir with a whisk to combine (the sugar will resemble moist sand). Caramelise the sugar for 5½ to 6 minutes over moderately high heat, stirring constantly with a whisk to break up any lumps (the sugar will first turn clear as it liquefies, then light brown as it caramelises). Remove the

saucepan from the heat, add the chocolate and stir to dissolve. Dip a wire whisk into the chocolate caramel and drizzle the hot caramel, in long thin lines, on to 4 non-stick baking sheets, one sheet at a time (move the whisk back and forth over the length of the baking sheets). Continue drizzling—making an effort to create as many individual long, thin and separate chocolate caramel strips as possible—until all the caramel is used. Allow the strips to harden at room temperature, about 15 minutes. Break the strips into the desired size voodoo needles (7.5 to 10cm/3 to 4in needles make for delightful sticking). The voodoo needles can be stored in a tightly sealed plastic container in the freezer until needed (which may be sooner than you think, especially if an intruder sticks a finger into the glaze).

FINISH ASSEMBLING THE CAKE

Remove the cake from the freezer. Pour the glaze over the top of the cake. Spread the reserved mousse evenly just on the sides of the cake. Use a palette knife to spread a smooth coating of glaze over the top and sides of the voodoo cake. Refrigerate the cake for 1 hour to set the glaze.

TO SERVE

Heat the blade of a serrated slicer under hot running water and wipe the blade dry before cutting each slice. Place a piece of Chocolate Voodoo Cake in the centre of each serving plate. Randomly stick the chocolate caramel voodoo needles into the cake slices (avoid thinking about your enemies at this time, if at all possible). Dispatch immediately.

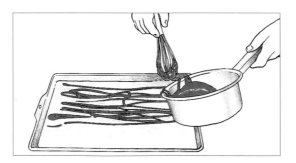

Dip a wire whisk into the chocolate caramel and drizzle the hot caramel, in long thin lines, on to the nonstick baking sheet.

Randomly stick the chocolate caramel voodoo needles into the cake slices.

MOCHA ALMOND PRALINE SNAP

SERVES 10

INGREDIENTS

ESPRESSO ALMOND MERINGUE

100g/3½oz toasted flaked almonds

250g/9oz caster sugar

3 tablespoons cornflour

10 size-3 egg whites

1 tablespoon instant espresso powder

¼ teaspoon cream of tartar

pinch of salt

1 teaspoon almond essence

ALMOND PRALINE

200g/7oz toasted flaked almonds

600g/1lb 5oz caster sugar

1½ teaspoons fresh lemon juice

EXQUISITE CHOCOLATE BUTTERCREAM

280g/10oz bittersweet chocolate, cut into 15g/½oz pieces

55g/2oz unsweetened chocolate, cut into 15g/½oz pieces

450g/1lb unsalted butter, cut into 16 equal pieces

6 size-3 egg whites

200g/7oz caster sugar

EQUIPMENT

Measuring jug, measuring spoons, 23 × 7.5cm/ 9 × 3in round springform cake tin, four 25 × 38cm/10 × 15in baking sheets, chef's knife, cutting board, baking parchment, food processor with metal blade, double boiler, whisk, instant-read thermometer, electric mixer with balloon whisk and flat beater, rubber spatula, piping bag, two 23 × 33cm/9 × 13in non-stick baking trays, 3 litre/5 pint saucepan, 3 small plastic containers with lids, small bowl, heat-resistant cling film, 5 litre/8 pint stainless steel bowl, large star nozzle, 3 litre/5 pint stainless steel bowl, serrated knife, large metal kitchen spoon, palette knife, serrated slicer

PREPARE THE ESPRESSO ALMOND MERINGUE LAYERS

Preheat the oven to 130°C/250°F/Gas ½.

Using the removable bottom of a 23 × 7.5cm/9 × 3in springform tin as a guide, trace a circle on each of 4 sheets of baking parchment (cut to fit the baking sheets) with a pencil. Place each sheet of parchment, with the pencilled mark face down, on a baking sheet.

Place the flaked almonds, 50g/2oz of the sugar and the cornflour in the bowl of a food processor fitted with a metal blade. Pulse the mixture until finely chopped. Set aside.

Heat 2.5cm/1in of water in the bottom half of a double boiler over moderately high heat. Place the egg whites, the remaining 200g/7oz sugar, the espresso powder, cream of tartar and salt in the top half of the double boiler. Heat the egg white mixture to a temperature of 50°C/120°F while gently and constantly whisking, about 2½ to 3 minutes. Transfer the mixture to the bowl of an electric mixer fitted with a balloon whisk. Whisk on high until stiff but not dry, about 3 to 3½ minutes. Add the almond essence and whisk on high for 15 seconds. Remove the bowl from the mixer and use a rubber spatula to fold in the finely chopped almond mixture.

Fill a piping bag (with no nozzle) with about ¼ of the meringue. Fill a traced circle with meringue: start in the centre and pipe a 1.5cm/½in wide spiral towards the outside of the circle. Fill the piping bag again and repeat this procedure with each of the 3 remaining circles (each circle should be filled with about one quarter of the original amount of meringue). Place the meringues on the centre and bottom shelves of the preheated oven and bake for 1 hour (rotate the meringues from centre to bottom after 30 minutes). Reduce the oven temperature to 120°C/225°F/Gas ¼ and bake for an additional 2 hours. Remove from the oven and allow to cool on the baking sheets for 30 minutes before handling.

MAKE THE ALMOND PRALINE

Evenly divide and spread the almonds over two 23 × 33cm/9 × 13in non-stick baking trays. Set aside.

Place the caster sugar and lemon juice in a 3 litre/5 pint saucepan. Stir with a whisk to combine (the sugar will resemble moist sand).

Caramelise the sugar for about 10 minutes over moderately high heat, stirring constantly with a whisk to break up any lumps (the sugar will first turn clear as it liquefies, then light brown as it caramelises). Remove the saucepan from the heat. Carefully pour the caramelised sugar over the almonds, evenly dividing it between the 2 baking trays, covering as many of the nuts as possible (the more nuts covered the better). Pick up the baking trays by the edges and gently rock them to allow the caramelised sugar to flow over the almonds; move quickly but carefully because the sugar will stop flowing as it cools. Allow the praline to harden at room temperature for about 15 minutes.

Place the praline from 1 baking sheet on a cutting board. Use a sharp chef's knife to chop the praline into 3mm/⅛in pieces (later this praline will be incorporated with some of the exquisite chocolate buttercream), which can be stored in a tightly sealed plastic container in the freezer until needed. Break 10 irregular 4cm/1½in pieces from the remaining sheet of praline (these will be used to garnish the top of the snap). Store in a tightly sealed plastic container in the freezer until needed.

The remaining praline should be broken into 5 to 7.5cm/2 to 3in pieces. Place these pieces in the bowl of a food processor fitted with a metal blade. Pulse until very finely chopped (the finely chopped praline will be used to decorate the sides of the snap) and store in a tightly sealed plastic container in the freezer until needed.

PREPARE THE EXQUISITE CHOCOLATE BUTTERCREAM

Heat 2.5cm/1in of water in the bottom half of a double boiler over moderate heat. Place the bittersweet chocolate and unsweetened chocolate in the top half of the double boiler. Tightly cover the top with heat-resistant cling film and allow to heat for 8 to 10 minutes. Remove from the heat and stir until smooth. Transfer to a small bowl and set aside until needed. (This is done to dissipate the heat in the chocolate. If the chocolate is too warm it may melt the butter when the two are combined.)

Place the butter in the bowl of an electric mixer fitted with a flat beater. Beat the butter on low for 2 minutes, then on medium for 3 minutes. Scrape down the sides of the bowl. Beat on high for about 5 minutes or until light and fluffy. Transfer the whisked butter to a 5 litre/8 pint stainless steel bowl and set aside during the next step.

Heat 2.5cm/1in of water in the bottom half of a double boiler over moderate heat. Place the egg whites and caster sugar in the top half of the double boiler. Heat the egg white mixture to a temperature of 50°C/120°F while gently and constantly whisking, about 2½ to 3 minutes. Transfer the mixture to the bowl of an electric mixer fitted with a balloon whisk. Whisk on high until stiff peaks form, about 4 to 4½ minutes. Remove the bowl from the mixer.

Fold the melted chocolate into the whisked butter, using a rubber spatula to combine thoroughly. Fold in the whisked egg whites until thoroughly combined. Transfer 250ml/8fl oz buttercream to a piping bag fitted with a large star nozzle. Refrigerate until needed. Transfer 750ml/1¼ pints of buttercream to a 3 litre/5 pint stainless steel bowl. Add the (3mm/⅛in) chopped pralines to the bowl and combine (this becomes 1 litre/2 pints of almond praline brittle buttercream).

Hold remaining 750ml/1.5 pints of buttercream until needed.

BEGIN ASSEMBLING THE MOCHA ALMOND PRALINE SNAP

Trim each meringue with a serrated knife so that it will fit perfectly inside a 23 × 7.5cm/9 × 3in springform tin. Place a trimmed meringue, top side up, inside the tin. Spoon one third of the almond praline brittle buttercream on top of the meringue and spread evenly to the edges. Place another meringue inside the tin on top of the first layer of buttercream, gently pressing into place. Spoon ½ of the remaining almond praline buttercream on top of the meringue in the tin and spread evenly to the edges. Top the buttercream layer with the third meringue, gently pressing into place. Spoon the remaining almond praline buttercream over the meringue in the tin, spreading evenly to the edges. Top the last layer of almond praline buttercream with the last meringue, placing it bottom side up (so the smoothest surface is facing up). Press down gently on the last layer to level it in place. Chill in the freezer for 1 hour.

FINISH ASSEMBLING THE CAKE

Remove the springform tin from the freezer. Release the sides of the springform tin. Use a palette knife to cover the top and sides of the layered meringue gâteau with the remaining Exquisite Chocolate Buttercream, spreading it evenly. Press a thick coating of finely chopped almond praline on the sides of the cake, coating evenly. Pipe a circle of 10 buttercream stars along the outside edge of the top of the cake. Decorate each star with an irregular piece of almond praline. Refrigerate for 30 minutes before cutting and serving.

TO SERVE

Heat the blade of the serrated slicer under hot running water and wipe the blade dry before cutting each slice. Serve immediately.

CHOCOLATE PECAN BOURBON BASH

SERVES 12

INGREDIENTS

PECAN CAKE

240g/8½oz unsalted butter (15g/½oz melted)

340g/12oz toasted pecans, finely chopped

225g/8oz plain flour

1½ teaspoons bicarbonate of soda

½ teaspoon salt

340g/12oz soft light brown sugar

3 size-3 eggs

125ml/4fl oz sour mash bourbon whiskey

1 teaspoon pure vanilla essence

185ml/6fl oz hot water

CHOCOLATE GANACHE

500ml/16fl oz whipping cream

55g/2oz unsalted butter

50g/scant 2oz caster sugar

500g/1lb 2oz bittersweet chocolate, cut into
15g/½oz pieces

115g/4oz unsweetened chocolate, cut into
15g/½oz pieces

115g/4oz toasted pecans, chopped into 3mm/⅛in
pieces

CHOCOLATE BOURBON MOUSSE

340g/12oz bittersweet chocolate, cut into
15g/½oz pieces

55g/2oz unsweetened chocolate, cut into
15g/½oz pieces

185ml/6fl oz whipping cream

3 tablespoons sour mash bourbon whiskey

5 size-3 egg whites

2 tablespoons caster sugar

CHOCOLATE BOURBON SAUCE

Chocolate Bourbon Sauce (see page 131), warm

EQUIPMENT

Measuring jug, measuring spoons, baking tray, food processor with metal blade, chef's knife, cutting board, small non-stick pan, pastry brush, 23 × 7.5cm/9 × 3in round springform cake tin, sieve, greaseproof paper, electric mixer with flat beater, rubber spatula, wooden cocktail stick, 3 litre/5 pint saucepan, three 3 litre/5 pint stainless steel bowls, whisk, serrated slicer, palette knife, round cake card, double boiler, heat-resistant cling film, 5 litre/8 pint stainless steel bowl, large metal kitchen spoon, serrated knife

MAKE THE PECAN CAKE

Preheat the oven to 150°C/300°F/Gas 2.

Lightly coat the inside of a 23 × 7.5cm/9 × 3in springform tin with melted butter. Press a thin coating of 55g/2oz finely chopped pecans on to the buttered bottom of the tin. Set aside.

Combine together in a sieve the flour, bicarbonate of soda and salt. Sift on to greaseproof paper and set aside.

Place the remaining 225g/8oz butter and the light brown sugar in the bowl of an electric mixer fitted with a flat beater. Beat on low for 2 minutes. Scrape down the sides of the bowl. Add the remaining 285g/10oz finely chopped pecans and mix on low for 1 minute. Add the eggs, half of the sour mash bourbon whiskey (4 tablespoons) and the vanilla essence and beat on medium for 2 minutes. Scrape down the sides of the bowl. Operate the mixer on low, while slowly adding the sifted dry ingredients; allow to mix for 15 seconds. Add the hot water, increase the speed to medium and beat for an additional 10 seconds before removing the bowl from the mixer. Use a rubber spatula to finish mixing until smooth and thoroughly combined.

Immediately pour the mixture into the prepared springform tin, spreading evenly. Place the tin on a baking tray. Put the baking tray on the centre shelf in the preheated oven. Bake for 1 hour and 10 minutes to 1 hour and 15 minutes or until a wooden cocktail stick inserted in the centre of the cake comes out clean. Remove the cake from the oven and cool in the tin for 30 minutes at room temperature. Remove the side of the tin (wash and dry the side for use later) and refrigerate the cake for 30 minutes.

PREPARE THE CHOCOLATE GANACHE

While the cake is cooling, heat the whipping cream, butter and caster sugar in a 3 litre/5 pint saucepan over moderately high heat. When hot, stir to dissolve the sugar. Bring to the boil. Place the bittersweet chocolate and unsweetened chocolate in a 3 litre/5 pint stainless steel bowl. Pour the boiling cream over the chocolate and allow to stand for 5 minutes, then stir until smooth.

Remove 250ml/8fl oz ganache and combine with the chopped pecans. Hold this mixture at room temperature to use for the filling. Also hold the remaining ganache at room temperature until needed.

Remove the chilled cake from the refrigerator. Use a slicer to trim off just enough of the top of the cake to make an even surface. Slice the cake horizontally into 3 equal layers, leaving the bottom layer on the bottom of the springform tin. Sprinkle the remaining sour mash bourbon whiskey on both the bottom and the centre layer. Reassemble the springform tin. Pour the ganache and pecan mixture over the cake layer in the bottom of the tin. Use a palette knife to spread the ganache evenly over the surface of the cake. Top with the centre cake layer and press down gently but firmly to level the cake. Place the top layer on a cake card, then place the cake layers in the freezer for at least 30 minutes.

PREPARE THE CHOCOLATE BOURBON MOUSSE

Heat 2.5cm/1in of water in the bottom half of a double boiler over moderate heat. Place the bittersweet chocolate and unsweetened chocolate in the top half of the double boiler. Tightly cover the top with heat-resistant cling film. Heat for 7 to 8 minutes, then remove from the heat and stir until smooth. Transfer to a 5 litre/8 pint stainless steel bowl and set aside until needed.

Using a hand-held whisk, whip the cream and sour mash bourbon whiskey in a well-chilled stainless steel bowl until stiff. In a separate bowl, whisk the egg whites until soft peaks form. Add the caster sugar and continue to whisk until stiff peaks form. Add one third of the whipped cream to the melted chocolate and whisk vigorously until smooth. Place the remaining whipped cream and the whisked egg whites on top of the chocolate and use a rubber spatula to fold all together until smooth and completely combined.

Remove the cake layers from the freezer. Spoon the mousse on top of the centre cake layer in the springform tin and spread evenly to the edges. Place the remaining cake layer on top of the mousse and press gently to level. Place the cake in the freezer for 20 minutes.

ASSEMBLE THE BASH

Remove the cake from the freezer and cut around the edge to release the cake from the side of the springform tin. Spoon 250ml/8fl oz of chocolate ganache on to the cake and smooth it over the top and sides of the cake. Refrigerate the cake for 15 to 20 minutes to set the ganache. Pour the remaining chocolate ganache over the cake, once again using a palette knife to spread the ganache evenly over the top and sides. (If the ganache has become too firm to pour, set the bowl of ganache over a pan of hot tap water or place the bowl on a warm heating pad. It should take less than a minute or two for the ganache to attain 'pourable' consistency.) Refrigerate the cake for 1 hour before serving.

TO SERVE

Heat the blade of the serrated slicer under hot running water and wipe the blade dry before cutting each slice. Allow the slices to stand at room temperature for 15 to 20 minutes before serving.

Before placing the Chocolate Pecan Bourbon Bash slices on to (25cm/10in diameter) plates, flood the centre of each plate with 3 to 4 tablespoons warm Chocolate Bourbon Sauce, then place a slice of bash in the centre of each plate. Serve immediately.

THE CHEF'S TOUCH

If you are a teetotaler then you should probably refer to some other recipe. For those who do enjoy 'a taste' every now and then, however, this is one bash you do not want to miss. There should be no substitutions for the sour mash bourbon whiskey in this case. Go with the flow or flip to another page.

Toasting the pecans improves their flavour and eliminates any moisture the nuts may have acquired in storage. Toast the nuts on a baking sheet in a 170°C/325°F/Gas 3 oven for 10 to 12 minutes. Be sure to allow the nuts to cool thoroughly before chopping. Use a food processor with a metal blade to chop the nuts finely. A chef's knife will work well for chopping the pecans into 3mm/$\frac{1}{8}$in pieces.

The bash certainly can be prepared in one afternoon; however, you may want to spread the production over two days. On day 1, bake and cool the pecan cake. After the whole cake is thoroughly cooled, wrap with cling film and refrigerate until the next day. On day 2, prepare the ganache, the mousse and the sauce, then complete the assembly of the cake.

After assembly, you can keep the bash in the refrigerator for two to three days before serving. Allow the slices to stand at room temperature for 15 to 20 minutes before serving.

In keeping with the Bacchanalian nature of this dessert, add a final touch of bourbon whiskey–infused whipped cream. I suggest a dollop or two—or even three. (Whisk 375ml/12fl oz whipping cream and 6 tablespoons sour mash bourbon whiskey in a well-chilled stainless steel bowl until stiff.) And if you reach this part of the recipe, I am certain that suggesting a shot of good sour mash bourbon whiskey to accompany this cake will not be taken amiss.

GOOEY CHOCOLATE PEANUT BUTTER BROWNIE CAKE

SERVES 12

INGREDIENTS

GOOEY BROWNIE CAKES

250g/9oz unsalted butter (30g/1oz melted)

340g/12oz bittersweet chocolate, cut into 15g/½oz pieces

200g/7oz caster sugar

3 size-3 eggs

1½ teaspoons pure vanilla essence

75g/2½oz plain flour

1 teaspoon baking powder

250g/9oz creamy peanut butter

CHOCOLATE PEANUT BUTTER GANACHE

375ml/12fl oz whipping cream

3 tablespoons caster sugar

30g/1oz creamy peanut butter

500g/1lb 2oz bittersweet chocolate, cut into 15g/½oz pieces

225g/8oz toasted unsalted peanuts, chopped into 3mm/⅛in pieces

EQUIPMENT

Measuring jug, measuring spoons, three 23 × 4cm/ 9 × 1½in round cake tins, pastry brush, baking parchment, double boiler, heat-resistant cling film, whisk, electric mixer with flat beater, rubber spatula, 3 round cake cards, serrated knife, palette knife, 3 litre/5 pint saucepan, 3 litre/5 pint stainless steel bowl, serrated slicer

MAKE THE GOOEY BROWNIE CAKES

Preheat the oven to 150°C/300°F/Gas 2.

Lightly coat the inside of three 23 × 4cm/9 × 1½in cake tins with melted butter. Line each tin with baking parchment, then lightly coat the parchment with more melted butter. Set aside.

Heat 2.5cm/1in of water in the bottom half of a double boiler over moderate heat. Place the bittersweet chocolate and the remaining 225g/8oz butter in the top half. Tightly cover the top with heat-resistant cling film. Allow to heat for 8 to 10 minutes. Remove from the heat and stir until smooth. Set aside until needed.

Place the sugar, eggs and vanilla essence in the bowl of an electric mixer fitted with a flat beater. Beat on medium for 2 minutes. Use a rubber spatula to scrape down the sides of the bowl. Beat on high for 2 minutes. Scrape down the bowl. Add the melted chocolate and beat on medium until the chocolate is thoroughly incorporated, about 15 seconds. Add the flour and baking powder and beat on low for 1 minute. Remove the bowl from the mixer and use a rubber spatula to combine thoroughly.

Divide the mixture among the prepared tins, spreading evenly. Place 1 of the tins on the centre shelf and the remaining 2 tins on the bottom shelf of the preheated oven. Bake for 20 to 22 minutes or until the cakes are set but not dry (a wooden cocktail stick inserted in the centre of the cakes should hold some residual mixture). Rotate the brownie cakes from top to bottom about halfway through the baking time.

Remove the brownie cakes from the oven and allow to cool in the tins at room temperature for 10 to 15 minutes. Turn out each brownie cake on to an individual cake card. (These baked brownie cake layers are very delicate, so use a knife to cut around the edge of the cakes inside the tins; this will ensure that the cake does not tear when removed from its tin.) Remove the parchment from each brownie cake. Place the brownie cakes in the refrigerator to cool for 10 minutes. Remove 2 of the brownie cakes from the refrigerator and use a palette knife to spread 125g/4½oz of peanut butter in an even layer over each cake. Place these 2 brownie cake layers in the freezer while preparing the ganache.

PREPARE THE CHOCOLATE PEANUT BUTTER GANACHE

Heat the cream, caster sugar and creamy peanut butter in a 3 litre/5 pint saucepan over moderately high heat. When hot, stir to dissolve the sugar and blend in the peanut butter. Bring to the boil. Place the bittersweet chocolate in a 3 litre/5 pint stainless steel bowl. Pour the boiling cream over the chocolate and allow to stand for 5 minutes. Stir until smooth.

ASSEMBLE THE CAKE

Remove the two brownie cakes from the freezer. Pour 250ml/8fl oz of ganache over each and use a palette knife to spread the ganache to the edges. Refrigerate the ganache-covered cake layers for 10 minutes (to allow the ganache to become firm).

Remove all the brownie cake layers from the refrigerator. Stack the 2 ganache-coated layers on top of each other, then top with the uncoated layer and gently press into place. Place the assembled brownie cake in the freezer for 10 minutes (lacking freezer space, you may opt to chill the cake in the refrigerator for about 30 minutes).

Using a palette knife, evenly spread 125ml/
4fl oz ganache around the sides of the cake. Pour
the remaining ganache on to the top of the cake
and use a palette knife to spread the ganache to the
edges. If your kitchen is cool, the ganache may
become firm and difficult to pour. If this happens,
warm the bowl of ganache over a pan of hot tap
water or set the bowl on a warm heating pad. The
ganache should attain the proper viscosity in a
minute or two. Use a whisk to stir the ganache
gently until smooth.

Press the chopped peanuts into the ganache on
the side of the cake, coating evenly. Refrigerate the
cake for 10 minutes before cutting and serving.

TO SERVE

Heat the blade of the serrated slicer under hot running water and wipe the blade dry before making
each slice. Allow the slices to stand at room temperature for at least 1 hour before serving. The
longer the cake is held at room temperature the
gooier the texture will be. The cake may be refrigerated for 2 to 3 days after assembly. Remember,
the gooier the better.

FALLEN ANGEL CAKE WITH GOLDEN HALOS AND SINFUL CREAM

SERVES 6 TO 10

INGREDIENTS

FALLEN ANGEL CAKE

225g/8oz unsalted butter (15g/½oz melted)

225g/8oz bittersweet chocolate, cut into 15g/½oz pieces

6 size-3 egg yolks

150g/5½oz caster sugar

8 size-3 egg whites

2 tablespoons unsweetened cocoa powder

2 tablespoons icing sugar

GOLDEN HALOS

200g/7oz caster sugar

5 tablespoons warm water

SINFUL CREAM

500ml/16fl oz whipping cream

1 tablespoon caster sugar

3 tablespoons sour mash bourbon whiskey

EQUIPMENT

Measuring jug, measuring spoons, 23 × 7.5cm/ 9 × 3in round springform cake tin, pastry brush, baking parchment, double boiler, heat-resistant cling film, electric mixer with flat beater and balloon whisk, rubber spatula, 3 litre/5 pint stainless steel bowl, whisk, 3 baking sheets, wooden cocktail stick, 6 litre/10 pint saucepan, 1.5 litre/ 2½ pint saucepan, 23cm/9in stainless steel kitchen spoon, sieve, serrated slicer

PREPARE THE FALLEN ANGEL CAKE

Preheat the oven to 170°C/325°F/Gas 3.

Coat the inside of a 23 × 7.5cm/9 × 3in spring-form tin with 2 teaspoons melted butter. Line the tin with baking parchment. Coat the parchment with the remaining melted butter. Set aside.

Heat 2.5cm/1in of water in the bottom half of a double boiler over moderate heat. Place the bittersweet chocolate and the remaining 210g/7½oz butter in the top half. Tightly cover the top with heat-resistant cling film. Heat for 10 to 12 minutes. Remove from the heat and stir until smooth. Set aside until needed.

Place the egg yolks and caster sugar in the bowl of an electric mixer fitted with a flat beater. Beat the mixture on high until it becomes lemon-coloured and slightly thickened, about 3 minutes. Scrape down the sides of the bowl. Set the mixer on medium and leave the yolks to beat while whisking the egg whites.

Whisk the egg whites in a 3 litre/5 pint stainless steel bowl until stiff but not dry (about 4 minutes if whisking by hand and less time if using a hand-held electric mixer).

Remove the bowl with the egg yolks from the mixer. Use a rubber spatula to fold in the melted chocolate. Add one third of the beaten egg whites and stir to incorporate, then gently fold in the remaining egg whites. Pour the mixture into the springform tin, spreading evenly. Place on a baking sheet (this is insurance against spills) on the centre shelf of the pre-heated oven. Bake for 52 to 54 minutes or until a long wooden cocktail stick or wooden skewer inserted in the centre of the cake comes out fairly clean. (The skewer should hold some residual mixture, but should not be wet. Traditionally cakes are baked until a skewer inserted in the centre of the cake is clean and dry when removed. Our fallen angel cake is pulled from the oven about 10 to 15 minutes before

that point in order to maintain a heightened degree of moisture.) Remove the baked cake from the oven and allow to cool in the springform tin for 15 minutes. Release the cake from the springform tin and turn out on to a cake card. Remove the parchment and hold the cake at room temperature.

PREPARE THE GOLDEN HALOS

Line two baking sheets with baking parchment. Fill a 6 litre/10 pint saucepan ⅓ full with water. Heat the water and keep at a simmer while preparing the syrup.

Heat the caster sugar and water in a 1.5 litre/ 2½ pint saucepan over moderately high heat. Use a 23cm/9in long stainless steel kitchen spoon to stir the sugar mixture while it is heating. Intermittently, use a water-dampened pastry brush to 'wash' the inside of the saucepan at the edge of the liquefied sugar (this deters crystal formation around the inside of the pan). Heat the sugar syrup for about 16 minutes or until it acquires a light golden colour. Remove the saucepan from the heat and carefully place it in the pan of simmering water (expect a bit of sizzling at this moment). Working quickly, drizzle a spoonful (using the same spoon used to stir the sugar) of sugar syrup in a circular motion on to the parchment to create each halo. The halos will harden at cool room temperature in a matter of minutes. Hold the halos at room temperature until ready to serve the completed dessert. If the weather is hot and humid, I recommend placing the halos in the freezer.

MAKE THE SINFUL CREAM

Place the cream, caster sugar and sour mash bourbon whiskey in the well-chilled bowl of an electric mixer fitted with a well-chilled balloon whisk. Whip on high until soft peaks are formed, about 45 to 60 seconds.

THE FINISHING TOUCHES

Place the unsweetened cocoa and the icing sugar in a sieve. Lightly and evenly dust the cake with the cocoa and sugar.

TO SERVE

Heat the blade of the serrated slicer under hot running water and wipe the blade dry before cutting each slice.

For each serving of cake, portion a large heaping spoonful of sinful cream into the centre of a 25cm/10in plate. Nestle a slice of cake on to each cloud of cream, and crown the cake with a golden halo.

THE CHEF'S TOUCH

Our Fallen Angel Cake is named for the precipitous fall it undergoes after being removed from the oven. Do not despair when this happens—it gives the cake its interesting appearance and dense texture.

The preparation of the sugar halos may seem a bit daunting if you have never worked with cooked sugar. I recommend a little practice—you are sure to be rewarded for your effort.

Work quickly when preparing the halos. If the sugar becomes too stiff to spoon on to the parchment, remove the pan of sugar from the simmering water. Heat the pan of sugar over moderately high heat until the sugar is viscous enough to drizzle.

The halos can be prepared several days in advance. Store the halos in a sealed plastic container in your freezer. Place a piece of parchment in between each halo to prevent sticking. Remove the halos from the freezer immediately before serving the fallen angel cake.

The cake is at its best when served within an hour or so after being removed from the oven. Once the cake has cooled to room temperature, you can store it in the refrigerator for two to three days. Before serving bring the cake to room temperature for at least an hour.

I would not discourage a sip or two of Tennessee bourbon whiskey to help you enjoy this dessert.

WHITE AND DARK CHOCOLATE PATTY CAKE

SERVES 12

INGREDIENTS

WHITE CHOCOLATE PATTY CAKE

85g/3oz unsalted butter (30g/1oz melted)

340g/12oz white chocolate, cut into 15g/½oz pieces

2 tablespoons water

10 size-3 egg yolks

150g/5½oz caster sugar

6 size-3 egg whites

55g/2oz plain flour, sifted

DARK CHOCOLATE MOUSSE

400g/14oz bittersweet chocolate, cut into 15g/½oz pieces

115g/4oz unsweetened chocolate, cut into 15g/½oz pieces

125ml/4fl oz strong black coffee

55g/2oz white chocolate, cut into 15g/½oz pieces

500ml/16fl oz whipping cream

4 size-3 egg whites

2 tablespoons caster sugar

WHITE AND DARK CHOCOLATE GANACHES

225g/8oz white chocolate, cut into 15g/½oz pieces

300ml/½ pint whipping cream

225g/8oz bittersweet chocolate, chopped into 5mm/¼in pieces

EQUIPMENT

Measuring jug, measuring spoons, small non-stick pan, sieve, greaseproof paper, chef's knife, cutting board, pastry brush, two 23 × 4cm/9 × 1½in round cake tins, baking parchment, double boiler, heat-resistant cling film, 2 whisks, electric mixer with flat beater and balloon whisk, rubber spatula, 5 litre/8 pint stainless steel bowl, wooden cocktail stick, 2 round cake cards, 3 litre/5 pint stainless steel bowl, 23 × 7.5cm/9 × 3in round springform cake tin, large metal kitchen spoon, 1 litre/2 pint bowl, serrated knife, palette knife, piping bag, medium star nozzle, serrated slicer

BEGIN PREPARING THE WHITE CHOCOLATE PATTY CAKE

Preheat the oven to 170°C/325°F/Gas 3.

Lightly coat the inside of two 23 × 4cm/9 × 1½in cake tins with melted butter. Line each tin with baking parchment, then lightly coat the parchment with more melted butter. Set aside.

Heat 2.5cm/1in of water in the bottom half of a double boiler over moderate heat. Place the remaining 55g/2oz butter, the white chocolate and the water in the top half of the double boiler. Tightly cover the top with heat-resistant cling film. Allow to heat for 10 to 12 minutes. Remove from heat, discard the cling film, stir until smooth and set aside until needed.

Place the egg yolks and 100g/3½oz of the sugar in the bowl of an electric mixer fitted with a flat beater. Beat on high for 2 minutes. Use a rubber spatula to scrape down the sides of the bowl. Continue to beat on high for 2 minutes or until slightly thickened and lemon-coloured. Adjust the mixer speed to low and leave the yolks to beat while whisking the egg whites (if this is not done, the yolks will develop undesirable lumps).

Whisk the egg whites in a 5 litre/8 pint stainless steel bowl until soft peaks form, about 3 minutes. Gradually add the remaining sugar while continuing to whisk the egg whites until stiff but not dry, about 2 to 3 more minutes.

Add the melted chocolate to the beaten egg yolks and beat on medium until completely incorporated, about 30 seconds. Remove the bowl from the mixer. Using a rubber spatula, fold the sifted plain flour into the beaten egg yolk and chocolate mixture. Add one third of the whisked egg whites and stir to incorporate, then gently fold in the remaining egg whites.

Divide the mixture between the prepared tins, spreading evenly, and bake on the centre shelf in the preheated oven for about 26 to 30 minutes or until a wooden cocktail stick inserted in the centre of the cake comes out clean. Remove the cakes from the oven and allow to cool in the tins for 20 minutes. Turn out the cakes on to cake cards and cool to room temperature, about 20 minutes. Remove the parchment and refrigerate the cakes, on the cake cards, until needed.

PREPARE THE DARK CHOCOLATE MOUSSE

Heat 2.5cm/1in of water in the bottom half of a double boiler over moderate heat. Place the bittersweet chocolate, unsweetened chocolate, black coffee and white chocolate in the top half of the double boiler. Tightly cover the top with heat-resistant cling film. Allow to heat for 12 to 14 minutes. Remove from heat and stir until smooth. Transfer to a 3 litre/5 pint stainless steel bowl, then set aside at room temperature until needed.

Place the cream in the well-chilled bowl of an electric mixer fitted with a well-chilled balloon whisk. Whip on high until stiff, about 1 minute. Set aside in the refrigerator until needed.

Whisk the egg whites in a 5 litre/8 pint stainless steel bowl until soft peaks form, about 3 minutes. Add the caster sugar and continue to whisk until stiff but not dry, 1½ to 2 minutes longer. Fold one quarter of the egg whites into the melted chocolate mixture. Then add the egg white and chocolate mixture to the remaining egg whites, followed by the remaining whipped cream. Fold all together gently but thoroughly. Refrigerate the chocolate mousse until needed.

BEGIN ASSEMBLING THE PATTY CAKE

Place one of the inverted white chocolate cakes inside a 23 × 7.5cm/9 × 3in springform tin. Use your fingers gently to pat down the edges of the cake (to create as flat a surface as possible).

Spoon the dark chocolate mousse on top of the cake and spread evenly. Place the remaining cake on top of the mousse, and once again gently pat down the edges to create a flat surface. Wrap the entire cake (tin and all) with cling film and place in the freezer for 2 hours.

MAKE THE WHITE AND DARK CHOCOLATE GANACHES

Heat 2.5cm/1in of water in a double boiler over moderate heat. Place the white chocolate in the top half of the double boiler. Tightly cover the top with heat-resistant cling film. Allow to heat for 6 minutes, then remove from heat and stir until smooth. Heat the cream in a 1.5 litre/2½ pint saucepan over moderate heat. Bring to the boil. Place the chopped bittersweet chocolate in a 1 litre/2 pint bowl. Pour 125ml/4fl oz cup boiling cream over the melted white chocolate and the remaining cream over the chopped bittersweet chocolate. Stir both until smooth. Refrigerate the white chocolate ganache for at least 1 hour. Set aside the dark chocolate ganache at room temperature until needed.

FINISH ASSEMBLING THE PATTY CAKE

Remove the cake from the freezer. Remove the cling film. Cut around the edge to release the cake from the side of the springform tin. Using a palette knife, smooth 3 to 4 tablespoons dark chocolate ganache on the top and sides of the cake (consider this the under-coat of ganache). Refrigerate the cake for 10 minutes to firm the ganache.

Pour the remaining dark chocolate ganache over the cake and use a palette knife to spread the ganache over the top and sides of the cake. Refrigerate the cake for 10 to 15 minutes to set the ganache before decorating with the white chocolate ganache.

Fill a piping bag fitted with a medium star nozzle with the white chocolate ganache. Pipe a circle of white chocolate stars (each touching the other) along the outside edge of the top of the cake. Then pipe a second circle of stars inside the first (once again each star touching the other). Refrigerate the cake for at least 30 minutes before cutting and serving.

TO SERVE

Heat the blade of the serrated slicer under hot running water and wipe the blade dry before cutting each slice. Allow the slices to stand at room temperature for 10 to 15 minutes before serving.

THE CHEF'S TOUCH

I happened upon pastry chef Tim O'Connor patting down the edges of a white chocolate mousse cake one day and joked in passing that we should call it a patty cake rather than a mousse cake. As they say in show business, a legend was born—or so we hope.

Be sure to use good white chocolate (Droste's is our choice) for this recipe. Look for white chocolate with cocoa butter as the second ingredient, after sugar. Lesser quality white chocolate has been manufactured with tropical oils, which impart absolutely no chocolate flavour to the product.

When you prepare this recipe, you may notice that the melted white chocolate, butter, and water starts out smooth, then gets very grainy. Don't worry—keep stirring and it will become (and remain) smooth in just a minute or so.

After assembly, you can keep the patty cake in the refrigerator for up to two days before serving.

A cup of French roast coffee would be my choice for a beverage to accompany the winsome patty cake. This robust coffee works well with the particular sweetness of the dessert.

CHOCOLATE CARAMEL HAZELNUT DAMNATION

SERVES 12 TO 16

INGREDIENTS

CARAMEL SAUCE

250ml/8fl oz whipping cream

30g/1oz unsalted butter

¼ teaspoon salt

400g/14oz caster sugar

½ teaspoon fresh lemon juice

CARAMEL CHOCOLATE CHEESECAKE

1 teaspoon melted unsalted butter

115g/4oz toasted hazelnuts, finely chopped

125ml/4fl oz hot strong black coffee

125ml/4fl oz caramel sauce

115g/4oz bittersweet chocolate, cut into 15g/½oz pieces

55g/2oz unsweetened chocolate, cut into 15g/½oz pieces

450g/1lb cream cheese, softened

100g/3½oz caster sugar

¼ teaspoon salt

3 size-3 eggs

½ teaspoon pure vanilla essence

HAZELNUT PRALINE

75g/2½oz whole toasted hazelnuts

100g/3½oz caster sugar

¼ teaspoon fresh lemon juice

CHOCOLATE FUDGE CAKE

115g/4oz plus 1 teaspoon (5g) unsalted butter

170g/6oz plus 1 tablespoon plain flour

1 teaspoon bicarbonate of soda

¼ teaspoon salt

55g/2oz unsweetened chocolate, cut into 15g/½oz pieces

340g/12oz soft light brown sugar

2 size-3 eggs

½ teaspoon pure vanilla essence

125ml/4fl oz soured cream

125ml/4fl oz hot water

CHOCOLATE CARAMEL GANACHE

250ml/8fl oz whipping cream

340g/12oz bittersweet chocolate, cut into 15g/½oz pieces

125ml/4fl oz caramel sauce

115g/4oz toasted hazelnuts, finely chopped

CHOCOLATE CARAMEL MOUSSE

115g/4oz bittersweet chocolate, cut into 15g/½oz pieces

30g/1oz unsweetened chocolate, cut in half

3 tablespoons caramel sauce

185ml/6fl oz whipping cream

4 size-3 egg whites

2 tablespoons caster sugar

EQUIPMENT

Measuring jug, measuring spoons, baking tray, 2 large 100% cotton tea towels, food processor with metal blade, 1.5 litre/2½ pint saucepan, 3 litre/5 pint saucepan, whisk, 23 × 5cm/9 × 2in round cake tin, 23 × 7.5cm/9 × 3in round spring-form cake tin, double boiler, heat-resistant cling film, electric mixer with flat beater, rubber spatula, instant-read thermometer, pie tin, sieve, greaseproof paper, wooden cocktail stick, round cake card, four 3 litre/5 pint stainless steel bowls, 1 litre/2 pint plastic container, large metal kitchen spoon, serrated knife, palette knife, serrated slicer

PREPARE THE CARAMEL SAUCE

Heat the cream, butter and salt in a 1.5 litre/2½ pint saucepan over moderate heat. Bring to a simmer, then adjust the heat to keep the cream hot until needed. Combine the sugar and the lemon juice in a 3 litre/5 pint saucepan. Stir with a whisk to combine (the sugar will resemble moist sand). Caramelise the sugar for 7 to 8 minutes over moderately high heat, stirring constantly with a whisk to break up any lumps (the sugar will first turn clear as it liquefies, then light brown as it caramelises). Remove the saucepan from the heat. Carefully pour one third of the hot cream mixture into the caramelised sugar (this will cause frenetic bubbling); use a whisk to stir the caramel until the bubbling has subsided. Add the remaining cream and stir until smooth. This recipe should yield 500ml/16fl oz of caramel sauce. Set aside until needed during the preparation of the other components of the damnation cake.

Preheat the oven to 150°C/300°F/Gas 2.

Place a 23 × 5cm/9 × 2in cake tin partially filled with 1 litre/1⅔ pints of water on the bottom shelf of the oven (the bottom shelf should be at least 7.5cm/3in below the centre shelf). This creates the desired moist baking environment for the cheesecake.

PREPARE THE CARAMEL CHOCOLATE CHEESECAKE

Lightly coat the bottom of a 23 × 7.5cm/9 × 3in springform tin with 1 teaspoon melted butter. Press the finely chopped hazelnuts on to the buttered bottom of the tin. Set aside.

Heat 2.5cm/1in of water in the bottom half of a double boiler over moderate heat. Place the coffee, 125ml/4fl oz caramel sauce, the bittersweet chocolate and unsweetened chocolate in the top half of the double boiler. Tightly cover the top with heat-resistant cling film. Heat for 6 minutes, then remove from the heat and stir until smooth. Set aside until needed.

Place the softened cream cheese, sugar and salt in the bowl of an electric mixer fitted with a flat beater. Beat on low for 1 minute. Scrape down the sides of the bowl, then beat on medium for an additional 2 minutes. Scrape down the bowl. Add the eggs, one at a time, beating on medium for 15 seconds after each addition. Scrape down the bowl after each addition. Add the vanilla essence and the melted chocolate mixture and beat on medium for 10 seconds. Remove the bowl from the mixer. Use a rubber spatula to finish mixing until smooth and thoroughly combined. (This repetitive beating, alternated by scraping down the bowl, will give the cake a silky smooth texture.) Pour the cheesecake mixture into the prepared springform tin, spreading evenly.

Place the springform tin on the centre shelf of the preheated oven and bake the cheesecake for about 1 hour or until the internal temperature reaches 76°C/170°F. Turn off the oven and allow the cheesecake to remain in the oven for an additional 30 minutes. Remove from the oven and cool at room temperature for 30 minutes. (Don't forget to remove the cake tin with the water from the oven.) Refrigerate the cheesecake in the springform tin for at least 1 hour before assembling the cake.

PREPARE THE HAZELNUT PRALINE

While the cheesecake is baking, place the whole hazelnuts in a pie tin, grouping the nuts together, side by side. Combine the sugar and lemon juice in a 1.5 litre/2½ pint saucepan. Stir with a whisk to combine (the sugar will resemble moist sand). Caramelise the sugar for 4 to 4½ minutes over moderately high heat, stirring constantly with a whisk to break up any lumps (the sugar will first turn clear as it liquefies, then light brown as it caramelises). Remove the saucepan from the heat. Carefully pour the caramelised sugar over the hazelnuts, covering as many of the nuts as possible. Place the pie tin in the freezer to harden the praline for about 15 minutes.

Remove the praline from the freezer and break into 5 to 6cm/2 to 2½in pieces. Place the broken praline pieces in the bowl of a food processor fitted with a metal blade. Finely chop the praline. Keep

the praline in a tightly sealed plastic container in the freezer until needed.

Adjust oven temperature to 170°C/325°F/Gas 3.

PREPARE THE CHOCOLATE FUDGE CAKE

Coat the inside of a 23 × 5cm/9 × 2in cake tin with 1 teaspoon butter, then flour the pan with 1 tablespoon plain flour, shaking out the excess. Set aside.

Sift together the remaining 170g/6oz flour, the bicarbonate of soda and salt on to greaseproof paper. Set aside.

Heat 2.5cm/1in of water in the bottom half of a double boiler over moderate heat. Place the unsweetened chocolate in the top half of the double boiler. Tightly cover the top with heat-resistant cling film and allow to heat for 4 to 5 minutes. Remove from the heat and stir until smooth.

Place the brown sugar and the remaining 115g/4oz butter in the bowl of an electric mixer fitted with a flat beater. Beat on low for 2 minutes and then on medium for 2 minutes. Scrape down the sides of the bowl, then beat on high for 2 additional minutes. Add the eggs, one at a time, scraping down the bowl and beating on medium for 30 seconds after each addition. Add the melted chocolate and vanilla essence and beat on low for 30 seconds. Scrape down the bowl. While operating the mixer on low, add one third of the sifted dry ingredients and half of the soured cream. Allow to mix for 30 seconds. Add another one third of the dry ingredients and the remaining soured cream and mix for another 30 seconds. Add the remaining sifted dry ingredients and the hot water. Increase the mixer speed to medium and beat for 10 seconds. Remove the bowl from the mixer. Use a rubber spatula to finish mixing until smooth and thoroughly combined. Immediately pour the cake mixture into the prepared tin and spread evenly. (Move quickly—once the hot water is added to the mixture, the raising action of the bicarbonate of soda will be activated. If you take too long getting the tin into the oven, the soda will lose its 'punch'.) Bake on the centre shelf in the preheated oven for 45 minutes or until a wooden cocktail stick inserted in the centre of the cake comes out clean. Remove from

the oven and allow to cool in the tin for 15 minutes at room temperature. Turn out on to a cake card and refrigerate for 30 minutes.

PREPARE THE CHOCOLATE CARAMEL GANACHE

Heat the whipping cream in a 1.5 litre/2½ pint saucepan over moderately high heat. Bring to the boil. Place the bittersweet chocolate and 125ml/4fl oz caramel sauce in a 3 litre/5 pint stainless steel bowl. Pour the boiling cream over the chocolate and caramel sauce and allow to stand for 5 minutes. Stir until smooth.

Remove 250ml/8fl oz chocolate caramel ganache and combine with the finely chopped hazelnuts. Keep this mixture at room temperature to use for the filling. The remaining ganache should also be kept at room temperature until needed.

PREPARE THE CHOCOLATE CARAMEL MOUSSE

Heat 2.5cm/1in of water in the bottom half of a double boiler over moderate heat. Place the bittersweet chocolate, unsweetened chocolate and 3 tablespoons caramel sauce in the top half of the double boiler. Tightly cover the top with heat-resistant cling film. Allow to heat for 6 to 8 minutes. Remove from heat and stir until smooth. Transfer to a 3 litre/5 pint stainless steel bowl and set aside until needed.

Using a hand-held whisk, whip the whipping cream in a well-chilled 3 litre/5 pint stainless steel bowl until stiff. In a separate bowl, whisk the egg whites until soft peaks form. Add the caster sugar and continue to whisk until stiff peaks form. Use a rubber spatula to fold one third of the egg whites into the chocolate and caramel mixture. Spoon the whipped cream and then the remaining egg whites on top of the mixture and fold all together until smooth and completely combined.

BEGIN ASSEMBLING THE CHOCOLATE CARAMEL HAZELNUT DAMNATION

Remove the Chocolate Fudge Cake from the refrigerator. Turn the cake over. Using a slicer, trim off just enough of the top of the cake to make an even surface. Slice the cake horizontally into 2 equal layers. Remove the cheesecake from the refrigerator. Do not remove the cheesecake from the springform tin (it will be used to build the damnation cake, layer upon layer). Use your fingertips gently to press down on the outside edges of the cheesecake (to create as flat a surface as possible). Pour the ganache and hazelnut mixture over the cheesecake. Use a palette knife to spread the ganache evenly over the surface of the cheesecake. Then invert the top half of the fudge cake on to this ganache layer, pressing down gently to level the cake layer.

Spoon the Chocolate Caramel Mousse on to the inverted cake layer and spread evenly. Place the bottom half of the fudge cake on the mousse layer, pressing down gently to level the cake layer. Place the entire cake in the freezer for 30 minutes or refrigerate for 1 hour.

COMPLETE THE ASSEMBLY

Remove the cake from the refrigerator. Using a knife, cut around the inside edge of the tin, then release the cake from the side of the springform tin (leave the cake on the bottom of the tin). Use a palette knife to smooth the top and sides of the cake with 3 to 4 tablespoons ganache. Pour the remaining ganache over the cake. Using a palette knife, evenly spread the ganache over the top and sides of the cake. (If the ganache has become too firm to pour, set the bowl of ganache over a pan of hot tap water or set the bowl on a warm heating pad. The ganache will become 'pourable' in a minute or two. Stir until smooth.) Press the reserved chopped praline on to the sides of the cake, coating evenly. Refrigerate the cake for 1 hour before serving.

TO SERVE

Heat the blade of the serrated slicer under hot running water and wipe the blade dry before cutting each slice. Allow the slices to stand at room temperature for 30 minutes before serving.

Use the remaining caramel sauce to decorate the dessert plates. Warm the sauce to a 'pourable' consistency, then use a spoon and eclectically drizzle caramel sauce over each plate.

THE CHEF'S TOUCH

Our first pastry chef at the Trellis, Don Mack, shared my fondness for tagging desserts with wicked appellations. For Don, naming this dessert was (as we say in our kitchen) a 'no brainer'. The name makes sense because a lot of damned hard work goes into the preparation. However, the pleasure that will be your reward for making Damnation is certain to be heavenly.

This recipe calls for about 310g/11oz of whole toasted hazelnuts. To skin the nuts (if not done already), first toast them on a baking tray at 170°C/325°F/Gas 3 for 18 to 20 minutes (be certain not to over-toast or they will become bitter). Remove the toasted nuts from the oven and immediately cover with a damp 100% cotton tea towel. Invert another baking tray over the first one to hold in the steam (this makes the nuts easier to skin). After 5 minutes, remove the skins from the nuts by placing small quantities inside a folded dry tea towel and rubbing vigorously between the hands. If skinned hazelnuts are purchased, toast at 170°C/325°F/Gas 3 for 10 to 12 minutes, then allow the nuts to cool before using. Place 225g/8oz of cooled hazelnuts in the bowl of a food processor fitted with a metal blade; process until finely chopped. The remaining nuts will be used whole.

Consider preparing Damnation over a period of two or three days. The Hazelnut Praline can be prepared several days in advance. Keep the chopped praline in a tightly sealed plastic container in the freezer until needed. The cheesecake and fudge cake can be prepared up to two days in advance. (Don't forget that the caramel sauce needs to be prepared before doing the cheesecake. The remaining sauce can be kept, covered with cling film, in the refrigerator until needed for the Chocolate Caramel Ganache and the Chocolate Caramel Mousse. Be sure to bring the refrigerated caramel sauce to room temperature before using.) On the chosen day, prepare the Chocolate Caramel Ganache and the Chocolate Caramel Mousse. Assemble the cake as directed in the recipe.

Use several cocktail sticks inserted in the side of the chocolate fudge cake as guides to help halve the cake accurately.

After assembly, the Damnation can be kept in the refrigerator for two to three days before serving. Allow the slices to stand at room temperature for 30 minutes before serving.

I suggest a glass of deep purple vintage port to ensure your salvation.

FRUITFUL FINALES

'How sweet it is.'
—JACKIE GLEASON

CHILLED FRUIT SOUP WITH POACHED APPLES, CRISPY CROUTONS
AND JONNY'S CIDER ICE CREAM

MY CHERRY CLAFOUTI

CHOCOLATE DRENCHED FRUIT

LEMON AND FRESH BERRY 'SHORTCAKE' WITH ROSE'S LEMON LUSCIOUS ICE CREAM

WARM ORANGE SEGMENTS AND SLICED STRAWBERRIES WITH CINNAMON HONEY
SCONES AND VANILLA CUSTARD

OVEN-ROASTED PEACHES WITH VERY BERRY YOGURT

CRANBERRY AND TOASTED WALNUT CROSTATA

STRAWBERRY RHUBARB VANILLA CUSTARD TART

CHILLED FRUIT SOUP
WITH POACHED APPLES, CRISPY CROUTONS AND JONNY'S CIDER ICE CREAM

SERVES 6

INGREDIENTS

POACHED APPLES

500ml/16fl oz cranberry juice cocktail
200g/7oz caster sugar
250ml/8fl oz port
3 cinnamon sticks, 7.5cm/3in each
8 whole cloves
3 Granny Smith apples

FRUIT SOUP

2 Granny Smith apples
170g/6oz blueberries
170g/6oz strawberries
250ml/8fl oz cranberry juice cocktail
50g/scant 2oz caster sugar
2 tablespoons fresh lemon juice

CRISPY APPLE CAKE CROUTONS

115g/4oz plus 1 teaspoon (5g) unsalted butter
210g/7½oz plus 1 teaspoon plain flour
½ teaspoon fresh lemon juice
1 Granny Smith apple
¾ teaspoon baking powder
½ teaspoon bicarbonate of soda
½ teaspoon ground cinnamon
¼ teaspoon salt
200g/7oz caster sugar
2 size-3 eggs
½ teaspoon pure vanilla essence

JONNY'S CIDER ICE CREAM

Jonny's Cider Ice Cream (see page 79)

EQUIPMENT

Measuring jug, measuring spoons, 3 litre/5 pint saucepan, kitchen spoon, paring knife, corer, cutting board, medium sieve, 3 litre/5 pint stainless steel bowl, cling film, 5 litre/8 pint stainless steel bowl, food processor with metal blade, 1 litre/2 pint non-reactive container, 23 × 12.5 × 7.5cm/9 × 5 × 3in loaf tin, fine sieve, greaseproof paper, electric mixer with flat beater, rubber spatula, non-stick baking sheet, wooden cocktail stick, serrated slicer, slotted spoon, ice cream scoop

POACH THE APPLES

Heat the cranberry juice cocktail, sugar, port, cinnamon sticks and cloves in a 3 litre/5 pint saucepan over moderately high heat. When hot, stir to dissolve the sugar. Bring to the boil, then adjust the heat and allow to simmer for 15 minutes.

While the cranberry juice mixture is simmering, peel, core and halve the Granny Smith apples. Place the peeled apple halves in the simmering liquid. Adjust the heat as necessary to allow the apple halves to poach gently for 30 minutes, turning them after 15 minutes (a spicy potpourri aroma will fill your kitchen during the simmering of the apples). Remove from the heat and allow the apples to steep in the poaching liquid for 1 hour at room temperature. Transfer the apples to a 3 litre/5 pint stainless steel bowl. Strain the poaching liquid over the apples (discard the cinnamon sticks and whole cloves). Cover the top with cling film and refrigerate for at least 3 hours before serving.

PREPARE THE FRUIT SOUP

Peel, core and quarter the Granny Smith apples and chop into 5mm/¼in pieces. Heat the chopped apples, blueberries, strawberries, cranberry juice cocktail, sugar and lemon juice in a 3 litre/5 pint saucepan over moderately high heat. When hot, stir to dissolve the sugar.

Bring the fruit and juice mixture to the boil, then adjust the heat and allow to simmer for 20 to 22 minutes or until the liquid is slightly thickened. Remove from the heat and cool in an iced-water bath to a temperature of 5 to 7°C/40 to 45°F. Place the cooled mixture in the bowl of a food processor fitted with a metal blade. Process until smooth and frothy, about 2 minutes (this should yield about 750ml/1¼ pints). Transfer the fruit soup to a non-reactive container, cover with cling film and refrigerate until ready to serve.

PREPARE THE CRISPY APPLE CAKE CROUTONS

Preheat the oven to 180°C/350°F/Gas 4.

Lightly coat the inside of a 23 × 12.5 × 7.5cm/9 × 5 × 3in loaf tin with 1 teaspoon butter. Flour the pan with 1 teaspoon flour and shake out the excess. Set aside.

In a stainless steel bowl, acidulate 250ml/8fl oz of water with the lemon juice. Peel, core and quarter the Granny Smith apple and chop into 5mm/¼in pieces. Immediately place in the acidulated water. Set aside.

Combine together in a sieve the remaining 210g/7½oz flour, the baking powder, bicarbonate of soda, cinnamon and salt. Sift on to greaseproof paper and set aside.

Place the remaining 115g/4oz butter and the sugar in the bowl of an electric mixer fitted with a flat beater. Mix on medium for 3 minutes. Scrape down the sides of the bowl. Mix on high for an additional 2 minutes. Scrape down the sides of the bowl. Add the eggs, one at a time, beating on high for 30 seconds and scraping down the bowl after each addition. Add the vanilla essence and beat on high for 30 seconds. Drain and rinse the chopped apples. Add the chopped apples and beat on medium for 30 seconds. Add the sifted dry ingredients and mix on low for 30 seconds. Remove the bowl from the mixer and use a rubber spatula to finish mixing until smooth and thoroughly combined.

Immediately pour the apple cake mixture into the prepared loaf tin. Place the loaf tin on a baking sheet on the centre shelf of the preheated oven and bake for 40 to 42 minutes or until a wooden cocktail stick inserted in the centre of the cake comes out clean. Remove the cake from the oven. Allow the cake to cool in the tin for 30 minutes. Remove from the tin and allow to cool to room temperature before slicing.

TO SERVE

Cut the cake into 2.5cm/1in slices. Trim the crust from the cake slices. Cut the slices into 2.5cm/1in cubes. Toast the cake cubes on a non-stick baking sheet in a preheated 180°C/350°F/Gas 4 oven for 15 to 18 minutes until golden brown. Keep the croutons warm while assembling the dessert.

Portion 125ml/4fl oz chilled fruit soup into each of six 23 or 25cm/9 or10in soup plates.

Remove the poached apples from the refrigerator. Use a slotted spoon to remove the apples from the poaching liquid (discard the liquid). Cut each half into a quarter. Make a fan out of each quarter: cut 5mm/¼ in slices from end to end, then gently press down on the slices to produce a fan effect.

Place a fan of sliced apples to the left and right of the centre of the plate, then place a large scoop of Jonny's Cider Ice Cream into the centre, between the apples. Sprinkle a few croutons on to each portion. Serve immediately.

THE CHEF'S TOUCH
My first encounter with the diverting concept of soup as dessert occurred a few years ago at Cakebread Cellars in Napa Valley, California. Invited by vintner Jack Cakebread and his wife Dolores, I joined four other chefs in a wine country culinary exposition called An American Harvest Workshop. We spent our days gathering the best foods of Napa and Sonoma county farms, returning in the evening to the winery's kitchen to prepare dinner for 60 to 80 people. On one night, noted chef Guenter Seeger, of the Ritz-Carlton Buckhead in Atlanta, Georgia, intrigued the diners with a grape soup with cabernet and cognac parfait. It was an extraordinary dessert. Later, I encouraged our pastry chef to develop a dessert soup for one of the Trellis' preview dinners.

This particular recipe for Chilled Fruit Soup with Poached Apples and Crispy Croutons was developed specifically for this book by my assistant Jon Pierre Peavey. Jon Pierre has, I believe, brought together an amalgam of tastes and textures that play off each other like the players in a good string quartet do.

The poached apples can be prepared several days in advance of serving the Chilled Fruit Soup. Keep the apples, covered by the strained poaching liquid, refrigerated in a non-reactive container.

The Chilled Fruit Soup is best served within forty-eight hours of preparation.

Although the apple cake can be baked several hours (even a day) ahead, it is best to wait until just a few minutes before serving the dessert to cut the apple cake and bake the croutons. To make life simpler, the cake can be baked and allowed to cool then covered with cling film and refrigerated until ready to serve the dessert. At that time, the croutons can be cut and toasted as described in the recipe.

A rather subjective beverage choice to accompany the Chilled Fruit Soup would be a 1984 Cakebread Cellars Rutherford Reserve. (Good luck finding this wine. You may need to visit Jack at Cakebread—he may still have a bottle or two on hand.) A late harvest zinfandel would also do nicely.

MY CHERRY CLAFOUTI

SERVES 8

INGREDIENTS

CITRUS SHORTBREAD CRUST

45g/1½oz unsalted butter, melted
12 Citrus Shortbread Biscuits (see page 133),
    broken into quarters

MY CHERRY FILLING

140g/5oz dried cherries
4 tablespoons cherry brandy
250ml/8fl oz whipping cream
100g/3½oz caster sugar
3 size-3 eggs

MY, MY CHERRY TOPPING

70g/2½oz dried cherries, chopped
250ml/8fl oz whipping cream

EQUIPMENT

Measuring jug, measuring spoons, small non-stick
pan, chef's knife, cutting board, pastry brush,
24 × 2cm/9½ × ¾in round loose-based tart tin,
food processor with metal blade, 3 litre/5 pint
stainless steel bowl, small stainless steel bowl, small
saucepan, cling film, 3 litre/5 pint saucepan, whisk,
medium sieve, rubber spatula, baking sheet, electric
mixer with balloon whisk, serrated slicer

ASSEMBLE THE CITRUS
SHORTBREAD CRUST

Lightly coat the inside of a 24 × 2cm/9½ × ¾in
loose-based tart tin with 15g/½oz melted butter.
Set aside.

In a food processor fitted with a metal blade,
chop the shortbread biscuits in two batches until
they are crumbs, about 20 to 25 seconds per batch.

Transfer the crumbs to a 3 litre/5 pint stainless steel
bowl. Combine the biscuit crumbs with the
remaining 30g/1oz melted butter. Mix by hand
until the crumbs bind together. Press the crumbs
around the buttered side of the tart tin, then on to
the buttered bottom. Place the tin in the freezer
until needed.

PREPARE MY CHERRY
FILLING

Preheat the oven to 170°C/325°F/Gas 3.

Place the dried cherries in a small stainless steel
bowl. Heat the cherry brandy in a small saucepan
over moderately high heat. When hot, immediately pour over the dried cherries. Cover with
cling film and allow to stand at room temperature
until needed.

Heat the cream and half of the sugar in a
3 litre/5 pint saucepan over moderate heat. When
hot, stir to dissolve the sugar. Bring to the boil.

While the cream is heating to the boil, whisk the
eggs and remaining sugar in a 3 litre/5 pint stainless
steel bowl (to prevent lumps, continue to whisk the
eggs until the cream boils). As soon as the cream
mixture begins to boil, pour it into the egg and
sugar mixture and stir to combine. Set aside for a
few moments.

Thoroughly drain the brandy-steeped cherries
(save this brandy for the cherry topping). Sprinkle
the cherries over the bottom of the shortbread crust.
Pour the cream and egg mixture over the cherries in
the tart tin and use a rubber spatula to spread the
cherries out evenly. Place the tin on a baking sheet
on the centre shelf of the preheated oven and bake
for 30 minutes or until the filling has set. Remove
the clafouti from the oven and allow to cool at
room temperature for 30 minutes. Loosely cover
the cooled clafouti with cling film and refrigerate
for 2 hours before serving.

PREPARE MY, MY CHERRY
TOPPING

In a small bowl, toss the chopped dried cherries
with the reserved cherry brandy. Set aside.

Place the cream in the well-chilled bowl of an
electric mixer fitted with a well-chilled balloon
whisk. Whip on high until stiff, about 1 minute.
Remove the bowl from the mixer and use a rubber
spatula to fold in the brandy-marinated chopped
cherries. Refrigerate the topping until ready to cut
and serve the clafouti.

TO SERVE

Heat the blade of the serrated slicer under hot running water and wipe the blade dry before cutting
each slice. Serve with a dollop or two—or three—
of My, My Cherry Topping.

THE CHEF'S TOUCH

*This is not your traditional clafouti. I must
admit that for some time I thought a clafouti
less than worthy, even if it is a classic French
dessert. Invigorating what I considered a
wimpy dessert with a funny name involved
little more, however, than adding brandy and
a surfeit of whipped cream.*

*The dried cherries for the filling can be
steeped in other brandies; even grappa (why
not be iconoclastic?) would work.*

*The cherry topping can be prepared
using a hand-held electric mixer, or by hand
using a wire whisk (preparation time may
increase slightly).*

*After assembly, My Cherry Clafouti can be
held in the refrigerator for twenty-four hours.*

*I would feel very content if I were offered
a shot of cherry brandy to accompany My
Cherry Clafouti.*

CHOCOLATE DRENCHED FRUIT

SERVES 12

INGREDIENTS

1.12 kg/2½lb bittersweet chocolate, cut into
15g/½oz pieces
450g/1lb red seedless grapes, stalks removed,
washed and dried
340g/12oz dried pineapple slices
340g/12oz dried peach halves
340g/12oz dried pear halves
675g/1½lb strawberries with stalks, lightly rinsed
and dried

EQUIPMENT

Chef's knife, paper towels, double boiler, heat-
resistant cling film, rubber spatula or whisk,
instant-read thermometer, 3 litre/5 pint stainless
steel bowl, fork, 2 baking sheets, baking parchment,
large circular serving platter

COMMENCE THE DELUGE OF CHOCOLATE

Heat 2.5cm/1in of water in the bottom half of a
double boiler over moderate heat. Place 450g/1lb
bittersweet chocolate in the top half of the double
boiler. Tightly cover the top with heat-resistant
cling film. Allow to heat for 12 minutes. Remove
from the heat and allow to stand for 5 minutes
before removing the cling film. Use a rubber spatula or whisk to stir the chocolate until smooth, and
continue to stir until the temperature of the chocolate is reduced to 32°C/90°F.

Line two baking sheets with baking parchment.
Place the grapes in a stainless steel bowl. Pour the
melted chocolate over the grapes. Use a fork to
transfer the chocolate-drenched grapes, one at a
time, on to the parchment-lined baking sheets.
Refrigerate the chocolate-drenched grapes for 10 to
15 minutes or until the chocolate has hardened.
Transfer the chocolate-covered grapes to the centre
of a large serving platter and refrigerate.

Heat 2.5cm/1in of water in the bottom half of a
double boiler over moderate heat. Place 450g/1lb
bittersweet chocolate in the top half of the double
boiler. Tightly cover the top with heat-resistant
cling film. Allow to heat for 12 minutes. Remove
from the heat and allow to stand for 5 minutes
before removing the cling film. Use a rubber spatula or whisk to stir the chocolate until smooth, and
continue to stir until the temperature of the chocolate is reduced to 32°C/90°F.

One at a time, dip 2 to 2.5cm/¾ to 1in of each
dried fruit into the melted chocolate. Allow excess
chocolate to drip back into the top half of the double boiler before placing the drenched fruit on to
parchment-lined baking sheets. Refrigerate the
chocolate-drenched fruit for 10 to 15 minutes or
until the chocolate has hardened. Transfer the
chocolate-covered fruit to the large serving platter,
arranging the fruit near the outside edge of the platter, and return to the refrigerator.

Heat 2.5cm/1in of water in the bottom half of a
double boiler over moderate heat. Place the remaining 225g/8oz bittersweet chocolate in the top half of
the double boiler. Tightly cover the top with heat-
resistant cling film. Allow to heat for 8 minutes.
Remove from the heat and allow to stand for 5 minutes before removing the cling film. Use a rubber
spatula or whisk to stir the chocolate until smooth,
and continue to stir until the temperature of the
chocolate is reduced to 32°C/90°F.

Holding the strawberries by the stalk, dip 2 to
2.5cm/¾ to 1in of each berry, one at a time, into
the melted chocolate. Allow excess chocolate to
drip back into the rest before placing the drenched
strawberries on to parchment-lined baking sheets.
Refrigerate the chocolate-drenched berries for 10
to 15 minutes or until the chocolate has hardened.
Transfer the chocolate-covered berries to the serving platter, placing them in between the grapes and
the dried fruit, and return to the refrigerator.

Keep the drenched fruit refrigerated until 10 to
15 minutes before serving.

THE CHEF'S TOUCH

*I suggest that you consider serving the
drenched fruit with a variety of dessert
sauces as well as fruit purées. The fruit and
sauces can be offered family-style, or you
may wish to arrange artful presentations of
drenched fruit on individual plates that
have been flooded with a sauce or purée of
your choice.*

*If the chocolate begins to stiffen during
the drenching, place the top half of the double boiler on a warm heating pad or in a pan
of hot tap water. Stir the chocolate for a few
minutes until the viscosity is correct, and
continue to drench the fruit.*

*White chocolate can also be melted and
used for drenching fruit. Depending on the
quality, it may melt a bit faster than dark
chocolate. I have found that the higher the
cocoa butter content, the faster the chocolate will melt; as top-quality white chocolate has a high percentage of cocoa butter,
it will melt rather quickly. When melting
450g/1lb of white chocolate, allow to heat
for 9 minutes (rather than the 12 minutes
specified for the bittersweet chocolate).
Remove from the heat and immediately stir
until smooth, then continue to stir until the
temperature of the chocolate is reduced to
32 to 33°C/90 to 92°F.*

*You may wish to double dip the fruit;
that is, to dip in white chocolate first, refrigerate until hard, and then completely or
partially dip the fruit in dark chocolate,
depending on the effect desired.*

*The dried fruit will keep for several days
in a sealed container in the refrigerator. The
strawberries and grapes should be enjoyed
within twenty-four hours of drenching.*

*If a chocolate bacchanal is not for you, then
you probably should skip this recipe. If you are
still with me, however, I suggest offering a
selection of port to complete the indulgence.*

LEMON AND FRESH BERRY 'SHORTCAKE'

WITH ROSE'S LEMON LUSCIOUS ICE CREAM

SERVES 8

INGREDIENTS

LEMON POPPY SEED 'SHORTCAKE'

115g/4oz plus 1 teaspoon (5g) unsalted butter, softened

250g/9oz plus 1 teaspoon plain flour

½ teaspoon baking powder

½ teaspoon bicarbonate of soda

¼ teaspoon salt

250g/9oz caster sugar

3 size-3 eggs

2 teaspoons poppy seeds

125ml/4fl oz buttermilk

2 tablespoons fresh lemon juice

2 teaspoons finely chopped lemon zest

½ teaspoon pure lemon essence

STRAWBERRY COULIS

340g/12oz fresh strawberries

50g/scant 2oz caster sugar

1 teaspoon fresh lemon juice

WHIPPED CREAM

375ml/12fl oz whipping cream

ROSE'S LEMON LUSCIOUS ICE CREAM

Rose's Lemon Luscious Ice Cream (see page 72)

FRESH BERRY GARNISH

340g/12oz fresh strawberries, quartered

170g/6oz fresh blackberries

170g/6oz fresh red raspberries

3 teaspoons poppy seeds

EQUIPMENT

Measuring jug, measuring spoons, vegetable peeler, chef's knife, cutting board, pastry brush, 23 × 12.5 × 7.5cm/9 × 5 × 3in loaf tin, sieve, greaseproof paper, electric mixer with flat beater and balloon whisk, rubber spatula, wooden cocktail stick, food processor with metal blade, 2 litre/3¼ pint stainless steel bowl, serrated slicer, ice cream scoop

PREPARE THE LEMON POPPY SEED 'SHORTCAKE'

Preheat the oven to 170°C/325°F/Gas 3.

Lightly coat the inside of a 23 × 12.5 × 7.5cm/9 × 5 × 3in loaf tin with 1 teaspoon butter. Flour the tin with 1 teaspoon flour and shake out the excess. Set aside.

Combine together in a sieve the remaining 250g/9oz plain flour, the baking powder, bicarbonate of soda and salt. Sift on to greaseproof paper and set aside.

Place the remaining 115g/4oz butter and the sugar in the bowl of an electric mixer fitted with a flat beater. Mix on low for 2 minutes. Scrape down the sides of the bowl. Mix on low for an additional 2 minutes (this mixing on low is necessary to dissolve the sugar). Scrape down the sides of the bowl. Increase the speed to medium and beat for 3 minutes. Scrape down the sides of the bowl. Increase mixer speed to high and beat for 3 minutes, then scrape down the bowl.

Add the eggs, one at a time, beating on medium for 2 minutes and scraping down the sides of the bowl after each addition. Now beat on medium for an additional 8 minutes. Scrape down the sides of the bowl. Add the poppy seeds. Operate the mixer on low while gradually adding the sifted dry ingredients. Once all of the dry ingredients have been incorporated, about 45 seconds, turn off the mixer. Add the buttermilk, then mix on medium for 20 seconds. Add the lemon juice, lemon zest and lemon essence and mix on medium for 20 seconds. Remove the bowl from the mixer and use a rubber spatula to finish mixing this delightfully aromatic mixture, until smooth and thoroughly combined.

Immediately pour the 'shortcake' mixture into the prepared loaf tin. Place the loaf tin on a baking sheet on the centre shelf of the preheated oven and bake for about 1 hour or until a wooden cocktail stick inserted in the centre of the 'shortcake' comes out clean. Remove the 'shortcake' from the oven. Allow the 'shortcake' to cool in the tin for 20 minutes. Remove from the tin and allow to cool to room temperature.

MAKE THE STRAWBERRY COULIS

In the bowl of a food processor fitted with a metal blade, process the stemmed strawberries with the sugar and lemon juice until smooth, about 20 seconds (this should yield about 375ml/12fl oz strawberry coulis). Transfer the coulis to a stainless steel bowl, cover with cling film and refrigerate until needed.

MAKE THE WHIPPED CREAM

Place the whipping cream in the well-chilled bowl of an electric mixer fitted with a well-chilled balloon whisk. Whip on high until stiff peaks form, about 1 minute. Cover with cling film and refrigerate until needed.

TO SERVE

Use a serrated slicer to cut the 'shortcake' into 16 slices, each 1cm/½in thick.

Drizzle 1 tablespoon of strawberry coulis on to each dessert plate. Place a slice of 'shortcake' on the sauce in the centre of each plate. Top each slice of 'shortcake' with 3 small scoops of Rose's Lemon Luscious Ice Cream.

Now top the ice cream with a second slice of 'shortcake'. Equally divide the berries on to each plate around the 'shortcake'. Drizzle 2 tablespoons of strawberry coulis over the cake and berries on each plate. Top each 'shortcake' with a heaping tablespoon of whipped cream and for the final touch, sprinkle ½ teaspoon of poppy seeds over each portion of whipped cream. Serve immediately.

THE CHEF'S TOUCH

If you have been searching for a twist on the standard shortcake recipe, seek no more. This confluence of 'shortcake', berries and Rose's Lemon Luscious Ice Cream is a wonderful variation on a traditional American theme.

The 'shortcake' can be prepared two to three days before serving the dessert. Wrap the thoroughly cooled cake in cling film and refrigerate until needed. For enhanced flavour, consider toasting the sliced 'shortcake' before serving.

Although the suggested berries work well with the cake and ice cream, use whatever is available. Also, if you like more berries per serving, don't be bashful—serve more.

My mother loves shortcake, and often served it when we were growing up in Woonsocket, Rhode Island. Mom would probably suggest a sparkling cold glass of milk to go along with this dessert. Now that I have lived in Virginia for more than 25 years, my suggestion would be a tall glass of iced tea.

WARM ORANGE SEGMENTS AND SLICED STRAWBERRIES

WITH CINNAMON HONEY SCONES AND VANILLA CUSTARD

SERVES 8

INGREDIENTS

CINNAMON HONEY SCONES

275ml/9fl oz buttermilk

85g/3oz clear honey

565g/1¼lb plain flour

1½ tablespoons baking powder

1½ tablespoons caster sugar

1 teaspoon salt

¾ teaspoon ground cinnamon

115g/4oz chilled unsalted butter, cut into
    8 equal pieces

VANILLA CUSTARD

375ml/12fl oz whipping cream

2 size-3 eggs

2 tablespoons caster sugar

1 teaspoon pure vanilla essence

WARM ORANGES AND STRAWBERRIES

30g/1oz unsalted butter

2 tablespoons caster sugar

8 navel oranges, peeled and cut into segments

340g/12oz strawberries, quartered

EQUIPMENT

Measuring jug, measuring spoons, chef's knife, paring knife, cutting board, whisk, small bowl, electric mixer with flat beater, rolling pin, 6cm/2½in pastry cutter, 2 non-stick baking sheets, 2 litre/3 pint saucepan, 3 litre/5 pint stainless steel bowl, instant-read thermometer, 5 litre/8 pint stainless steel bowl, large non-stick sauté pan, rubber spatula, aluminium foil

MAKE THE CINNAMON HONEY SCONES

Preheat the oven to 170°C/325°F/Gas 3.

Whisk the buttermilk and honey together in a small bowl. Set aside for a few minutes.

Put 530g/1lb 3oz flour, the baking powder, sugar, salt and cinnamon into the bowl of an electric mixer fitted with a flat beater. Mix on low for 30 seconds to combine the ingredients. Add the chilled butter pieces and mix on low for 2 minutes or until the butter is 'rubbed' into the flour and the mixture develops a mealy texture. Add the buttermilk and honey mixture and mix on low for 10 seconds. Increase the mixer speed to medium and mix until the dough comes together, about 10 seconds (for tender scones, avoid overmixing). Transfer the dough from the mixing bowl to a clean, dry, lightly floured work surface.

Roll out the dough (using the extra 35g/1oz flour as necessary to prevent sticking) to a thickness of 2cm/¾in. Cut the dough into 8 rounds using a 6cm/2½in pastry cutter (if things get a little sticky, dip the cutter in flour before making each cut). Form the remaining dough into a ball. Roll out the dough to a thickness of 2cm/¾in. Cut the dough into 4 rounds using the pastry cutter. Once again, form the remaining dough into a ball. Roll out the dough to a thickness of 2cm/¾in. Cut the dough into 4 rounds. Divide the 16 scones between 2 non-stick baking sheets, about 5cm/2in apart. Bake the scones on the centre shelf of the preheated oven for 13 to 14 minutes or until lightly browned (rotate the baking sheets from one side of the oven to the other about halfway through the baking

time). Remove the scones from the oven. The scones can be served immediately, or allowed to cool and stored for up to three days in a sealed plastic bag. Warm the scones before serving.

PREPARE THE VANILLA CUSTARD

Heat the whipping cream in a 2 litre/3 pint saucepan over moderately high heat. Bring to the boil. While the cream is heating, whisk the eggs and sugar in a 3 litre/5 pint stainless steel bowl for 2 minutes. Pour the boiling cream into this mixture and stir gently to combine. Return the mixture to the saucepan and heat over moderately high heat, stirring constantly. Bring to a temperature of 82°C/180°F, about 1½ minutes.

Remove from the heat and cool in an iced-water bath to a temperature of 5°C/40°F, about 10 minutes. When cold, stir in the vanilla essence (this should yield about 500ml/16fl oz sauce). Transfer to a plastic container. Close tightly and refrigerate until ready to use.

PREPARE THE WARM ORANGES AND STRAWBERRIES

Heat the butter and sugar in a large non-stick sauté pan over moderately high heat, constantly stirring to dissolve the sugar. When the mixture begins to bubble, add the oranges and strawberries and heat for about 2 minutes or until warmed through (use a rubber spatula to stir the fruit gently while heating). Remove the pan from the heat. Cover the pan with foil to keep the fruit warm for a few minutes.

TO SERVE

Split all the scones in half and keep warm. Portion 3 tablespoons of vanilla custard on each dessert plate. Place 2 warm scone halves (the bottom halves) in the centre of each dessert plate. Portion 2 tablespoons of warm oranges and strawberries on to each. Then top with the remaining scone halves. Finish by drizzling ½ tablespoon of vanilla custard on to the top of each scone. Serve immediately.

THE CHEF'S TOUCH

This dessert is easy to take for granted because it is so simple to prepare, and the flavours and textures are so familiar that you may think you have enjoyed it before. This is comfort food at its best.

My assistant Jon Pierre Peavey made a lot of scones as a teenager in Wisconsin. He urged me to emphasise how important it is to handle the dough as little as possible in order to achieve tender scones. So, once again let me say, do not overmix the dough.

The oranges can be segmented several hours or even the day before serving the dessert (be sure to store in a covered non-reactive container in the refrigerator until needed). Drain the orange segments in a colander before warming them.

For a special final touch, shake some ground cinnamon over each scone.

Pressed apple juice, hot or cold, works very nicely with this dessert, especially if you are inclined to lace it with calvados or apple brandy.

OVEN-ROASTED PEACHES WITH VERY BERRY YOGURT

SERVES 8

INGREDIENTS

VERY BERRY YOGURT

340g/12oz blueberries

340g/12oz strawberries

50g/scant 2oz caster sugar

250g/9oz red raspberries

750ml/1¼ pints plain low-fat yogurt

BRANDIED PEACH COULIS

3 medium ripe peaches, unpeeled, stoned and cut
into 8 slices each

115g/4oz soft light brown sugar

250ml/8fl oz water

4 tablespoons brandy

OVEN-ROASTED PEACHES

140g/5oz unsalted butter (30g/1oz melted)

100g/3½oz caster sugar

140g/5oz soft light brown sugar

2 size-3 eggs

1 teaspoon finely chopped orange zest

½ teaspoon pure vanilla essence

140g/5oz plain flour

¾ teaspoon bicarbonate of soda

4 tablespoons buttermilk

4 medium ripe peaches, halved and stoned

EQUIPMENT

Measuring jug, measuring spoons, stainless steel
chef's knife, cutting board, small non-stick pan,
vegetable peeler, 3 litre/5 pint saucepan, rubber
spatula, food processor with metal blade, medium
sieve, two 3 litre/5 pint stainless steel bowls, 5 litre/
8 pint stainless steel bowl, cling film, 2 litre/3 pint
plastic container with lid, pastry brush, 8 individual
soufflé dishes, each 250ml/8fl oz capacity, electric
mixer with flat beater, 2 baking sheets, palette knife

MAKE THE VERY BERRY YOGURT

Heat the blueberries, strawberries and sugar in a
3 litre/5 pint saucepan over moderate heat. As the
mixture gets hot, the sugar will dissolve and the
berries will liquefy and begin to boil (after about
10 minutes). Allow the mixture to boil, stirring
occasionally, for a further 20 minutes or until it
becomes very thick. Wonderful aromas will perme-
ate your kitchen during this time. Remove the mixture from the heat and cool in an iced-water bath to
a temperature of 5 to 7°C/40 to 45°F, about 20
minutes. Transfer the cold berry mixture to the
bowl of a food processor fitted with a metal blade.
Process until smooth, about 30 seconds (don't
overprocess or the mixture will get foamy). Pass
the berry purée through a sieve into a 3 litre/5
pint stainless steel bowl (this should yield about
300ml/½ pint of intensely coloured berry purée).
Add the whole red raspberries and the yogurt and
stir to combine. Cover the bowl with cling film and
refrigerate until needed.

PREPARE THE BRANDIED PEACH COULIS

Heat the stoned and sliced peaches, light brown
sugar and water in a 3 litre/5 pint saucepan over
moderately high heat. When hot, stir to dissolve the
sugar. Bring to the boil, then adjust the heat and
allow the mixture to simmer for about 20 minutes
or until thick. Remove from the heat. Cool in an
iced-water bath to a temperature of 5 to 7°C/40 to
45°F, about 20 minutes. Transfer the cold peach
mixture to the bowl of a food processor fitted with
a metal blade. Add the brandy and process the mixture until smooth, about 1 minute (this should
yield about 440ml/14fl oz coulis). Transfer the
Brandied Peach Coulis to a plastic container. Close
tightly and refrigerate until needed.

ROAST THE PEACHES

Preheat the oven to 180°C/350°F/Gas 4.

Lightly coat the inside of each soufflé dish with
melted butter.

Place the remaining 115g/4oz butter, the caster
sugar and 30g/1oz light brown sugar in the bowl of
an electric mixer fitted with a flat beater. Beat on
medium for 3 minutes. Scrape down the sides of the
bowl. Once again beat on medium for 3 minutes,
then scrape down the sides of the bowl. Add 1 egg
and beat on high for 30 seconds, then scrape down
the sides of the bowl. Add the remaining egg and
beat on high for 30 seconds, then scrape down the
sides of the bowl. Add the finely chopped orange
zest and the vanilla essence and beat on high for 30
seconds. Add the flour and bicarbonate of soda and
mix on low for 15 seconds. Add the buttermilk and
continue to mix on low for an additional 30 seconds. Remove the bowl from the mixer and use a
rubber spatula to finish mixing until smooth and
thoroughly combined.

Evenly divide the mixture among the prepared
soufflé dishes (about 2 heaping tablespoons per
dish). Place a peach half, cut side up, on the mixture in each dish, pushing down gently until the
peach is even with the mixture, yet still exposed.
Sprinkle the remaining 110g/4oz light brown sugar
over the peach halves. Place 4 soufflé dishes on
each of 2 baking sheets and bake on the centre
shelf of the preheated oven for 24 to 26 minutes or
until golden brown and bubbly on top. Remove
from the oven and allow to cool for 8 to 10 minutes before removing the oven-roasted peaches
from the soufflé dishes.

TO SERVE

Portion 125ml/4fl oz of Very Berry Yogurt into each of eight 23 or 25cm/9 or 10in soup plates. Drizzle 2 tablespoons of Brandied Peach Coulis over the Very Berry Yogurt on each plate. Using a palette knife, remove the Oven-Roasted Peaches (along with the baked batter that surrounds each peach), one at a time, from the soufflé dishes and set each in the centre of the yogurt on each plate. Serve immediately.

THE CHEF'S TOUCH

This recipe has made a convert out of me, since I have always scorned yogurt. Something about the word itself made it a target of my humour for years. But since my friend Judith Choate put together a book of yogurt recipes (Cooking with Yogurt), I have developed more respect for the tangy and healthful substance. It receives homage here because this Very Berry Yogurt is flat-out delicious.

Preparation of this dessert can be spread out over a couple of days. Both the Very Berry Yogurt and the Brandied Peach Coulis can be prepared a day or two in advance.

Once removed from the oven, the Oven-Roasted Peaches need to cool in the soufflé dishes for 8 to 10 minutes before handling—otherwise the baked batter that surrounds the peaches will fall apart when removed from the soufflé dishes. The peaches will stay warm and delicious in the soufflé dishes for up to 30 minutes after being removed from the oven. This dessert is best served warm, but it is also quite delicious at room temperature.

Although peaches may be available almost year round now, their accessibility does not always translate into deliciousness. They are best in the warm months of the year when picked as ripe as possible, from as close to your home as possible. Finally, select ripe peaches with smooth and blemish-free skins.

My wife, Connie, and I recently served this dessert at our home for a small dinner party. It was Connie's idea to accompany the dessert with Bellinis—Italian Spumante infused with peach nectar—a very agreeable selection indeed.

CRANBERRY AND TOASTED WALNUT CROSTATA

SERVES 8

INGREDIENTS

WALNUT PASTRY DOUGH

210g/7½oz plain flour

1 tablespoon plus 1 teaspoon caster sugar

½ teaspoon salt

55g/2oz toasted walnuts, finely chopped

55g/2oz chilled unsalted butter, cut into
    4 equal pieces

2 size-3 egg yolks

3 tablespoons iced water

CRANBERRY WALNUT FILLING

250ml/8fl oz whipping cream

50g/scant 2oz caster sugar

140g/5oz dried unsweetened cranberries

170g/6oz toasted walnuts

¼ teaspoon ground cinnamon

EQUIPMENT

Measuring jug, measuring spoons, food processor
with metal blade, electric mixer with flat beater,
small bowl, whisk, heat-resistant cling film,
3 litre/5 pint saucepan, rubber spatula, 23cm/9in
pie tin, baking parchment, 25 × 38cm/10 × 15in
baking tray, pastry brush, serrated knife

MAKE THE WALNUT PASTRY DOUGH

Place 175g/6½oz flour, 1 teaspoon sugar and the salt
in the bowl of an electric mixer fitted with a flat
beater. Mix on low for 15 seconds to combine the
ingredients. Add all but 2 tablespoons of the chopped
walnuts (the reserved walnuts will be sprinkled on
the pastry just prior to baking) and combine on low
for 15 seconds. Add the chilled butter and mix on
low for 1½ to 2 minutes or until the mixture develops a coarse texture. In a small bowl, whisk together
1 egg yolk with the iced water. Add the egg-and-
water mixture to the mixing bowl and mix on
low for 1 minute or until a loose dough is formed.
Remove the dough from the mixer and form it into
a smooth round ball. Wrap in cling film and refrigerate for at least 2 hours. The filling should be prepared as soon as the dough is refrigerated.

PREPARE THE CRANBERRY WALNUT FILLING

Heat the whipping cream and sugar in a 3 litre/
5 pint saucepan over moderate heat. When hot, stir
to dissolve the sugar. Bring to the boil, then adjust
the heat and allow to simmer for 6 minutes or until
slightly thickened. Remove from the heat and add

the cranberries, toasted walnuts and cinnamon; stir with a rubber spatula to combine thoroughly.

Line a 23cm/9in pie tin with heat-resistant cling film. Transfer the hot filling to the pie tin, spreading the mixture evenly to the edges. Refrigerate until ready to assemble the crostata.

ASSEMBLE AND BAKE THE CROSTATA

Preheat the oven to 190°C/375°F/Gas 5.

After the walnut dough has been refrigerated for 2 hours, transfer it to a clean, dry, lightly floured sheet of baking parchment. Roll out the dough (using the remaining 35g/1oz flour as necessary to prevent the dough from sticking) into a round about 35cm/14in in diameter and 3mm/⅛in thick. Place the rolled dough (leave it on the parchment) on a baking sheet. Invert the chilled cranberry and walnut mixture on to the centre of the rolled dough (discard the cling film). Fold the edges of the dough

towards the centre to enclose the cranberry and walnut mixture, leaving a 10cm/4in 'window' of fruit and nuts. Refrigerate for 10 minutes.

In a small bowl, whisk the remaining egg yolk. Brush the top of the crostata dough with the whisked yolk. Sprinkle the reserved finely chopped walnuts over the egg-washed dough, then sprinkle with the remaining tablespoon of sugar.

Place the baking sheet with the crostata on the centre shelf of the preheated oven and bake for 30 minutes or until golden brown. Remove the baked crostata from the oven and allow to stand at room temperature for 15 minutes before cutting and serving.

TO SERVE

Heat the blade of the knife under hot running water and wipe the blade dry before cutting each slice (as you would a pie or cake). Serve immediately while warm, or better yet, serve it with a scoop of Double Cappuccino Ice Cream (see page 77).

(see page 77)

STRAWBERRY RHUBARB VANILLA CUSTARD TART

SERVES 8

INGREDIENTS

TART PASTRY

175g/6oz plain flour

1 teaspoon caster sugar

½ teaspoon salt

115g/4oz chilled unsalted butter, cut into
   8 equal pieces

3 tablespoons iced water

ceramic baking beans

VANILLA CUSTARD CREAM

250ml/8fl oz creamy milk

125ml/4fl oz whipping or double cream

100g/3½oz caster sugar

2 size-3 eggs

5 tablespoons plain flour

15g/½oz unsalted butter, softened

1 teaspoon pure vanilla essence

RHUBARB FILLING

900g/2lb rhubarb, chopped into 1.5cm/½in pieces

100g/3½oz caster sugar

2 tablespoons fresh lemon juice

STRAWBERRY GLAZE AND TOPPING

900g/2lb strawberries

50g/scant 2oz caster sugar

EQUIPMENT

Measuring jug, measuring spoons, electric mixer with flat beater, cling film, rolling pin, 23 × 4cm/ 9 × 1½in loose-based round cake tin, paring knife, aluminium foil, baking sheet, 3 litre/5 pint saucepan, whisk, 3 litre/5 pint stainless steel bowl, rubber spatula, 5 litre/8 pint stainless steel bowl, instant-read thermometer, 1.5 litre/2½ pint saucepan, medium gauge sieve, small bowl, pastry brush, serrated slicer

MAKE THE TART PASTRY

Place 140g/5oz flour, the sugar and salt in the bowl of an electric mixer fitted with a flat beater. Mix on low for 15 seconds to combine the ingredients. Add the chilled butter and mix on low for 1½ minutes or until the butter is 'rubbed' into the flour and the mixture develops a very coarse texture. Add the iced water, 1 tablespoon at a time, mixing on low until the dough comes together, about 30 seconds. Remove the dough from the mixer and form it into a smooth round ball. Wrap in cling film and refrigerate for at least 2 hours.

Preheat the oven to 190°C/375°F/Gas 5.

After the dough has relaxed in the refrigerator for 2 hours, transfer it to a clean, dry, lightly floured work surface. Roll out the dough (using the remaining 35g/1oz flour as necessary to prevent the dough from sticking) into a round about 35cm/14in in diameter and 3mm/⅛in thick.

Line the cake tin with the dough, gently pressing the dough around the bottom and sides. Refrigerate for 5 to 10 minutes to firm the dough. Cut away the excess dough leaving a 2.5cm/1in border, which should be crimped around the top edge of the tin. Refrigerate for 15 minutes.

Line the dough with a piece of aluminium foil (use 2 pieces of foil if necessary); weight down the foil with ceramic baking beans. Place on a baking sheet and bake in the centre of the preheated oven for about 20 minutes or until the edges of the tart case are golden brown (rotate the pan 180° after 10 minutes). Remove the baked tart case from the oven; discard the foil and beans. Return the tart case to the oven and bake for an additional 2 minutes (so the bottom of the case can get some dry heat). Remove from the oven and allow to cool at room temperature while preparing the vanilla custard cream.

PREPARE THE VANILLA CUSTARD CREAM

Heat the milk and cream in a 3 litre/5 pint saucepan over moderate heat. Bring to the boil. While the milk mixture is heating, whisk the sugar and eggs in a stainless steel bowl for 3 minutes, then add the flour and whisk until smooth.

Pour the boiling milk mixture into the egg, sugar and flour mixture and stir to combine. Return to the saucepan and heat over moderate heat, stirring vigorously and constantly with a wire whisk, for 4 minutes or until the mixture thickens and the flour has cooked through. Remove the custard from the heat, add the butter and vanilla essence, and stir to combine.

Transfer the vanilla custard cream to the baked tart case and use a rubber spatula to spread the custard evenly to the edges. Refrigerate while preparing and cooling the rhubarb filling.

MAKE THE RHUBARB FILLING

Heat the sliced rhubarb with the sugar and lemon juice in a 3 litre/5 pint saucepan over moderate heat. Occasionally stir to dissolve the sugar while heating. Bring the mixture to the boil (because of the volume of rhubarb this will take about 8 to 9 minutes), then adjust the heat and allow to simmer for 40 minutes (stirring often) until the mixture is very thick, concentrated and 'rhubarby'. (The yield should be 500ml/16fl oz; any more means the cook became impatient and the mixture did not reduce in volume to the desired consistency.) Remove the filling from the heat and cool in an iced-water bath to a temperature of 5 to 7°C/40 to 45°F, about 15 to 20 minutes.

Remove the custard-filled tart case from the refrigerator. Spoon the rhubarb filling on to the custard and use a rubber spatula to spread evenly to the edges. Refrigerate the tart while preparing the strawberry glaze and topping.

PREPARE THE STRAWBERRY GLAZE

Heat one third of the strawberries and the sugar in a 1.5 litre/2½ pint saucepan over moderately high heat. Occasionally stir to dissolve the sugar while heating. Bring to the boil, then adjust the heat and allow to simmer for about 15 minutes or until the mixture is very thick. Remove from the heat and pass through a medium sieve into a small bowl, using a rubber spatula to press down on the seeds and pulp (discard the seeds and pulp). This should yield about 125ml/4fl oz strawberry glaze. Set aside for a few moments until needed.

COMPLETE THE FINISHING TOUCHES

Remove the tart from the refrigerator. Arrange the remaining whole strawberries, stalk side down, on the rhubarb filling in a ring along the outside edge of the tart. Continue to arrange rings of strawberries on the rhubarb filling until the filling is completely covered with whole berries.

Use a pastry brush to brush the strawberry glaze over the strawberries, covering the berries as well as any rhubarb filling that may be peeking through the sides of the berries. Refrigerate the tart for 1 hour before cutting and serving.

TO SERVE

Heat the blade of the slicer under hot running water and wipe the blade dry before cutting each slice. Serve immediately.

THE CHEF'S TOUCH

I thought about naming this dessert 'For Rhubarb Lovers Only', but I did not want to frighten away those souls with timid palates. After all, rhubarb's special flavour is remarkably piquant. Personally, I love how it awakens the palate. My only trepidation when eating this fruit, however, is that it is a member of the buckwheat family; having acquired late in life an allergy to buckwheat flour, I always eat my rhubarb tart one very cautious bite at a time.

Our Strawberry Rhubarb Vanilla Custard Tart has just the right balance of flavour even for those who are a bit shy when it comes to a tart pie.

Be certain to stir the rhubarb almost constantly while it is cooking as it will spatter quite a bit; the stirring helps lessen the spattering and will make cleaning your cooker a bit easier. You may also consider cooking the rhubarb filling in a larger saucepan or pot; this will also help keep the spattering down.

If you do not have any ceramic baking beans to hand, you can, of course, use uncooked rice or dried beans.

If the available strawberries are not the prettiest, or if the sizes of the berries are dramatically different, you may opt for slicing the berries and layering the sliced berries on top of the rhubarb filling in a starburst pattern.

Serve a very cold glass of mineral water with this strawberry rhubarb tart.

CHAPTER THREE

IRRESISTIBLE ICE CREAMS AND SORBETS

'Enjoy your ice cream while it's on your plate—that's my philosophy.'

—THORNTON WILDER

TRICK OR TREAT ICE CREAM

LATE HARVEST SORBET

HOLIDAY SUNDAE—ON MONDAY

ROSE'S LEMON LUSCIOUS ICE CREAM

SWEET DREAMS ICE CREAM SANDWICHES

LONG ISLAND ICED TEA SORBET

DOUBLE CAPPUCCINO ICE CREAM

JONNY'S CIDER ICE CREAM

BLACKBERRY CHOCOLATE PRALINE ICE CREAM

MAPLE SYRUP AND TOASTED WALNUT ICE CREAM

STRAWBERRY AND BANANA YIN YANG SORBET

ESPRESSO WITH A TWIST ICE CREAM

'WHAT A CHUNK OF CHOCOLATE' ICE CREAM TERRINE

TRICK OR TREAT ICE CREAM

YIELDS 3 LITRES/5 PINTS

INGREDIENTS

ORANGE CUSTARD ICE CREAM

750ml/1¼ pints orange juice

300g/10½oz caster sugar

4 tablespoons finely chopped orange zest

500ml/16fl oz whipping or double cream

250ml/8fl oz single or half cream

5 size-3 egg yolks

DARK CARAMEL SAUCE

250ml/8fl oz whipping cream

30g/1oz unsalted butter

100g/3½oz caster sugar

⅛ teaspoon fresh lemon juice

CHOCOLATE CREAM SAUCE

115g/4oz bittersweet chocolate, cut into
    15g/½oz pieces

125ml/4fl oz whipping cream

ADDED TREATS

170g/6oz plain chocolate chips

140g/5oz toasted unsalted peanuts

EQUIPMENT

Measuring jug, vegetable peeler, chef's knife, cutting board, measuring spoons, 3 litre/5 pint saucepan, whisk, two 3 litre/5 pint stainless steel bowls, 5 litre/8 pint stainless steel bowl, cling film, electric mixer with flat beater, rubber spatula, instant-read thermometer, ice cream maker, 1.5 litre/2½ pint saucepan, 4 litre/6½ pint plastic container with lid

PREPARE THE ORANGE CUSTARD ICE CREAM

Heat the orange juice, 200g/7oz sugar and the orange zest in a 3 litre/5 pint saucepan over moderately high heat. When hot, stir to dissolve the sugar. Bring to the boil. Allow to boil for 15 minutes (this will yield 560ml/scant 1 pint of slightly thickened syrup).

Cool the syrup in an iced-water bath to a temperature of 5 to 7°C/40 to 45°F, about 15 minutes. Cover with cling film and refrigerate until needed.

Heat the whipping cream and single cream in a 3 litre/5 pint saucepan over moderately high heat. Bring to the boil.

While the cream is heating, place the egg yolks and remaining 100g/3½oz sugar in the bowl of an electric mixer fitted with a flat beater. Beat on high for 2 to 2½ minutes. Scrape down the sides of the bowl, then beat on high until slightly thickened and lemon-coloured, 2½ to 3 minutes. (At this point, the cream should be boiling. If not, adjust the mixer speed to low and continue to mix until the cream boils. If the eggs are not mixed right up to the point the boiling cream is added, they will develop undesirable lumps.)

Pour the boiling cream into the beaten egg yolks and whisk to combine. Return to the saucepan and heat over moderately high heat, stirring constantly. Bring to a temperature of 85°C/185°F, about 1 minute. Remove from the heat and transfer to a 3 litre/5 pint stainless steel bowl. Cool in an iced-water bath to a temperature of 5 to 7°C/40 to 45°F, about 15 minutes.

When the mixture is cold, combine with the chilled orange syrup mixture, then freeze in an ice cream maker, following the manufacturer's instructions.

While the orange custard ice cream is freezing, prepare the sauces.

PREPARE THE DARK CARAMEL SAUCE

Heat the cream and butter in a 1.5 litre/2½ pint saucepan over low heat.

While the cream is heating, place the sugar and lemon juice in a 3 litre/5 pint saucepan. Stir with a whisk to combine (the sugar will resemble moist sand). Caramelise the sugar by heating for 4 minutes over moderately high heat, stirring constantly with a wire whisk to break up any lumps (the sugar will first turn clear as it liquefies, then light brown as it caramelises). Carefully (to avoid splattering) add the hot cream and butter, whisking briskly to combine. Remove from the heat and transfer the caramel sauce to a 3 litre/5 pint stainless steel bowl. Allow to cool to room temperature.

PREPARE THE CHOCOLATE CREAM SAUCE

Place the bittersweet chocolate in a 3 litre/5 pint stainless steel bowl. Heat the cream in a 1.5 litre/2½ pint saucepan over moderately high heat. Bring to the boil. Pour the boiling cream over the chocolate and allow to stand for 5 minutes. Stir with a whisk until smooth. Set aside until needed.

FINISH MAKING THE ICE CREAM

Transfer the semi-frozen orange custard ice cream to a plastic container. Immediately fold in the chocolate chips and peanuts. Add the caramel sauce. Using a large rubber spatula give the mixture two folds. Add the Chocolate Cream Sauce, and once again use a large rubber spatula to give the mixture 5 to 6 folds. Tightly cover the container and place it in the freezer for several hours before serving. Serve within 3 days.

Imagine combining the booty of the most puerile of feasts, Halloween, with a zippy orange-laced frozen custard and you'll conjure up the flavour of our Trick or Treat Ice Cream.

One medium orange should yield 3 tablespoons of zest, so you will need to zest 2 oranges to yield the required 4 tablespoons of finely chopped orange zest.

The egg yolks and sugar can be whisked using a hand-held electric mixer (mixing time may increase slightly) or by hand, using a wire whisk (mixing time may double). If either of these methods is used, be sure to continue whisking the egg yolks while waiting for the cream to come to the boil. If the eggs are not whisked right up to the point the boiling cream is added, they will develop undesirable lumps.

No evil will come to those who substitute their preferred treats for the ones we recommend when preparing ice cream. My assistant culinary wizard Jon Pierre Peavey suggests a panoply of goodies: chocolate-covered raisins, chocolate-covered peanuts, M&M's, miniature marshmallows and other kinds of chips (such as butterscotch or peanut butter).

LATE HARVEST SORBET

YIELDS 1.75 LITRES/SCANT 3 PINTS

INGREDIENTS

1 bottle (75cl) late harvest Riesling

200g/7oz caster sugar

125ml/4fl oz fresh orange juice

85g/3oz clear honey

4 tablespoons fresh lemon juice

675g/1½lb red seedless grapes, stalks removed and washed

EQUIPMENT

Measuring jug, 3 litre/5 pint saucepan, whisk, 3 litre/5 pint stainless steel bowl, 5 litre/8 pint stainless steel bowl, instant-read thermometer, hand-held blender, ice cream maker, 2 litre/3 pint plastic container with lid

PREPARE THE SORBET

Heat the late harvest Riesling, sugar, orange juice, honey and lemon juice in a 3 litre/5 pint saucepan over moderately high heat. When hot, stir to dissolve the sugar. Bring to the boil. Add the grapes (they go in whole) and bring to the boil. Allow to boil for 15 minutes (this will yield 1.5 litres/2½ pints of slightly thickened grape syrup mixture).

Cool the mixture in an iced-water bath to a temperature of 5 to 7°C/40 to 45°F, about 15 minutes. When the grape syrup mixture is thoroughly chilled, purée it using a hand-held blender. (If you do not have a hand-held blender, purée the mixture in a food processor fitted with a metal blade.)

Freeze the chilled grape syrup mixture in an ice cream maker, following the manufacturer's instructions. Transfer the semi-frozen Late Harvest Sorbet to a plastic container. Tightly cover the container and place it in the freezer for several hours before serving. Serve within 3 days.

> ### THE CHEF'S TOUCH
> *Grapes harvested late in the picking season have a high intensity of sugar that lends a lush honey-like flavour to late harvest wines. The German wine makers seem to have a deft touch with this style of wine. All of Germany's greatest wines are produced from the Riesling grape, and it is from this grape that prizes known by the designations Auslese, Beerenauslese and Trockenbeerenauslese are crafted— sweet nectar, to be sure. You may select any of these wines for this sorbet, although I suggest the more reasonably priced (they are all pricey) Auslese (we used a 1992 Schitt Sohne Auslese). Of course, you could also use your favourite late harvest wine from France or the New World (let me know if you choose Château Yquem— I'll invite myself over).*
>
> *Although all the wines mentioned above (including the wine required for the recipe) are vinified from white grapes, I use fresh red seedless grapes to give the sorbet its vibrant colour.*

HOLIDAY SUNDAE—ON MONDAY

YIELDS 12 TO 16 SUNDAES

INGREDIENTS

HARVEST PUMPKIN ICE CREAM
(YIELDS 2 LITRES/3 ¼ PINTS)

500ml/16fl oz whipping or double cream

375ml/12fl oz creamy milk

200g/7oz caster sugar

¼ teaspoon ground cinnamon

pinch of ground cloves

pinch of ground nutmeg

6 size-3 egg yolks

370g/13oz fresh pumpkin purée or canned
    pumpkin

BITTERSWEET CHOCOLATE
ICE CREAM
(YIELDS 1 LITRE/1 ⅔ PINTS)

500ml/16fl oz creamy milk

170g/6oz unsweetened chocolate, cut into
    15g/½oz pieces

115g/4oz bittersweet chocolate, cut into
    15g/½oz pieces

250ml/8fl oz whipping or double cream

200g/7oz caster sugar

6 size-3 egg yolks

CARAMEL ICE CREAM
(YIELDS 1.75 LITRES/SCANT 3 PINTS)

300g/10½oz caster sugar

¼ teaspoon fresh lemon juice

500ml/16fl oz whipping or double cream

500ml/16fl oz creamy milk

6 size-3 egg yolks

GOLDEN SUGAR SHARDS

200g/7oz caster sugar

¼ teaspoon fresh lemon juice

DOUBLE CHOCOLATE SAUCE

Double Chocolate Sauce (see page 130), warm

EQUIPMENT

Measuring jug, measuring spoons, 3 litre/5 pint
saucepan, whisk, electric mixer with flat beater,
rubber spatula, instant-read thermometer, three
3 litre/5 pint stainless steel bowls, 5 litre/8 pint
stainless steel bowl, ice cream maker, three 2 litre/
3 pint plastic containers with lids, heat-resistant
cling film, non-stick baking tray

PREPARE THE HARVEST
PUMPKIN ICE CREAM

Heat the cream, milk, 100g/3½oz of the sugar, the
cinnamon, cloves and nutmeg in a 3 litre/5 pint
saucepan over moderately high heat. When hot, stir
to dissolve the sugar. Bring to the boil.

While the cream is heating, place the egg yolks
and the remaining 100g/3½oz sugar in the bowl of
an electric mixer fitted with a flat beater. Beat on
high for 2 to 2½ minutes. Scrape down the sides of
the bowl, then beat on high until slightly thickened
and lemon-coloured, a further 2½ to 3 minutes.
(At this point, the cream should be boiling. If not,
adjust the mixer speed to low and continue to mix
until the cream boils. If the eggs are not mixed right
up to the point the boiling cream is added, they will
develop undesirable lumps.)

Pour the boiling cream into the beaten egg
yolks and whisk to combine. Return the mixture to
the saucepan and heat over moderately high heat,
stirring constantly. Bring to a temperature of
85°C/185°F, about 1 minute. Remove from the
heat and transfer to a 3 litre/5 pint stainless steel
bowl. Add the pumpkin purée and stir to combine.
Cool in an iced-water bath to a temperature of 5 to
7°C/40 to 45°F, about 15 minutes.

When the mixture is cold, freeze in an ice cream
maker, following the manufacturer's instructions.
Transfer the semi-frozen ice cream to a plastic container. Tightly cover the container, then place in the
freezer for several hours before serving. Serve
within 3 to 4 days.

PREPARE THE BITTERSWEET
CHOCOLATE ICE CREAM

Heat 2.5cm/1in of water in the bottom half of a
double boiler over moderate heat. Place 250ml/
8fl oz milk, the unsweetened chocolate and the
bittersweet chocolate in the top half of the double
boiler; tightly cover the top with heat-resistant
cling film. Allow to heat for 8 to 10 minutes.
Remove from the heat and stir until smooth. Keep
at room temperature until needed.

Heat the remaining 250ml/8fl oz milk, the
cream and 100g/3½oz of the sugar in a 3 litre/
5 pint saucepan over moderately high heat. When
hot, stir to dissolve the sugar. Bring to the boil.

While the cream is heating, place the egg yolks
and the remaining 100g/3½oz sugar in the bowl of
an electric mixer fitted with a flat beater. Beat on
high for 2 to 2½ minutes. Scrape down the sides of
the bowl, then beat on high until slightly thickened
and lemon-coloured, a further 2½ to 3 minutes.
(At this point, the cream should be boiling. If not,
adjust the mixer speed to low and continue to mix
until the cream boils. If the eggs are not mixed right
up to the point the boiling cream is added, they will
develop undesirable lumps.)

Pour the boiling cream into the beaten egg
yolks and whisk to combine. Return mixture to the
saucepan and heat over moderately high heat, stirring constantly. Bring to a temperature of 85°C/
185°F, about 1 minute. Remove from the heat and
transfer to a 3 litre/5 pint stainless steel bowl. Add
the melted chocolate–and–milk mixture and stir to
combine. Cool in an iced-water bath to a temperature of 5 to 7°C/40 to 45°F, about 30 minutes (this
mixture takes additional time to cool to the desired
temperature because it is very dense).

When the mixture is cold, freeze in an ice cream
maker, following the manufacturer's instructions.
Transfer the semi-frozen ice cream to a plastic container. Tightly cover the container and place it in
the freezer for several hours before serving. Serve
within 3 to 4 days.

PREPARE THE CARAMEL ICE CREAM

Place 200g/7oz of the sugar and the lemon juice in a 3 litre/5 pint saucepan. Stir with a whisk to combine (the sugar will resemble moist sand). Caramelise the sugar by heating for 4½ to 5 minutes over moderately high heat, stirring constantly with a wire whisk to break up any lumps (the sugar will first turn clear as it liquefies, then light brown as it caramelises).

Remove the saucepan from the heat. Immediately (and carefully) add 125ml/4fl oz of the cream and stir to combine (lots of steaming and bubbling will occur when you add the cream, so take care not to scald yourself). Transfer the caramel to a 5 litre/8 pint stainless steel bowl and allow to cool to room temperature.

Heat the remaining 375ml/12fl oz cream and the milk in a 3 litre/5 pint saucepan over moderately high heat. Bring to the boil.

While the cream is heating, place the egg yolks and the remaining 100g/3½oz sugar in the bowl of an electric mixer fitted with a flat beater. Beat on high for 2 to 2½ minutes. Scrape down the sides of the bowl, then beat on high until slightly thickened and lemon-coloured, a further 2½ to 3 minutes. (At this point, the cream should be boiling. If not, adjust the mixer speed to low and continue to mix until the cream boils. If the eggs are not mixed right up to the point the boiling cream is added, they will develop undesirable lumps.)

Pour the boiling cream into the beaten egg yolks and whisk to combine. Return to the saucepan and heat over moderately high heat, stirring constantly. Bring to a temperature of 85°C/185°F, about 1 minute. Remove from the heat and immediately add to the prepared caramel, whisking to combine. Cool in an iced-water bath to a temperature of 5 to 7°C/40 to 45°F, about 15 to 20 minutes.

When the mixture is cold, freeze in an ice cream maker, following the manufacturer's instructions. Transfer the semi-frozen ice cream to a plastic container. Tightly cover the container, then place in the freezer for several hours before serving. Serve within 3 to 4 days.

PREPARE THE GOLDEN SUGAR SHARDS

Place the sugar and lemon juice in a 3 litre/5 pint saucepan. Stir with a whisk to combine (the sugar will resemble moist sand). Caramelise the sugar by heating for 4½ to 5 minutes over moderately high heat, stirring constantly with a wire whisk to break up any lumps (the sugar will first turn clear as it liquefies, then light brown as it caramelises). Pour the caramelised sugar on to a non-stick baking tray and place in the freezer to harden, about 10 to 15 minutes. Turn the baking tray over and drop the hardened golden sugar on to a clean, dry, hard surface (a large cutting board will work) to break the sugar into irregular shaped shards. Store the Golden Sugar Shards in an airtight plastic container in the freezer until ready to use. (The shards will keep for several weeks if the container is tightly sealed.)

ASSEMBLE THIS KILLER SUNDAE

Place a large scoop of Harvest Pumpkin Ice Cream in the bottom of a large balloon wine glass. Next place a scoop (slightly smaller than the pumpkin ice cream) of Caramel Ice Cream on top of the pumpkin ice cream. Now place a scoop (about half the amount of the pumpkin ice cream) of Bittersweet Chocolate Ice Cream on top of the Caramel Ice Cream. Repeat for as many sundaes as desired. Sauce each sundae with 4 tablespoons of warm Double Chocolate Sauce and garnish with Golden Sugar Shards. Serve immediately.

ROSE'S LEMON LUSCIOUS ICE CREAM

YIELDS 2 LITRES/3 1/4 PINTS

INGREDIENTS

400g/14oz caster sugar

125ml/4fl oz water

1 tablespoon finely chopped lemon zest

750ml/1¼ pints whipping or double cream

250ml/8fl oz creamy milk

55g/2oz unsalted butter

8 size-3 egg yolks

250ml/8fl oz fresh lemon juice

EQUIPMENT

Measuring jug, measuring spoons, 1.5 litre/2½ pint saucepan, 3 litre/5 pint saucepan, whisk, electric mixer with flat beater, rubber spatula, instant-read thermometer, 3 litre/5 pint stainless steel bowl, small bowl, 5 litre/8 pint stainless steel bowl, ice cream maker, 2 litre/3 pint plastic container with lid

PREPARE THE ICE CREAM

Heat 100g/3½oz of the sugar, the water and the lemon zest in a 1.5 litre/2½ pint saucepan over moderately high heat. When hot, stir to dissolve the sugar. Bring to the boil, then allow to boil for 5 minutes until slightly thickened (this should yield 125ml/4fl oz syrup). Remove from the heat and cool to room temperature.

While the syrup is cooling, heat the cream, milk, 200g/7oz of the sugar and the butter in a 3 litre/ 5 pint saucepan over moderately high heat. When hot, stir to dissolve the sugar. Bring to the boil.

While the cream is heating, place the egg yolks and the remaining 100g/3½oz sugar in the bowl of an electric mixer fitted with a flat beater. Beat on high for 2 to 2½ minutes. Scrape down the sides of the bowl, then beat on high until slightly thickened and lemon-coloured, a further 2½ to 3 minutes. (At this point the cream should be boiling. If not, adjust the mixer speed to low and continue to mix until the cream boils. If the eggs are not mixed right up to the point when the boiling cream is added, they will develop undesirable lumps.)

Pour the boiling cream into the beaten egg yolks and whisk to combine. Return to the saucepan and heat over moderately high heat, stirring constantly. Bring to a temperature of 85°C/185°F, about 2 minutes. Remove from the heat and transfer to a 3 litre/5 pint stainless steel bowl. Cool in an iced-water bath to a temperature of 5 to 7°C/40 to 45°F, about 15 minutes.

When the mixture is cold, add the cooled lemon syrup and the fresh lemon juice and stir to combine. Freeze in an ice cream maker, following the manufacturer's instructions. Transfer the semi-frozen ice cream to a plastic container. Tightly cover the container, then place in the freezer for several hours before serving. Serve within 3 to 4 days.

THE CHEF'S TOUCH

When Rose Beranbaum came to Williamsburg to promote her newly released cookbook Rose's Melting Pot, *in March 1994, a book-signing was held at the Rizzoli bookstore next door to the Trellis. The following night, the Trellis celebrated the new spring menu with a preview dinner that concluded with the light and refreshing Rose's Lemon Luscious Ice Cream. Although we paired Rose's ice cream with delicate almond biscuits, you could also enjoy it with the Lemon and Fresh Berry 'Shortcake' (see page 54).*

For 250ml/8fl oz fresh lemon juice, squeeze 8 medium lemons (each lemon should weigh in at 85g/3oz). But before you squeeze, I recommend using the palm of your hand to firmly press down on each lemon, one at a time, and roll it back and forth on the work surface for a few seconds. This loosens the pulp and makes the juice flow more freely. Having performed this manoeuvre with all 8 lemons, cut each one in half and squeeze the juice out of each half, using a sieve to capture the seeds.

SWEET DREAMS ICE CREAM SANDWICHES

YIELDS 24 MINI SANDWICHES

INGREDIENTS

COGNAC ICE CREAM

250ml/8fl oz Cognac

500ml/16fl oz whipping or double cream

375ml/12fl oz creamy milk

200g/7oz caster sugar

6 size-3 egg yolks

4 tablespoons B & B (Benedictine and Brandy)

COCOA BISCUITS

170g/6oz plain flour

20g/¾oz unsweetened cocoa powder

¾ teaspoon baking powder

¼ teaspoon salt

225g/8oz unsalted butter

150g/5½oz caster sugar

4 size-3 eggs

1 teaspoon pure vanilla essence

CHOCOLATE MINT NIGHTCAPS

170g/6oz bittersweet chocolate, cut into
    15g/½oz pieces

185ml/6fl oz whipping cream

1 tablespoon chopped fresh mint

EQUIPMENT

Measuring jug, measuring spoons, chef's knife, cutting board, 1.5 litre/2½ pint saucepan, 3 litre/ 5 pint saucepan, whisk, electric mixer with flat beater, rubber spatula, instant-read thermometer, two 3 litre/5 pint stainless steel bowls, 5 litre/8 pint stainless steel bowl, ice cream maker, 2 litre/3 pint plastic container with lid, sieve, greaseproof paper, four 23 × 33cm/9 × 13in baking sheets, baking parchment, large flat plastic container with lid, medium sieve, ice cream scoop, piping bag, medium star or plain nozzle

PREPARE THE COGNAC ICE CREAM

Heat the Cognac in a 1.5 litre/2½ pint saucepan over moderately high heat. Bring to the boil. Allow to boil for 4 minutes (this will yield 125ml/4fl oz reduced Cognac and a marvellous aroma). Remove from the heat and cool to room temperature.

Heat the cream, milk and 100g/3½oz of the sugar in a 3 litre/5 pint saucepan over moderately high heat. When hot, stir to dissolve the sugar. Bring to the boil.

While the cream is heating, place the egg yolks and remaining 100g/3½oz sugar in the bowl of an electric mixer fitted with a flat beater. Beat on high for 2 to 2½ minutes. Scrape down the sides of the

bowl, then beat on high until slightly thickened and lemon-coloured, a further 2½ to 3 minutes. (At this point, the cream should be boiling. If not, adjust the mixer speed to low and continue to mix until the cream boils. If the eggs are not mixed right up to the point when the boiling cream is added, they will develop undesirable lumps.)

Pour the boiling cream into the beaten egg yolks and whisk to combine. Return to the saucepan and heat over moderately high heat, stirring constantly. Bring to a temperature of 85°C/185°F, about 1 minute. Remove from the heat and transfer to a 3 litre/5 pint stainless steel bowl. Cool in an iced-water bath to a temperature of 5 to 7°C/40 to 45°F, about 15 minutes.

When the mixture is cold, add the Cognac and the B & B and stir to combine. Freeze in an ice cream maker, following the manufacturer's instructions. Transfer the semi-frozen ice cream to a plastic container. Tightly cover the container, then place in the freezer for several hours before assembling the ice cream sandwiches.

PREPARE THE COCOA BISCUITS

While the ice cream is freezing, preheat the oven to 150°C/300°F/Gas 2.

Sift together the flour, cocoa, baking powder and salt on to greaseproof paper. Set aside.

Line 4 baking sheets with baking parchment.

Place the butter and sugar in the bowl of an electric mixer fitted with a flat beater. Beat on medium for 2 minutes. Scrape down the sides of the bowl and beat on high for an additional minute or until light in colour. Scrape down the bowl. While beating on medium, add the eggs, one at a time, stopping to scrape down the bowl after incorporating each addition. Add the vanilla essence and beat on medium for 30 seconds. Add the sifted dry ingredients and mix on medium for 30 seconds. Remove the bowl from the mixer. Use a rubber spatula to finish mixing until smooth and thoroughly combined.

Portion 12 biscuits per parchment-covered baking sheet by dropping 1 heaping teaspoon of mixture per biscuit on to each of the 4 baking sheets. Place the biscuits on the top and centre shelves of the preheated oven and bake for 7 to 8 minutes, rotating the sheets from top to centre about halfway through the baking time. Remove the biscuits from the oven and allow to cool for a few minutes on the baking sheets. When cool, remove from the baking sheets and store in an airtight container in the freezer until ready to use.

The ice cream sandwiches can be assembled when the Cognac ice cream is firm enough to scoop (this could take from 3 to 24 hours depending on the efficiency of your freezer—and how crowded it may be).

PREPARE THE CHOCOLATE MINT NIGHTCAPS

Place the chocolate pieces in a stainless steel bowl. Heat the cream with the chopped mint in a 1.5 litre/2½ pint saucepan over moderately high heat. Bring to the boil. Remove from the heat and pour through a medium sieve into the bowl of chocolate pieces (discard the mint). Stir with a whisk until smooth. Transfer the chocolate mixture to a baking sheet, using a rubber spatula to spread the chocolate to the edges. Place the baking sheet in the refrigerator for 30 minutes. While the chocolate mint mixture is cooling, assemble the ice cream sandwiches.

ASSEMBLE THE SWEET DREAMS ICE CREAM SANDWICHES

Place 12 biscuits upside down on a baking sheet lined with baking parchment. Portion a heaping scoop of Cognac Ice Cream on to each of the biscuits. Place a biscuit, top side up, on each portion. Gently press the biscuit into place. Place the sandwich in the freezer. Repeat this procedure with the remaining biscuits. Keep the sandwiches in the freezer until the chocolate mint mixture has been refrigerated for 30 minutes.

Remove the chocolate mint mixture from the refrigerator. Transfer the mixture to a piping bag fitted with a medium star or plain nozzle (depending on what form you prefer for the nightcap). Pipe a nightcap-shaped portion of chocolate (about a teaspoon) on to the centre of each biscuit (accomplish this effect by piping a small circle of chocolate, spiralling upwards, and then pulling away from the circle, allowing a strip of chocolate to taper to a point towards the edge of the biscuit.) Serve immediately, with your favourite postprandial (a complementary choice would be the same Cognac used in the ice cream).

LONG ISLAND ICED TEA SORBET

YIELDS 1.5 LITRES/2 ½ PINTS

INGREDIENTS

300g/10½oz caster sugar

250ml/8fl oz dark rum

250ml/8fl oz tequila

125ml/4fl oz fresh lemon juice

4 tablespoons lime juice cordial

1 teaspoon finely chopped fresh lemon zest

1 teaspoon finely chopped fresh lime zest

375ml/12fl oz cola

375ml/12fl oz water

4 tablespoons coffee liqueur

EQUIPMENT

Measuring jug, vegetable peeler, chef's knife, cutting board, measuring spoons, 3 litre/5 pint saucepan, whisk, 3 litre/5 pint stainless steel bowl, 5 litre/8 pint stainless steel bowl, instant-read thermometer, ice cream maker, 2 litre/3 pint plastic container with lid

PREPARE THE SORBET

Heat the sugar, dark rum, tequila, lemon juice, lime juice cordial, lemon zest and lime zest in a 3 litre/5 pint saucepan over moderately high heat. When hot, stir to dissolve the sugar. Bring to the boil. Allow to boil for 13 minutes. (This will yield 550ml/18fl oz of slightly syrupy, intoxicatingly aromatic, caramel-coloured, 'spiked' tea.)

Cool the mixture in an iced-water bath to a temperature of 5 to 7°C/40 to 45°F, about 15 minutes. When the mixture is thoroughly chilled, stir in the cola, water and coffee liqueur.

Freeze the Long Island iced tea mixture in an ice cream maker, following the manufacturer's instructions. Transfer the semi-frozen sorbet to a plastic container. Tightly cover the container, then place in the freezer for several hours before serving. Serve within 24 hours.

THE CHEF'S TOUCH

Trellis head bartender Luke Lambert is a bit taciturn when it comes to discussing his military service. The fact is, Colonel Lambert had a career in the US Air Force that spanned 30 years. But when he was not at the controls of various types of aircraft, Luke might be found pursuing his other love, the craft of mixology.

This sorbet recipe was developed with Luke's guidance. It is a high-flying concoction, revved up with plenty of spirit, although the heating of the primary intoxicants mitigates their effect. I am sure you will agree, however, that a few spoonfuls of this delightful sorbet gives a healthy boost to the spirit.

To take this sorbet recipe to a higher altitude, use Myers's dark rum, Cuervo Especial tequila, Coca-Cola Classic and Kahlua Licor de Cafe.

One whole medium-size lemon and one whole lime will each yield more zest than needed for this recipe. Use only the amount of zest specified—otherwise the balance of flavour will be altered.

You can find Rose's lime juice cordial in most supermarkets. You will certainly find it behind the bar as it is essential for preparing many cocktails.

DOUBLE CAPPUCCINO ICE CREAM

YIELDS 1.5 LITRES/2 ½ PINTS

INGREDIENTS

600ml/1 pint whipping or double cream
250ml/8fl oz creamy milk
150g/5½oz caster sugar
5 size-3 egg yolks
4 tablespoons espresso powder
pinch of ground cinnamon
125ml/4fl oz hot strong black coffee

EQUIPMENT

Measuring jug, measuring spoons, 3 litre/5 pint saucepan, whisk, electric mixer with flat beater, rubber spatula, instant-read thermometer, 3 litre/5 pint stainless steel bowl, small bowl, 5 litre/8 pint stainless steel bowl, ice cream maker, 2 litre/3 pint plastic container with lid

PREPARE THE ICE CREAM

Heat the cream, milk and 75g/2½oz of the sugar in a 3 litre/5 pint saucepan over moderately high heat. When hot, stir to dissolve the sugar. Bring to the boil.

While the cream is heating, place the egg yolks and the remaining 75g/3oz sugar in the bowl of an electric mixer fitted with a flat beater. Beat on high for 2 to 2½ minutes. Scrape down the bowl, then beat on high until slightly thickened and lemon-coloured, a further 2½ to 3 minutes. (At this point, the cream should be boiling. If not, adjust the mixer speed to low and continue to mix until the cream boils. If the eggs are not mixed right up to the point when the boiling cream is added, they will develop undesirable lumps.)

Pour the boiling cream into the beaten egg yolks and whisk to combine. Return to the saucepan and heat over moderately high heat, stirring constantly. Bring to a temperature of 85°C/185°F, about 1 minute. Remove from the heat and transfer to a 3 litre/5 pint stainless steel bowl. Place the espresso powder and the ground cinnamon in a separate small bowl. Pour in the hot black coffee and stir to dissolve the espresso powder. Pour the coffee and espresso mixture into the cream and egg yolk mixture. Cool in an iced-water bath to a temperature of 5 to 7°C/40 to 45°F, about 15 minutes.

Freeze the mixture in an ice cream maker, following the manufacturer's instructions. Transfer the semi-frozen ice cream to a plastic container. Tightly cover, then place in the freezer for several hours before serving. Serve within 5 days.

THE CHEF'S TOUCH

Sitting in an outdoor cafe slowly sipping a cappuccino may be the way to go on a cool autumn day, but when the temperature sky-rockets, it's a large bowl of ice cream for me.

For an Italianate flair, fold about 8 to 10 Sambuca Almond Biscotti (see page 132)—chopped into 1.5cm/½in pieces—into the semi-frozen ice cream just before placing it in the freezer to harden.

The egg yolks and sugar can be whisked using a hand-held electric mixer (mixing time may increase slightly) or by hand, using a wire whisk (mixing time may double). If either of these methods is used, be sure to continue whisking the yolks while waiting for the cream to come to the boil—otherwise you may end up with lumpy eggs.

JONNY'S CIDER ICE CREAM

YIELDS 2 LITRES/3 ¼ PINTS

INGREDIENTS

1 litre/1⅔ pints pressed apple juice
250ml/8fl oz bourbon whiskey
2 cinnamon sticks, 7.5cm/3in each
12 whole cloves
225g/8oz soft light brown sugar
500ml/16fl oz whipping or double cream
250ml/8fl oz whole milk
200g/7oz caster sugar
6 size-3 egg yolks

EQUIPMENT

Measuring jug, 3 litre/5 pint saucepan, whisk, two 3 litre/5 pint stainless steel bowls, 5 litre/8 pint stainless steel bowl, cling film, electric mixer with flat beater, rubber spatula, instant-read thermometer, ice cream maker, 2 litre/3 pint plastic container with lid

PREPARE THE ICE CREAM

Heat the apple juice, bourbon whiskey, cinnamon sticks and whole cloves in a 3 litre/5 pint saucepan over moderately high heat. Bring to the boil, then lower the heat to allow the mixture to simmer for 45 minutes (this should yield about 600ml/1 pint). Remove from the heat. Immediately add the brown sugar, stirring with a whisk to dissolve. Cool the mixture in an iced-water bath. When cool, cover with cling film and refrigerate until needed.

Heat the cream, milk and 100g/3½oz of the sugar in a 3 litre/5 pint saucepan over moderately high heat. When hot, stir to dissolve the sugar. Bring to the boil.

While the cream is heating, place the egg yolks and the remaining 100g/3½oz sugar in the bowl of an electric mixer fitted with a flat beater. Beat on high for 2 to 2½ minutes. Scrape down the sides of the bowl, then beat on high until slightly thickened and lemon-coloured, a further 2½ to 3 minutes. (At this point, the cream should be boiling. If not, adjust the mixer speed to low and continue to mix until the cream boils. If the eggs are not mixed right up to the point when the boiling cream is added, they will develop undesirable lumps.)

Pour the boiling cream into the beaten egg yolks and whisk to combine. Return to the saucepan and heat over moderately high heat, stirring constantly. Bring to a temperature of 85°C/185°F, about 1 minute. Remove from the heat and transfer to a 3 litre/5 pint stainless steel bowl. Cool in an iced-water bath to a temperature of 5 to 7°C/40 to 45°F, about 15 minutes.

When the mixture is cold, combine with the chilled juice mixture and freeze in an ice cream maker, following the manufacturer's instructions. Transfer the semi-frozen ice cream to a plastic container. Tightly cover the container, then place in the freezer for 24 hours before serving. Serve within 3 to 4 days.

THE CHEF'S TOUCH

You do not have to be a moonshiner to concoct (or enjoy) this delectation. Irish whiskey makes an interesting substitute for bourbon, as does apple brandy or calvados. French apple brandy blends well with the apple juice, as does grain alcohol (ouch) or rum. In fact, you can substitute almost anything you have a taste for—or should I say, have had a taste of. Seriously, though, most of the alcohol will evaporate during the simmering process, leaving the taste but not the punch. So, unless you become pixilated at the very thought of this type of concoction, do not fret about this dessert's intoxicating effect.

Select a good apple juice for this recipe. At the Trellis, we prefer an unfiltered freshly pressed apple juice. Although quite cloudy, it has a very pleasant flavour without any of the cloying sweetness found in many commercial brands. Seek out a small regional producer in your area (thank goodness for the resurgence in small producers pressing high-quality juices and fermented ciders).

The egg yolks and sugar can be whisked using a hand-held electric mixer (mixing time may increase slightly) or by hand, using a wire whisk (mixing time may double). If either of these methods is used, be sure to continue whisking the yolks while waiting for the cream to come to the boil—otherwise you may end up with lumpy eggs.

BLACKBERRY CHOCOLATE PRALINE ICE CREAM

YIELDS 1.75 LITRES/SCANT 3 PINTS

INGREDIENTS

CHOCOLATE PRALINE

115g/4oz toasted pecans

200g/7oz caster sugar

¼ teaspoon fresh lemon juice

30g/1oz unsweetened chocolate, chopped into 5mm/¼in pieces

BLACKBERRY ICE CREAM

340g/12oz fresh blackberries, rinsed

170g/6oz caster sugar

1 teaspoon fresh lemon juice

375ml/12fl oz whipping or double cream

250ml/8fl oz half cream

5 size-3 egg yolks

125ml/4fl oz buttermilk

EQUIPMENT

Measuring jug, measuring spoons, baking tray, colander, pie tin, 3 litre/5 pint saucepan, whisk, serrated slicer, cutting board, 2 litre/3 pint plastic container with lid, 1.5 litre/2½ pint saucepan, metal spoon, medium sieve, rubber spatula, 3 litre/5 pint stainless steel bowl, 5 litre/8 pint stainless steel bowl, cling film, electric mixer with flat beater, instant-read thermometer, ice cream maker

MAKE THE CHOCOLATE PRALINE

Place the toasted pecans in a pie tin, spreading them to the inside edges. Set aside.

Combine the sugar and lemon juice in a 3 litre/5 pint saucepan. Stir with a whisk to combine (the sugar will resemble moist sand). Caramelise the sugar by heating for 4½ to 5 minutes over moderately high heat, stirring constantly with a wire whisk to break up any lumps (the sugar will first turn clear as it liquefies, then light brown as it caramelises). Remove the saucepan from the heat, add the chopped chocolate and stir to dissolve. Immediately and carefully pour the caramelised mixture over the pecans, covering all the nuts. Place the pie tin in the freezer to harden the praline, about 15 minutes.

Remove the praline from the freezer. Use a serrated slicer to cut the praline into 3mm/⅛in pieces. Keep the praline in a tightly sealed plastic container in the freezer until needed.

PREPARE THE BLACKBERRY ICE CREAM

Heat the blackberries, 2 tablespoons of the sugar and the lemon juice in a 1.5 litre/2½ pint saucepan over moderate heat. As the mixture gets hot, the sugar will dissolve and the berries will liquefy and begin to boil, after about 5 minutes. Allow the mixture to boil for about 15 minutes longer or until it becomes very thick, stirring occasionally. Remove from the heat and pass through a sieve into a 2 litre/3 pint bowl, using a rubber spatula to press down on the seeds and pulp (discard the seeds and pulp). This should yield about 125ml/4fl oz blackberry purée. Cool the purée in an iced-water bath for about 10 minutes. When the purée is cold, cover with cling film and refrigerate until needed.

Heat the whipping cream, half cream and 4 tablespoons sugar in a 3 litre/5 pint saucepan over moderately high heat. When hot, stir to dissolve the sugar. Bring to the boil.

While the cream is heating, place the egg yolks and the remaining 100g/3½oz sugar in the bowl of an electric mixer fitted with a flat beater. Beat on high for 2 to 2½ minutes. Scrape down the sides of the bowl, then beat on high until slightly thickened and lemon-coloured, a further 2½ to 3 minutes. (At this point, the cream should be boiling. If not, adjust the mixer speed to low and continue to mix until the cream boils. If the eggs are not mixed right up to the point when the boiling cream is added, they will develop undesirable lumps.)

Pour the boiling cream into the beaten egg yolks and whisk to combine. Return to the saucepan and heat over moderately high heat, stirring constantly. Bring to a temperature of 85°C/185°F, about 1 minute. Remove from the heat and transfer to a 3 litre/5 pint stainless steel bowl. Cool in an iced-water bath to a temperature of 5 to 7°C/40 to 45°F, about 15 minutes.

When the mixture is cold, stir in the buttermilk and freeze in an ice cream maker, following the manufacturer's instructions. Transfer the semi-frozen ice cream to a plastic container. Use a rubber spatula to fold in the chocolate praline and then the blackberry purée. (Do not overmix—the idea is to contrast fanciful swirls of the purée with a homogeneously coloured base). Tightly cover the container, then place in the freezer for several hours before serving. Serve within 3 days.

THE CHEF'S TOUCH

In the hilly farm country north of Eau Claire, Wisconsin, stands of thorny blackberry bushes yield remarkably sweet and juicy (but diminutive) berries that can turn a picker's hands purple for 3 days. That's according to my assistant Jon Pierre Peavey, who is wont to rhapsodise about the bounties of his home state. As a young lad he spent many a pleasurable late summer day, pails tied to his waist, picking and eating the tiny berries that are known in those parts as black caps. He also assisted his mother in preparing creamy fresh blackberry ice cream. In this recipe Jon Pierre has elevated Mrs Peavey's creation into the realm of indulgence with the addition of the chocolate praline.

Blackberries, which are plentiful during the summer, are available year-round if you are willing to pay the price for imported fruit.

Rinse the berries before using by placing them in a colander and spraying with lukewarm water. Drain the berries on paper towels to remove excess moisture.

Enhance the flavour of the pecans and reduce moisture by toasting them on a baking sheet in a 170°C/325°F/Gas 3 oven for 10 to 12 minutes.

This prodigious batch of chocolate praline provides a generous amount of delicious crunch in every mouthful of this ice cream. If you prefer a less crunchy ice cream, simply divide the praline recipe in half. Of course, you can always prepare the praline recipe as listed, and use half the

amount of chopped praline, saving the remainder to sprinkle over your favourite ice cream or to eat alone (the praline will keep indefinitely in a tightly sealed plastic container in your freezer).

The egg yolks and sugar can be whisked using a hand-held electric mixer (mixing time may increase slightly) or by hand, using a wire whisk (mixing time may double). If either of these methods is used, be sure to continue whisking the yolks while waiting for the cream to come to the boil—otherwise you may end up with lumpy eggs.

For the final touch, garnish each portion of ice cream with fresh blackberries. Or, you can double the recipe for the blackberry purée and drizzle the extra purée over the ice cream.

MAPLE SYRUP AND TOASTED WALNUT ICE CREAM

YIELDS 2 LITRES/3¼ PINTS

INGREDIENTS

MAPLE GLAZED WALNUTS

125ml/4fl oz pure maple syrup
170g/6oz toasted walnut halves

MAPLE SYRUP ICE CREAM

500ml/16fl oz whipping or double cream
250ml/8fl oz half cream
250ml/8fl oz pure maple syrup
5 size-3 egg yolks
50g/scant 2oz caster sugar

EQUIPMENT

Measuring jug, 1.5 litre/2½ pint saucepan, metal spoon, pie tin, 2 litre/3 pint plastic container with lid, 3 litre/5 pint saucepan, whisk, electric mixer with flat beater, rubber spatula, instant-read thermometer, 3 litre/5 pint stainless steel bowl, 5 litre/8 pint stainless steel bowl, ice cream maker

GLAZE THE WALNUTS

Heat the maple syrup in a 1.5 litre/2½ pint saucepan over moderately high heat. When the syrup begins to boil, reduce the heat to moderate and allow the syrup to continue to boil and thicken for 10 minutes, stirring occasionally. Remove the very hot syrup from the heat. Immediately add the toasted walnuts. Use a metal spoon to stir the walnuts into the hot syrup. Transfer the glazed walnuts to a pie tin and place in the freezer to harden.

Remove the walnuts from the freezer. Use your hands to separate the walnuts and break into pieces no larger than the original size of the individual walnut halves. Keep the glazed walnuts in a tightly sealed plastic container in the freezer until needed.

PREPARE THE MAPLE SYRUP ICE CREAM

Heat the whipping cream, half cream and maple syrup in a 3 litre/5 pint saucepan over moderately high heat. When hot, stir to dissolve the sugar. Bring to the boil.

While the cream is heating, place the egg yolks and sugar in the bowl of an electric mixer fitted with a flat beater. Beat on high for 2 to 2½ minutes. Scrape down the sides of the bowl, then beat on high until slightly thickened and lemon-coloured, a further 2½ to 3 minutes. (At this point, the cream should be boiling. If not, adjust the mixer speed to low and continue to mix until the cream boils. If the eggs are not mixed right up to the point the boiling cream is added, they will develop undesirable lumps.)

Pour the boiling cream into the beaten egg yolks and whisk to combine. Return to the saucepan and heat over moderately high heat, stirring constantly. Bring to a temperature of 85°C/185°F, about 1 minute. Remove from the heat and transfer to a 3 litre/5 pint stainless steel bowl. Cool in an iced-water bath to a temperature of 5 to 7°C/ 40 to 45°F, about 15 minutes.

When the mixture is cold, freeze in an ice cream maker, following the manufacturer's instructions. Transfer the semi-frozen ice cream to a plastic container. Use a rubber spatula to fold in the glazed walnuts. Tightly cover the container, then place in the freezer for several hours before serving. Serve within 5 days.

> ### THE CHEF'S TOUCH
> *I have many delicious memories of licking Vermont maple syrup from my fingers as a youngster growing up in New England. Select your favourite pure maple syrup for this recipe. Be sure it is pure. I strongly recommend you do not use maple-flavoured syrup or pancake syrup (the former is primarily corn syrup with a modicum of maple syrup and the latter is corn syrup with artificial flavouring).*
>
> *Boiling the syrup for 10 minutes before adding the walnuts is quite important—less time and the walnuts will be a sticky mass.*
>
> *For optimum flavour, toast the walnuts on a baking sheet in a 170°C/325°F/Gas 3 oven for 12 to 14 minutes. Allow the nuts to cool thoroughly before you add them to the glaze.*
>
> *The glazed walnuts will keep indefinitely in a tightly sealed plastic container in the freezer.*
>
> *The egg yolks and sugar can be whisked using a hand-held electric mixer (mixing time may increase slightly) or by hand, using a wire whisk (mixing time may double). If either of these methods is used, be sure to continue whisking the yolks while waiting for the cream to come to the boil—otherwise you may end up with lumpy eggs.*

STRAWBERRY AND BANANA YIN YANG SORBET

YIELDS 2 LITRES/SCANT 3 PINTS

INGREDIENTS

675g/1½lb strawberries
900g/2lb medium-size bananas, unpeeled weight
1 medium-size lemon
500ml/16fl oz water
300g/10½oz caster sugar
4 tablespoons dark rum

EQUIPMENT

Measuring jug, measuring spoons, paring knife, colander, chef's knife, cutting board, two 3 litre/5 pint stainless steel bowls, vegetable peeler, 3 litre/5 pint saucepan, small sieve, whisk, hand-held blender, instant-read thermometer, ice cream maker, rubber spatula, 2 litre/3 pint plastic container with lid

PREPARE THE SORBET

Place the strawberries in a colander and spray with lukewarm water. Drain the berries on paper towels to remove excess moisture. Cut the strawberries into 5mm/¼in slices. Place the sliced berries in a 3 litre/5 pint stainless steel bowl and set aside until needed.

Cut the bananas into 5mm/¼in slices. Place the banana slices in a separate 3 litre/5 pint stainless steel bowl and set aside while preparing the sugar syrup.

Peel the coloured zest from the lemon using a vegetable peeler, being careful to remove only the coloured zest and not the bitter white pith that lies beneath. Use a sharp chef's knife to finely chop all the lemon zest. Transfer the lemon zest to a 3 litre/5 pint saucepan. Cut the peeled lemon in half. Squeeze the juice from the halves into the saucepan, using a small sieve to capture the seeds. Add the water and sugar to the saucepan and bring the mixture to the boil over moderately high heat (stir to dissolve the sugar). Allow the lemon sugar mixture to boil for 10 minutes (this should yield 500ml/16fl oz syrup). Remove from the heat, add the rum and stir to combine.

Pour 250ml/8fl oz of hot syrup over the strawberries and the remainder over the bananas. Stir the fruit with a rubber spatula. Allow the fruit to steep in the syrup for 40 minutes, stirring occasionally. Use a hand-held blender to purée each bowl of fruit. (If you do not have a hand-held blender, the fruit can be puréed in a food processor with a metal blade. If using a food processor, purée the bananas first. Remove the bananas from the bowl of the processor and then, without cleaning the blender, purée the strawberries. Return the puréed fruit to the separate bowls.) Cool the bowl of banana purée in an iced-water bath to a temperature of 5 to 7°C/40 to 45°F, about 15 minutes.

Freeze the banana purée in an ice cream maker, following the manufacturer's instructions. While the banana sorbet is freezing, cool the strawberry purée in an iced-water bath to a temperature of 5 to 7°C/40 to 45°F. Transfer the semi-frozen banana sorbet to a plastic container. Tightly cover the container, then place in the freezer while freezing the strawberry purée. Freeze the strawberry purée in an ice cream maker, following the manufacturer's instructions. Transfer the semi-frozen strawberry sorbet to the container of banana sorbet. Use a rubber spatula to swirl the strawberry purée (the yin) into the banana sorbet (the yang). Tightly cover the container, then place in the freezer for several hours before serving. Serve within 3 days.

THE CHEF'S TOUCH

The hand-held blender (not to be confused with a hand-held electric mixer) is a great tool. Electrically powered and economically priced, the blender can easily purée cooked or partially cooked fruit and vegetables, as well as many soups. And the best part is that it is easy to clean.

After peeling, 900g/2lb of medium-size bananas should yield about 620g/1lb 6oz of flesh. Select ripe bananas that are uniformly yellow in colour. Avoid bananas whose skin has green streaks (under-ripe) or lots of brown patches (over-ripe).

ESPRESSO WITH A TWIST ICE CREAM

YIELDS 1.75 LITRES/SCANT 3 PINTS

INGREDIENTS

1 medium-size lemon
400g/14oz caster sugar
250ml/8fl oz water
500ml/16fl oz creamy milk
250ml/8fl oz whipping or double cream
4 tablespoons freshly ground espresso beans
2 size-3 eggs
2 size-3 egg yolks

EQUIPMENT

Measuring jug, coffee grinder, vegetable peeler, chef's knife, cutting board, 1.5 litre/2½ pint saucepan, small sieve, 2 litre/3 pint stainless steel bowl, 5 litre/8 pint stainless steel bowl, cling film, 3 litre/5 pint saucepan, whisk, muslin, 3 litre/5 pint stainless steel bowl, electric mixer with flat beater, rubber spatula, instant-read thermometer, ice cream maker, 2 litre/3 pint plastic container with lid

PREPARE THE ICE CREAM

Peel the coloured zest from the lemon using a vegetable peeler. Remove the zest in long 2.5cm/1in wide strips, being careful to remove only the coloured zest and not the bitter white pith that lies beneath. Use a very sharp chef's knife to cut the strips of zest across into very thin shreds. Place the lemon shreds in a 1.5 litre/2½ pint saucepan. Cut the peeled lemon in half. Squeeze the juice from the halves into the saucepan, using a small sieve to capture the seeds. Add 200g/7oz of the sugar and the water to the saucepan and bring the mixture to the boil over moderately high heat (stir to dissolve the sugar). Allow the lemon sugar mixture to boil for 5 minutes (this should yield slightly more than 300ml/½ pint syrup). Remove from the heat and cool in an iced-water bath. When cool, cover with cling film and keep refrigerated until needed.

Heat the milk, cream and ground espresso beans in a 3 litre/5 pint saucepan over moderately high heat. Bring the mixture to the boil, stirring frequently with a whisk. Remove from the heat and strain, through several folds of muslin, into a 3 litre/5 pint stainless steel bowl (this should yield 660ml/22fl oz espresso-flavoured milk-and-cream mixture). Thoroughly wash and dry the saucepan. Return the mixture to the saucepan along with 100g/3½oz sugar. Bring to the boil over moderately high heat. (It should only take 2 minutes for the mixture to boil, so keep a close eye on it to make sure that the mixture does not boil over the sides of the pan.) Remove the saucepan from the heat and set aside while whisking the egg yolks.

Immediately place the eggs, egg yolks and the remaining 100g/3½oz sugar in the bowl of an electric mixer fitted with a flat beater. Beat the eggs on high for 2 to 2½ minutes. Scrape down the sides of the bowl, then beat on high until slightly thickened and lemon-coloured, a further 2½ to 3 minutes.

Pour the very hot cream into the beaten eggs and whisk to combine. Return to the saucepan and heat over moderately high heat, stirring constantly. Bring to a temperature of 85°C/185°F, about 1½ minutes. Remove from the heat and transfer to a 3 litre/5 pint stainless steel bowl. Cool in an iced-water bath to a temperature of 5 to 7°C/40 to 45°F, about 15 minutes.

When the mixture is cold, stir in the lemon sugar syrup. Freeze the mixture in an ice cream maker, following the manufacturer's instructions. Transfer the semi-frozen ice cream to a plastic container. Tightly cover the container, then place in the freezer for several hours before serving. Serve within 3 to 4 days.

THE CHEF'S TOUCH

My culinary peregrinations have found me enjoying espresso all over the world. I admit to being a purist, as I take my espresso without the addition of sugar, and I most certainly eschew the sometime offered twist of lemon. So why do I now offer this smooth and intensely flavoured frozen concoction with the aforementioned lemon twist? The answer is in the first spoonful.

For the record, 15g/½oz of whole espresso beans will yield 4 tablespoons ground espresso.

Before cutting the whole lemon in half, use the palm of your hand to press firmly on the lemon, and roll it back and forth on a countertop. This will break up the membrane inside the lemon so that the juice will come flowing out when the halves are squeezed.

The whole eggs, yolks and sugar can be whisked using a hand-held electric mixer (mixing time may increase slightly) or by hand, using a wire whisk (mixing time may double).

'WHAT A CHUNK OF CHOCOLATE' ICE CREAM TERRINE

SERVES 8 TO 10

INGREDIENTS

DARK CHOCOLATE NUT BARK

225g/8oz bittersweet chocolate, cut into
   15g/½oz pieces
70g/2½oz toasted unsalted peanuts
70g/2½oz raisins

WHITE CHOCOLATE ICE CREAM

225g/8oz white chocolate, cut into
   15g/½oz pieces
500ml/16fl oz half cream
250ml/8fl oz creamy milk
200g/7oz caster sugar
5 size-3 egg yolks

RED RASPBERRY SAUCE

Red Raspberry Sauce (see page 130)

EQUIPMENT

Measuring jug, baking tray, double boiler, heat-resistant cling film, rubber spatula, cutting board, chef's knife, 2 litre/3 pint plastic container with lid, 3 litre/5 pint saucepan, whisk, electric mixer with flat beater, instant-read thermometer, 3 litre/5 pint stainless steel bowl, 5 litre/8 pint stainless steel bowl, ice cream maker, 23 × 12.5 × 7.5cm/9 × 5 × 3in loaf tin, baking parchment, aluminium foil, serrated slicer

PREPARE THE DARK CHOCOLATE NUT BARK

Heat 2.5cm/1in of water in the bottom half of a double boiler over moderate heat. Place the bittersweet chocolate in the top half of the double boiler. Tightly cover the top with heat-resistant cling film. Heat for 8 to 10 minutes. Remove from the heat and stir until smooth. Add the peanuts and raisins and combine thoroughly. Pour the dark chocolate nut bark on to a baking tray. Use a rubber spatula to spread the nut bark out to a thickness of 1.5cm/½in (the nut bark should cover a 20 × 25cm/8 × 10in rectangular area). Place in the freezer for 15 minutes, or in the refrigerator for 40 minutes, until cold and solidified. Transfer the nut bark from the baking tray to a cutting board. Chop the nut bark into 5mm/¼in pieces. Keep the nut bark in a tightly sealed plastic container in the freezer until needed.

PREPARE THE WHITE CHOCOLATE ICE CREAM

Heat 2.5cm/1in of water in the bottom half of a double boiler over moderate heat. Place the white chocolate and 125ml/4fl oz half cream in the top half of the double boiler. Tightly cover the top with heat-resistant cling film. Allow to heat for 7 to 8 minutes. Remove from the heat and stir until smooth. Keep at room temperature until ready to use.

Heat the remaining 375ml/12fl oz half cream, the milk and 100g/3½oz sugar in a 3 litre/5 pint saucepan over moderately high heat. When hot, stir to dissolve the sugar. Bring to the boil.

While the cream is heating, place the egg yolks and the remaining 100g/3½oz sugar in the bowl of an electric mixer fitted with a flat beater. Beat on high for 2 to 2½ minutes. Scrape down the sides of the bowl, then beat on high until slightly thickened and lemon-coloured, a further 2½ to 3 minutes. (At this point, the cream should be boiling. If not, adjust the mixer speed to low and continue to mix until the cream boils. If the eggs are not mixed right up to the point the boiling cream is added, they will develop undesirable lumps.)

Pour the boiling cream into the beaten egg yolks and whisk to combine. Return to the saucepan and heat over moderately high heat, stirring constantly. Bring to a temperature of 85°C/185°F, about 1 minute. Remove from the heat and transfer to a 3 litre/5 pint stainless steel bowl. Add the melted white chocolate and cream mixture and stir to combine. Cool in an iced-water bath to a temperature of 5 to 7°C/40 to 45°F, about 20 minutes.

When the mixture is cold, freeze in an ice cream maker, following the manufacturer's instructions. While the ice cream is freezing, line the bottom and 2 narrow sides of a loaf tin with a single strip of baking parchment 10cm/4in wide and 45cm/18in long. Set aside until needed.

Transfer the semi-frozen white chocolate ice cream to a 3 litre/5 pint stainless steel bowl. Use a rubber spatula to fold the chopped nut bark into the ice cream. Now turn the ice cream into the loaf tin, spreading evenly. Cover the loaf tin with aluminium foil and freeze the ice cream terrine for 24 hours. Serve within 3 to 4 days.

TO SERVE

Remove the loaf tin from the freezer. Take off the aluminium foil. Briefly (that is, for a few seconds) dip the loaf tin in a sink containing 2.5cm/1in of very hot water. Turn out the terrine by inverting the tin on to a baking sheet lined with baking parchment; discard the used baking parchment. Then return the terrine to the freezer for 5 to 10 minutes.

This is the fun part: splatter 1 to 2 tablespoons of red raspberry sauce on to each of 8 to 10 large plates. Slice the ends from the terrine (go ahead and indulge yourself), and cut the terrine into 8 to 10 portions. Place a slice of terrine in the centre of each sauced plate and serve immediately.

THE CHEF'S TOUCH

The dark chocolate nut bark reminds me of one of my favourite childhood candies— Chunky—and Arnold Stang, the slightly oddball comedian who did their television commercials. Arnold's pitch included an enthusiastic exclamation, 'Chunky—what a chunk of chocolate!' I predict that you will have a similar exclamation after the first bite of this terrine.

Be sure to use unsalted peanuts for this recipe. Enhance their flavour by toasting them for 10 to 12 minutes in a 170°C/325°F/Gas 3 oven.

The egg yolks and sugar can be whisked with a hand-held electric mixer (mixing time may increase slightly) or by hand, using a wire whisk (mixing time may double). If either of these methods is used, be sure to continue whisking the yolks while waiting for the cream to come to the boil—otherwise you may end up with lumpy eggs.

'Splatter art' is what we call the random splashing of plates with sauces, melted chocolate, icing sugar or even cocoa powder. Avoid making a mess by placing the plate to be decorated into your kitchen sink or onto a large piece of baking parchment; then drop, scatter, splash, slosh or even spatter the sauce (or whatever) on to the plate. The effect is eclectic and tantalising, and the process is a lot of fun.

CHAPTER FOUR

NOSTALGIC INDULGENCES

'Cooking is like love, it should be entered into with abandon or not at all.'
—HARRIET VAN HORNE

MRS. D'S CHOCOLATE CARAMELS

VIRGINIA'S PRECIOUS FRUIT CAKE

WHISKEY SOAKED RAISIN BREAD PUDDING WITH JACK'S HONEY RAISIN SAUCE

'24' CARROT CAKE

TOASTED BRANDY AND SPICE CAKE

DAN'S BLUEBERRY SPONGE ROLL

AUNTIE EM'S ANGEL FOOD CAKE

CONNIE'S STICKY BUNS

MRS D'S CHOCOLATE CARAMELS

YIELDS 50 CARAMELS

INGREDIENTS

1 teaspoon melted unsalted butter

500ml/16fl oz whipping cream

200g/7oz caster sugar

250ml/8fl oz light corn syrup or liquid glucose

170g/6oz unsweetened chocolate, chopped into 5mm/¼in pieces

1 teaspoon pure vanilla essence

225g/8oz toasted walnut pieces

EQUIPMENT

Measuring jug, measuring spoons, small non-stick pan, chef's knife, cutting board, 25 × 38cm/10 × 15in baking tray, aluminium foil, pastry brush, 3 litre/5 pint saucepan, whisk, rubber spatula, serrated slicer

MAKE THE CHOCOLATE CARAMELS

Line a baking tray with aluminium foil. Lightly coat the foil with melted butter and set aside.

Heat the cream, sugar, corn syrup and chopped chocolate in a 3 litre/5 pint saucepan over moderate heat. When hot, stir to dissolve the sugar and chocolate. Bring the mixture to the boil (about 20 minutes), then adjust the heat to low and simmer gently for 40 minutes, stirring frequently, until quite thick. Remove from the heat. Add the vanilla essence and stir to combine. Add the chopped walnuts and stir with a rubber spatula to combine. Pour the mixture on to the foil-lined baking tray, using a rubber spatula to spread the mixture to the edges. Allow the mixture to stand at room temperature for 15 minutes, then refrigerate for 2 hours before cutting.

Turn the caramel out on to a cutting board. Use a serrated slicer to make 9 cuts across the width of the sheet of caramel at 4cm/1½in intervals. Then make 4 cuts across the length of the sheet at 5cm/2in intervals. Individually wrap each caramel in cling film or aluminium foil, and store in the refrigerator until ready to devour.

THE CHEF'S TOUCH

This recipe may upset consummate sweet makers. For starters, it's so simple. Furthermore, I don't tell you at what temperature to cook the caramel, only for how long. Well, folks, this is my mom's recipe and she has been making it for all of my 50 years, so I will refer you to Mrs D, if you feel like complaining. I do believe, though, that once these caramels are made, only kudos and proposals will be going her way (she is young and single, after all).

Toast the walnut pieces on a baking sheet in a 170°C/325°F/Gas 3 oven for 12 to 14 minutes. Allow the nuts to cool thoroughly before adding to the recipe.

For professional-looking caramels, heat the blade of the slicer under hot running water, then wipe the blade dry before making each cut across the caramel sheet. The caramels will have a clean, precise look.

For long-term storage, the individually wrapped caramels can be placed in a tightly sealed plastic container in the freezer. They will keep beautifully for several months that way. The one caveat with freezing: be sure to thaw the caramels before biting into them— a frozen caramel will keep your jaw tied up for more time than you might like.

VIRGINIA'S PRECIOUS FRUIT CAKE

SERVES 16 TO 24

INGREDIENTS

450g/1lb glacé cherries
560g/1¼lb plain flour
450g/1lb unsalted butter, cut into 16 equal pieces
500g/1lb 2oz caster sugar
6 size-3 eggs
2 teaspoons finely chopped lemon zest
1 teaspoon pure vanilla essence
½ teaspoon salt
450g/1lb toasted pecan halves

EQUIPMENT

Measuring jug, chef's knife, cutting board, vegetable peeler, measuring spoons, 2 baking sheets, 3 litre/5 pint stainless steel bowl, electric mixer with flat beater, rubber spatula, 25cm/10in non-stick angel cake tin or other deep ring tin, wooden skewer, serrated slicer

PREPARE THE FRUIT CAKE

Preheat the oven to 140°C/275°F/Gas 1.

Place the glacé cherries in a 3 litre/5 pint stainless steel bowl. Sprinkle 4 tablespoons flour over the cherries, then gently toss the cherries to coat lightly.

Place the butter and sugar in the bowl of an electric mixer fitted with a flat beater. Beat on medium for 3 minutes. Scrape down the sides of the bowl. Increase the speed to high and beat for 4 more minutes, then once again scrape down the sides of the bowl. Add the eggs, one at a time, beating on high for 1 minute and scraping down the bowl after each addition. Add the lemon zest and the vanilla essence and beat on high for 1 minute. Operate the mixer on low while gradually adding the remaining flour and the salt. Allow to mix until combined, about 30 seconds. Scrape down the sides of the bowl. Add the cherries and 340g/12oz of the pecans and mix on low for 15 seconds. Remove the bowl from the mixer and use a rubber spatula to finish mixing until thoroughly combined.

Immediately transfer the fruit cake mixture to the angel cake tin, then arrange the remaining pecan halves, smooth side down, on top of the mixture (gently press down on each pecan to set them ever so slightly into the mixture). Bake on the centre shelf of the preheated oven for about 2½ hours or until a wooden skewer inserted in the centre of the cake comes out clean. Remove the cake from the oven and allow to cool in the tin for 1 hour at room temperature. Turn out the cake from the tin. Allow the cake to cool at room temperature for 1 additional hour before slicing.

TO SERVE

Use a serrated slicer to cut the fruit cake into 2.5 to 4cm/1 to 1½in thick slices, depending on the desired number of servings. Serve immediately.

WHISKEY SOAKED RAISIN BREAD PUDDING

WITH JACK'S HONEY RAISIN SAUCE

SERVES 10

INGREDIENTS

WHISKEY SOAKED RAISINS

210g/7½oz raisins

125ml/4fl oz sour mash bourbon whiskey

BUTTERY BUN DOUGH

Buttery Bun Dough (see page 102)

2 teaspoons melted unsalted butter

CUSTARD

200g/7oz caster sugar

4 size-3 eggs

500ml/16fl oz half cream

½ teaspoon pure vanilla essence

1 teaspoon ground cinnamon

225g/8oz toasted walnuts, chopped into 5mm/¼in pieces

JACK'S HONEY RAISIN SAUCE

280g/10oz raisins

250ml/8fl oz sour mash bourbon whiskey

170g/6oz clear honey

EQUIPMENT

Measuring jug, measuring spoons, small non-stick sauté pan, baking tray, plastic container with lid, cling film, 100% cotton tea towel, pie tin, pastry brush, 23 × 12.5 × 7.5cm/9 × 5 × 3in loaf tin, small bowl, whisk, serrated slicer, cutting board, baking parchment, 5 litre/8 pint stainless steel bowl, instant-read thermometer, 1.5 litre/2½ pint saucepan, double boiler, paring knife

SOAK THE RAISINS IN WHISKEY

Combine the raisins and bourbon whiskey in a plastic container with a tight-fitting lid. Allow to stand at room temperature for 6 hours or overnight.

MAKE THE BUTTERY BUN DOUGH

Preheat the oven to 170°C/325°F/Gas 3.

Prepare the Buttery Bun Dough. Remove the bowl with the prepared dough from the mixer. Cover the dough with cling film and refrigerate for 1 hour. Remove the bowl from the refrigerator. Discard the film and cover the bowl of dough with a tea towel, then place in a warm location and allow the dough to rise for about 1 hour or until it has doubled in volume. Knock back the dough to its original size, transfer the dough to a pie tin, tightly cover with cling film and place in the freezer for 15 minutes.

Lightly coat the inside of a 23 × 12.5 × 7.5cm/ 9 × 5 × 3in loaf tin with 1 teaspoon melted butter. Set aside.

Remove the dough from the freezer. Use your hands to flatten the dough into a 20 × 25cm/8 × 10in rectangle on a clean, dry, lightly floured work surface, using the 4 tablespoons flour (from the Buttery Bun Dough recipe) as necessary. Starting from the narrow end, roll up the dough into a tight spiral to form it into 20cm/8in long loaf. Place the loaf in the buttered loaf tin. Whisk the remaining egg and milk (from the Buttery Bun Dough recipe), and gently and lightly brush the top of the dough with this egg wash.

Bake on the centre shelf of the preheated oven for 40 minutes. Remove from the oven and allow the baked loaf to cool in the tin for 15 minutes before removing. Remove the baked loaf from the tin and allow to cool to room temperature before cutting. Using a serrated slicer, first cut the loaf into 2.5cm/1in thick slices; then cut the slices into 2.5cm/1in cubes (don't trim off the crust). Cover with cling film and refrigerate until needed.

Lightly coat the inside of a clean 23 × 12.5 × 7.5cm/9 × 5 × 3in loaf tin with the remaining tea-spoon melted butter. Line the bottom and long sides (not the narrow ends) of the loaf tin with a 20 × 30cm/8 × 12in strip of baking parchment. Set aside.

PREPARE THE CUSTARD

Combine the sugar and eggs in a 5 litre/8 pint stainless steel bowl and whisk lightly to combine. Add the cream, vanilla essence and cinnamon and whisk to combine. Set aside.

ASSEMBLE AND BAKE THE BREAD PUDDING

Preheat the oven to 150°C/300°F/Gas 2.

Add the whiskey-soaked raisins to the custard and stir to combine. Now add the cubed loaf and the toasted walnut pieces. Use your hands to toss the ingredients together gently but thoroughly. Transfer the bread pudding mixture to the loaf tin, a handful at a time, gently pressing the bread pieces into the corners of the tin. Pour any custard remaining in the bowl over the ingredients in the loaf tin.

Bake the bread pudding on the centre shelf of the preheated oven for 1½ hours or until the internal temperature of the pudding reaches 60°C/140°F. Remove the baked bread pudding from the oven and keep in the tin for 1 hour before slicing and serving.

WHILE THE PUDDING BAKES, PREPARE JACK'S HONEY RAISIN SAUCE

Heat the raisins and bourbon whiskey in a 1.5 litre/ 2½ pint saucepan over moderate heat. Bring the mixture to the boil, then adjust the heat and allow to simmer gently for 20 minutes. Remove the saucepan from the heat. Add the honey and stir to incorporate. Keep the sauce warm in a double boiler until needed. You may also cool the sauce in an iced-water bath to a temperature of 5 to 7°C/40 to 45°F. When cold, transfer to a plastic container, cover tightly, and refrigerate until needed. Jack's Honey Raisin Sauce can be kept refrigerated for several days (the sauce will get sweeter by the day). Heat the sauce before serving—actually, it is also delicious cold or at room temperature, especially on a scoop or two of White Chocolate Ice Cream (see page 86).

TO SERVE

Remove the bread pudding from the loaf tin: use a thin-bladed paring knife to loosen the ends of the pudding away from the narrow ends of the tin, then grasp the baking parchment and lift the pudding out of the tin. Discard the baking parchment. Use a serrated slicer to cut the warm bread pudding into 10 2cm/¾in thick slices.

Serve each slice of bread pudding with 2 tablespoons of warm Honey Raisin Sauce.

'24' CARROT CAKE

SERVES 10 TO 12

INGREDIENTS

CARROT CAKE

240g/8½oz unsalted butter (15g/½oz melted)
170g/6oz grated carrot
155g/5½oz diced fresh pineapple
70g/2½oz dried apricots, finely chopped
70g/2½oz sultanas
125ml/4fl oz orange juice
55g/2oz toasted hazelnuts, finely chopped
420g/15oz plain flour
2 teaspoons bicarbonate of soda
1 teaspoon ground cinnamon
½ teaspoon salt
400g/14oz caster sugar
3 size-3 eggs

CREAM CHEESE ICING

675g/1½lb cream cheese, softened
4 tablespoons orange liqueur
1 teaspoon pure vanilla essence
55g/2oz icing sugar
70g/2½oz dried apricots, finely chopped
55g/2oz toasted hazelnuts, finely chopped

CARROT TOP GARNISH

115g/4oz grated carrot

EQUIPMENT

Measuring spoons, small non-stick sauté pan, vegetable peeler, hand grater, measuring jug, chef's knife, cutting board, baking tray, pastry brush, 2 23 × 5cm/9 × 2in round cake tins, baking parchment, 3 litre/5 pint stainless steel bowl, cling film, sieve, greaseproof paper, electric mixer with flat beater, rubber spatula, wooden cocktail stick, 2 round cake cards, palette knife, serrated slicer

PREPARE THE CARROT CAKE

Preheat the oven to 170°C/325°F/Gas 3.

Lightly coat the inside of 2 23 × 5cm/9 × 2in cake tins with melted butter. Line each tin with baking parchment, then lightly coat the parchment with more melted butter. Set aside.

Combine together in a 3 litre/5 pint stainless steel bowl the grated carrot, diced pineapple, finely chopped apricots, raisins, orange juice and finely chopped hazelnuts. Tightly cover the top with cling film and set aside at room temperature until needed.

Combine together in a sieve the flour, bicarbonate of soda, ground cinnamon and salt. Sift on to greaseproof paper and set aside.

Place the 225g/8oz remaining butter and the sugar in the bowl of an electric mixer fitted with a flat beater. Beat on medium for 3 minutes. Scrape down the sides of the bowl. Increase the speed to high and beat for 3 additional minutes. Scrape down the sides of the bowl.

Add the eggs, one at a time, beating on high for 1 minute and scraping down the sides of the bowl after each addition. Operate the mixer on low while gradually adding the sifted dry ingredients. Allow to mix for 30 seconds. Add the fruit-and-nut mixture and mix on low for 20 seconds. Remove the bowl from the mixer and use a rubber spatula to finish mixing until thoroughly combined.

Immediately divide the carrot cake mixture between the prepared tins, spreading evenly. Bake on the centre shelf in the preheated oven for about 50 minutes or until a wooden cocktail stick inserted in the centre of the cake comes out clean. Remove the cakes from the oven and cool in the tins for 20 minutes at room temperature. Turn out the cakes on to cake cards. Carefully remove the baking parchment. Allow the cakes to continue to cool at room temperature for 1 hour. While the cakes are cooling, move on to the next step.

MAKE THE CREAM CHEESE ICING

Place the *softened* cream cheese in the bowl of an electric mixer fitted with a flat beater. Beat on low for 1 minute. Scrape down the sides of the bowl and the beater. Increase the speed to medium and beat for 3 additional minutes. Scrape down the sides of the bowl. Add the orange liqueur and vanilla essence and beat on medium for 30 seconds (if you enjoy the fragrance of a tropical paradise that rises from the mixing bowl, wait until you taste the icing). Sift in the icing sugar and mix on low for 30 seconds. Scrape down the sides of the bowl. Now beat on high until the icing is light and smooth, about 3 minutes. Remove the bowl from the mixer. Transfer 250ml/8fl oz of the icing to a small bowl; add the diced apricots and chopped hazelnuts to this icing and use a rubber spatula to combine thoroughly. Set both icings aside at room temperature until ready to ice the cake (remember, the cakes need to be out of the tin and at room temperature for 1 hour before being iced).

ASSEMBLE THE CAKE

Spoon the apricot and hazelnut cream cheese icing on to one of the inverted cake layers. Use a palette knife to spread the icing evenly to the edges. Place the other inverted cake layer on top of the iced layer and press gently into place. Use a palette knife to spread the plain cream cheese icing evenly over the top and side of the cake. Refrigerate the cake for 1 hour before serving.

TO SERVE

Cut the carrot cake with a serrated slicer, heating the blade of the slicer under hot running water and wiping the blade dry before making each slice. Equally divide the grated carrot among the cake slices, sprinkling it on top. Serve immediately.

THE CHEF'S TOUCH

My assistant Jon Pierre Peavey developed a similar version of this cake for his sister Melanie's wedding several years ago. Jon named it '24' Carrot Cake because of its golden interior. For the nuptial celebration, Melanie had requested a dense and moist cake, but did not want a dark interior (something about her light-hearted personality suggested this) or an overly spiced flavour that would overwhelm the champagne bubbles. No need to wait for a

wedding to feel blissful, though—this cake will ring your chimes any day of the year.

A word about carrots: select small to medium carrots (they tend to be sweeter). You'll need about 340g/12oz of carrots, as purchased, to yield the total amount of grated carrot for this recipe. When choosing the carrots, pass over those that are cracked and have a withered appearance.

The carrots can be grated several hours before being used. Refrigerate the grated carrots in a

stainless steel bowl, tightly covered with cling film (do not store grated carrots in water, as this will diminish the flavour).

You may substitute dark raisins for the sultanas. The sultanas, however, contribute to the sunny blond interior of the cake, and tend to be moister and plumper than the dark variety.

The best beverage to enjoy with carrot cake is a vivacious Australian or New Zealand sparkling wine.

TOASTED BRANDY AND SPICE CAKE

SERVES 24

INGREDIENTS

575g/1¼lb plain flour
½ teaspoon bicarbonate of soda
½ teaspoon ground mace
½ teaspoon salt
450g/1lb unsalted butter
600g/1lb 5 oz caster sugar
5 size-3 eggs
2 tablespoons brandy
250ml/8fl oz creamy milk

EQUIPMENT

Measuring jug, measuring spoons, sieve, greaseproof paper, electric mixer with flat beater, rubber spatula, 25cm/10in non-stick angel cake tin or other deep ring tin, wooden skewer, serrated slicer, cutting board, 2 baking sheets

PREPARE THE CAKE

Preheat the oven to 170°C/325°F/Gas 3.

Combine together in a sieve the flour, bicarbonate of soda, mace and salt. Sift on to greaseproof paper and set aside.

Place the butter and sugar in the bowl of an electric mixer fitted with a flat beater. Mix on low for 2 minutes. Scrape down the sides of the bowl. Increase the speed to medium and beat for 3 minutes. Scrape down the sides of the bowl again, then beat on medium for an additional 3 minutes. Scrape down the sides of the bowl, then beat on high for 3 minutes. Scrape down the sides of the bowl. Add the eggs, one at a time, beating on medium for 1 minute and scraping down the bowl after each addition. Continue to beat on medium for an additional 4 minutes. Scrape down the sides of the bowl. Add the brandy and beat on medium for 2 minutes. Operate the mixer on low while adding one third of the sifted dry ingredients and 125ml/4fl oz milk; allow to mix for 30 seconds.

Add another one third of the sifted dry ingredients and the remaining 125ml/4fl oz milk and mix for another 30 seconds. Add the remaining dry ingredients and mix for an additional 30 seconds before removing the bowl from the mixer. Use a rubber spatula to finish mixing until smooth and thoroughly combined.

Immediately turn the cake mixture into the angel cake tin and bake on the centre shelf of the preheated oven for 1 hour and 35 minutes to 1 hour and 40 minutes or until a wooden skewer inserted in the centre of the cake comes out clean. Remove the cake from the oven and allow to cool in the tin for 15 to 20 minutes. Turn out the cake from the tin. Allow the cake to cool at room temperature for 1 hour before slicing.

TO SERVE

Preheat the grill to high.

Use a serrated slicer to cut the cake into 24 slices, each 2.5cm/1in thick (measured from the outside edge of the cake). Divide the cake slices between 2 baking sheets. Place under the grill, one at a time, and toast the slices for about 1 minute on each side or until golden brown and warm throughout. Remove from the oven and serve immediately, one slice per portion.

THE CHEF'S TOUCH

Probably not too many kitchens in America have a recipe file without a recipe for a 'pound' cake such as this. Its simplicity and infallibility no doubt contribute to this cake's popularity.

Pound cake garnered its name from an 'original' recipe reputed to have a pound of each of the primary ingredients (if you count flour, butter, sugar and eggs you end up with a 4-pound cake). There seems to be no shortage of variations on a theme for pound cake. Although this recipe doesn't add up poundwise, it surpasses most with its light texture and iconoclastic flavours of mace and brandy.

One of the secrets of baking a moist pound cake is to use a non-stick ring tin versus a loaf tin. It was tradition in my wife Connie's family that a pound cake had to be baked in one of those tins 'with the holes in them', according to Connie's cousin Letha. As Connie's mother, Virginia, sagely surmised, 'It seems to me that a pound cake baked in a loaf tin either is too gooey in the centre or too dry if cooked through'. We experimented, and Virginia is right.

The substantial amount of mixture for this cake fills the tin to near capacity. The baked result of this extravagance is a high, crested golden brown crust that lifts itself away from the tin with little regard to previously established pound cake behaviour.

Although the cake is delicious at room temperature, toasting the slices enhances both the flavour and the texture. For added pleasure I recommend serving the toasted slices of cake with White Chocolate Ice Cream (see page 86) and fresh berries (see what is available at the market).

If the cake is not to be polished off the day it is baked, cover with cling film (after it has cooled) and keep at cool room temperature for two to three days.

A cold glass of milk is a perfect accompaniment for this nostalgic cake, but with a Dessert To Die For, why be prosaic? Try a glass of glistening golden Sauternes.

DAN'S BLUEBERRY SPONGE ROLL

SERVES 8

INGREDIENTS

BLUEBERRY FILLING

340g/12oz fresh blueberries
150g/5½oz caster sugar
1 teaspoon fresh lemon juice
170g/6oz red raspberries

REALLY MOIST SPONGE

130g/4½oz unsalted butter (15g/½oz melted)
200g/7oz caster sugar
5 size-3 eggs
1 teaspoon pure vanilla essence
½ teaspoon almond essence
115g/4oz plain flour, sifted
½ teaspoon salt
2 tablespoons icing sugar

BITTER ALMOND BUTTERCREAM

2oog/7oz flaked almonds
340g/12oz unsalted butter, softened
3 size-3 egg whites
150g/5½oz caster sugar
½ teaspoon pure vanilla essence
½ teaspoon almond essence
2 tablespoons unsweetened cocoa powder

FRESH BLUEBERRY COULIS

340g/12oz fresh blueberries
50g/scant 2oz caster sugar

EQUIPMENT

Measuring jug, measuring spoons, sieve, greaseproof paper, 3 litre/5 pint saucepan, whisk, 3 litre/5 pint stainless steel bowl, 5 litre/8 pint stainless steel bowl, instant-read thermometer, cling film, 26 × 39cm/10½ × 15½in swiss roll tin, pastry brush, baking parchment, electric mixer with flat beater and balloon whisk, rubber spatula, sharp paring knife, palette knife, 2 baking sheets, double boiler, medium sieve, serrated slicer

PREPARE THE BLUEBERRY FILLING

Heat the blueberries, sugar and lemon juice in a 3 litre/5 pint saucepan over moderate heat. As the mixture heats, the sugar will dissolve and the blueberries will liquefy and begin to boil, after about 7 minutes. Allow the mixture to boil for about 20 minutes or until it becomes very thick, stirring frequently. Remove the mixture from the heat, add the raspberries and cool in an iced-water bath to a temperature of 5 to 7°C/40 to 45°F, about 20 minutes. Cover the blueberry filling with cling film and set aside at room temperature until needed.

MAKE THE REALLY MOIST SPONGE

Preheat the oven to 170°C/325°F/Gas 3.

Lightly but thoroughly coat the bottom and sides of the swiss roll tin with melted butter. Line the tin with baking parchment, then lightly coat the parchment with more melted butter. Set aside.

Place the remaining 115g/4oz butter and the caster sugar in the bowl of an electric mixer fitted with a flat beater. Beat on medium for 2 minutes. Scrape down the sides of the bowl, then beat on high for 3 minutes. Scrape down the sides of the bowl. Add eggs, one at a time, beating on medium for 1 minute and scraping down the sides of the bowl after each addition. Add the vanilla essence and almond essence and beat on high for 1 additional minute. Gradually add the sifted flour and the salt and mix on low for 40 seconds. Remove the bowl from the mixer and use a rubber spatula to finish mixing until smooth and thoroughly combined.

Pour the cake mixture into the prepared swiss roll tin, spreading evenly to the edges. Place the tin on the centre shelf of the preheated oven and bake for 14 to 15 minutes or until the edges of the sponge start to brown and pull away from the sides of the tin. Remove the sponge from the oven.

Sift the icing sugar over a large (approximately 45 × 55cm/18 × 22in) sheet of baking parchment.

Invert the still very warm sponge on to the paper (first use a sharp knife to loosen the sponge from the tin). Remove the lining parchment carefully from the sponge. Using a palette knife, spread the blueberry filling over the sponge. Spread evenly to the edges. Starting with the long side nearest you, roll up the sponge away from you, using the parchment to help lift the sponge over on to itself. Continue to roll up the sponge to the opposite end, making a tight roll. Now wrap the parchment around the sponge roll. Place on a baking sheet and refrigerate for 1 hour or until firm.

PREPARE THE BITTER ALMOND BUTTERCREAM

Preheat the oven to 170°C/325°F/Gas 3.

Toast the flaked almonds on a baking sheet in the preheated oven for 25 minutes or until uniformly dark brown (but not burnt). Remove from the oven and allow to cool to room temperature. Set the nuts aside until needed.

Place the butter in the bowl of an electric mixer fitted with a flat beater. Beat the butter on low for 2 minutes, then on medium for 3 minutes. Scrape down the sides of the bowl. Beat on high until light and fluffy, about 3 minutes. Transfer the butter to a 5 litre/8 pint stainless steel bowl and set aside until needed.

Heat 2.5cm/1in of water in the bottom half of a double boiler over moderate heat. Place the egg whites and caster sugar in the top half of the double boiler. Gently whisk the egg whites as they heat, to reach a temperature of 49°C/120°F, about 2 minutes. Transfer the heated egg whites to the *clean* bowl of an electric mixer fitted with a balloon whisk. Whisk on high until stiff peaks form, about 4 minutes. Add the vanilla essence and almond essence and whisk on high for 30 seconds. Remove the bowl from the mixer. Sift the cocoa on to the whisked egg white mixture. Use a rubber spatula to fold the cocoa into the egg whites. Gently but thoroughly fold the egg white–and–cocoa mixture into the butter. Set aside for a few moments.

ASSEMBLE DAN'S BLUEBERRY SPONGE ROLL

Remove the sponge roll from the refrigerator. Unwrap the roll and discard the parchment. Carefully place the sponge roll, seam side down, on a clean baking sheet or a large platter. Using a palette knife, evenly spread the bitter almond buttercream over the top and sides, but not the ends (and not the seam side bottom), of the sponge roll. Now gently and evenly press the toasted almonds into the buttercream on the top and sides of the sponge roll. Refrigerate for at least 1 hour before serving.

MAKE THE FRESH BLUEBERRY COULIS

Heat the blueberries and sugar in a 3 litre/5 pint saucepan over moderate heat. As the mixture heats, the sugar will dissolve and after about 5 minutes the blueberries will liquefy and begin to boil.

Remove the mixture from the heat and pass through a medium sieve into a small stainless steel bowl. Use a rubber spatula to press the berries through the sieve, releasing as much berry juice as possible. Discard the pulp from the sieve.

Cool in an iced-water bath to a temperature of 5 to 7°C/40 to 45°F, about 15 to 20 minutes. The coulis can be used immediately or transferred to a plastic container (tightly covered) and kept refrigerated for 4 to 5 days.

TO SERVE

Use a serrated slicer to trim a 5mm/¼in thick slice from each end of the sponge roll. Cut the roll into 8 slices, each 3cm/1¼in thick. Heat the blade of the serrated slicer under hot running water and wipe the blade dry before cutting each slice.

Drizzle 2 tablespoons of blueberry coulis on to each serving plate. Stand a slice of sponge roll in the centre of each plate and serve immediately.

THE CHEF'S TOUCH

My literary agent Dan Green encouraged me to include a sponge roll as one of the Nostalgic Indulgences. I'm always fascinated by people's favourite childhood confections (my favourite was my mother's peanut fudge). For Dan, the luscious spiral of jam in a sponge roll conjures up memories—and temptations—that took root during his childhood.

The allure of this sponge roll is indeed the luscious, jewel-toned fresh blueberry filling. I recommend indulging in this sponge roll only when fresh blueberries are available.

For convenience, you may want to prepare the blueberry filling before assembling the sponge roll. Refrigerate the cooled filling, tightly covered in a plastic container, for up to a week before using.

Be sure to use a swiss roll tin and not a baking tray. A regular baking tray is too shallow at only 1.5cm/½in deep, whereas a swiss roll tin is from 2 to 2.5cm/¾ to 1in deep.

The Bitter Almond Buttercream recipe produces a significant amount of buttercream, and all of it is needed to apply the lavish coating that makes this sponge roll so delectable. If you have difficulty applying all the buttercream to the sponge roll at once, consider spreading a thin layer, refrigerating the roll for a few minutes, and then applying a couple more layers (refrigerating between applications).

For a more artistic look, try placing the toasted almonds one by one in a pattern into the buttercream (sounds crazy, but like Michelangelo hanging from the ceiling of the Sistine Chapel, some artistic endeavours are worth the effort).

This is an extraordinary sponge roll, and I recommend an extraordinary American sparkling wine to accompany it: a Cuvee de Pinot from Jack Davies' Schramsberg winery. Its ripe flavour and beautiful amber colour complement the luscious, multi-textured sponge roll.

AUNTIE EM'S ANGEL FOOD CAKE

YIELDS 6 MINI CAKES

INGREDIENTS

MINI ANGEL FOOD CAKES

10 size-3 egg whites

1 teaspoon cream of tartar

¼ teaspoon salt

200g/7oz caster sugar

3 tablespoons finely chopped orange zest

1 tablespoon orange liqueur

115g/4oz plain flour, sifted

CARAMEL PINEAPPLE SAUCE

185ml/6fl oz whipping cream

250g/9oz caster sugar

½ teaspoon fresh lemon juice

1 large pineapple (about 1.6kg/3½lb), peeled and core removed, cut into 5mm/¼in slices

WARM STRAWBERRIES

30g/1oz unsalted butter

2 tablespoons caster sugar

675g/1½ lb strawberries, cut into 5mm/¼ in slices

DOUBLE CHOCOLATE SAUCE

½ recipe of Double Chocolate Sauce (see page 130), warm

EQUIPMENT

Measuring spoons, measuring jug, vegetable peeler, chef's knife, cutting board, sieve, greaseproof paper, electric mixer with balloon whisk, rubber spatula, 6 individual non-stick angel cake tins or other ring tins, small plastic knife, 1.5 litre/2½ pint saucepan, 3 litre/5 pint saucepan, whisk, 3 litre/5 pint stainless steel bowl, 5 litre/8 pint stainless steel bowl, instant-read thermometer, large non-stick sauté pan

PREPARE THE MINI ANGEL FOOD CAKES

Preheat the oven to 180°C/350°F/Gas 4.

Place the egg whites, cream of tartar and salt in the bowl of an electric mixer fitted with a balloon whisk. Whisk on medium for 1 minute or until foamy. Increase the speed to high and whisk for 2 more minutes or until soft peaks form. Gradually add the caster sugar while whisking on high until stiff but not dry, about 4 minutes. Add the orange zest and orange liqueur and whisk on high for an additional 20 seconds (gradually move the speed to high to prevent spewing the orange liqueur from the bowl). Remove the bowl from the mixer. Using a rubber spatula, fold in the flour, combining thoroughly.

Use a tablespoon to divide the cake mixture evenly among the individual tins (about 8 heaping tablespoons per tin), filling them to just below the rim. Use the back of the spoon to smooth the top of the mixture in each tin. Place the tins on the centre shelf of the preheated oven. Bake for 30 minutes or until golden brown and the tops are dry to the touch.

Remove from the oven and invert the tins over the tops of small bottles or funnels (the inverted cakes should be suspended high enough so that they do not touch the surface below). Allow to cool for 30 minutes at room temperature. To remove the cakes, use a small plastic knife to 'cut' around the edge of each cake to loosen it from the side and centre funnel of each tin; then gently twist each cake to free it from the tin without tearing the delicate outer crust. Set the cakes aside at room temperature until needed.

MAKE THE CARAMEL PINEAPPLE SAUCE

Heat the cream in a 1.5 litre/2½ pint saucepan over low heat.

While the cream is heating, place the sugar and the lemon juice in a 3 litre/5 pint saucepan. Stir with a whisk to combine (the sugar will resemble moist sand). Caramelise the sugar by heating for 7 minutes over moderately high heat, stirring constantly with a wire whisk to break up any lumps (the sugar will first turn clear as it liquefies, then light brown as it caramelises).

Slowly and carefully add the hot cream, whisking briskly to combine. Immediately add the pineapple pieces and stir to combine. Adjust the heat as necessary to allow the sauce to simmer for 20 minutes, stirring frequently, until the sauce becomes slightly thickened. Remove from the heat and transfer to a stainless steel bowl, then cool in an iced-water bath to a temperature of 5 to 7°C/40 to 45°F. The cooled caramel pineapple sauce can be kept at room temperature while preparing the warm strawberries, or cover with cling film and refrigerate for up to 3 to 4 days.

TO SERVE

Heat the butter and sugar in a large non-stick sauté pan over moderately high heat, constantly stirring to dissolve the sugar. When the mixture begins to bubble, add the strawberries and heat for 2 minutes or until warmed through (use a rubber spatula to stir the strawberries gently while heating). Remove the tin from the heat.

Portion 3 to 4 heaping tablespoons of caramel pineapple sauce on to each dessert plate. Place a mini angel food cake in the centre of each plate. Spoon 2 to 3 tablespoons of warm Double Chocolate Sauce on to the top and side of each cake, allowing some of the sauce to spill into the centre of the cake. Portion 3 tablespoons of warm strawberries directly on top of the caramel pineapple sauce and around each cake. Serve immediately.

THE CHEF'S TOUCH

These mini cakes are elevated above the commonplace with a zestful orange infusion and the company of Caramel Pineapple Sauce, warm strawberries and decadent Double Chocolate Sauce.

Legend has it that thrifty Pennsylvania Dutch cooks developed angel food as a way to use the surfeit of egg whites that remained after producing the yolk-rich noodles they favoured. Although it is nice to know the genesis, don't wait until you make noodles to prepare these cakes. A few yolks are a worthy sacrifice for the small indulgence of supernal angel food.

Do use freshly separated egg whites for the preparation of these cakes. Some cooks are fond of saving egg whites in the freezer or refrigerator for long periods of time. Don't do it, or your angel will not be as heavenly.

One medium orange should yield the necessary zest for this recipe.

Once cooled, the mini cakes can be covered with cling film and kept at cool room temperature for two to three days.

Given Auntie Em's predilection for stepping out in borrowed red 10cm/4in high heels, her preference for a refreshing glass of orange juice as an accompaniment to her angel food may seem mundane. Knowing her as I do, however, I wouldn't be surprised to find her juice laced with vodka.

CONNIE'S STICKY BUNS

YIELDS 6 BUNS

INGREDIENTS

BUTTERY BUN DOUGH

2 tablespoons caster sugar

125ml/4fl oz warm water

2 tablespoons dried yeast

5 size-3 eggs

560g/1¼lb plain flour, plus 4 tablespoons for rolling

1 teaspoon salt

225g/8oz unsalted butter, softened, cut into 16 equal pieces

1 tablespoon creamy milk

CINNAMON WALNUT FILLING

115g/4oz toasted walnuts, chopped

225g/8oz soft light brown sugar

1 teaspoon ground cinnamon

STICKY GLAZE

115g/4oz unsalted butter, softened

4 tablespoons (85g/3oz) pure maple syrup

115g/4oz soft dark brown sugar

115g/4oz toasted walnuts, chopped

EQUIPMENT

Measuring spoons, measuring jug, baking sheet, chef's knife, cutting board, electric mixer with flat beater and dough hook, whisk, cling film, 2 small stainless steel bowls, rubber spatula, 6 individual soufflé dishes, each 250ml/8fl oz capacity, pastry brush, serrated slicer, 100% cotton tea towel, wooden skewer

PREPARE THE BUTTERY BUN DOUGH

Preheat the oven to 170°C/325°F/Gas 3.

In the bowl of an electric mixer, dissolve the caster sugar in the warm water. Add the yeast and stir gently to dissolve. Allow the mixture to stand and foam for 3 minutes.

Attach the mixing bowl to the electric mixer fitted with a flat beater. Add 4 of the eggs on top of the yeast mixture, then add the flour and, finally, add the salt. Combine on low speed for 1 minute. Remove the beater and replace it with the dough hook. Mix on medium low until the dough forms a smooth ball, about 3 minutes. Adjust the mixer speed to medium and add the butter, one piece at a time, being sure that each piece is thoroughly incorporated (this takes about 1 minute for each) before adding the next. (If the dough creeps to the top of the dough hook—which often happens to me—stop the mixer and pull the dough off the hook and back into the bowl.) Continue to add the butter until all of it has been thoroughly incorporated into the dough.

Remove the bowl from the mixer and take out the dough hook. Cover the bowl with cling film and refrigerate for 1 hour.

MAKE THE CINNAMON WALNUT FILLING

Place the chopped walnuts, light brown sugar and cinnamon in a small bowl. Use a rubber spatula to stir the mixture until thoroughly combined. Set aside at room temperature until needed.

MAKE THE STICKY GLAZE

Place the butter in the bowl of an electric mixer fitted with a flat beater. Beat on high for 2 minutes. Scrape down the sides of the bowl. Add the maple syrup and dark brown sugar and beat on medium for 1 minute or until thoroughly combined.

Generously coat the inside of 6 individual soufflé dishes with the glaze, using 3 tablespoons for each dish. Evenly divide the chopped walnuts among the soufflé dishes, sprinkling the nuts over the bottom. Place the prepared dishes on a baking sheet and set aside until needed.

ASSEMBLE AND BAKE THE STICKY BUNS

Make an egg wash by whisking together the remaining egg and the tablespoon of milk from the Buttery Bun Dough recipe.

Transfer the dough (after it has been refrigerated for 1 hour) to a clean, dry work surface sprinkled with the 4 tablespoons flour. Use your hands to flatten the dough into a 25 × 35cm/10 × 14in rectangle, then gently and lightly brush the entire surface of the dough with the egg wash (there will be some wash left over). Evenly sprinkle the cinnamon walnut filling over the egg-washed surface of the dough, leaving a 2.5cm/1in wide border along the long edge nearest you. Now roll up the dough, from the other long edge, towards you (creating a spiral of dough around the filling).

Use a serrated slicer to cut the rolled dough across into 6 pieces, each 2cm/¾in wide (although the dough was only 35cm/14in long, it stretches out and gets longer—about 40cm/16in—when rolled). Place the pieces, cut side up, in the prepared soufflé dishes. Use your fingers to gently press down on the dough to eliminate any large gaps between the dough and the inside surface of the dish.

Cover with a tea towel and allow to rise in a warm location for 30 minutes or until the dough reaches about 2.5cm/1in above the top edge of the soufflé dishes. Place the baking sheet with the soufflé dishes in the preheated oven and bake for 35 minutes or until golden brown and a wooden skewer inserted in the centre comes out clean. Remove the buns from the oven and allow them to cool in the soufflé dishes for 10 to 15 minutes before turning out.

TO SERVE

If serving warm from the oven, turn out the sticky buns from the soufflé dishes on to individual serving plates. Use a rubber spatula to spread the glaze remaining in the soufflé dishes on to the tops of the buns. Serve immediately. The buns can be kept at room temperature for several hours, then reheated in a 150°C/300°F/Gas 2 oven for several minutes or until warm throughout. For reheating, place the buns on a baking sheet covered with parchment.

THE CHEF'S TOUCH

I consider this recipe to be the most decadent of our nostalgic indulgences, especially when the buns are served warm from the oven with Maple Syrup and Toasted Walnut Ice Cream (see page 82).

Before chopping, toast the walnuts on a baking sheet in a 170°C/325°F/Gas 3 oven for 12 to 14 minutes. (Cool the nuts thoroughly before chopping.)

Leave the sticky buns in the soufflé dishes for 10 to 15 minutes after baking in order to set the glaze on the buns; if the buns are removed from the dishes too soon, the glaze will dribble off the buns in thin rivulets.

My wife, Connie, recommends enjoying a cold glass of skimmed milk with the sticky buns. Tea or coffee are fine too.

CHAPTER FIVE

DROP-DEAD DELECTATIONS

'Nothing succeeds like excess.'

—OSCAR WILDE

AUTUMNAL PASTICHE

CHERRY BOMB WITH CHERRIES AND BERRIES

WILD ORCHID

CHOCOLATE MADONNA

CHOCOLATE EXQUISITE PAIN

CHOCOLATE RESURRECTION

PILLAR OF CHOCOLATE WITH COCOA THUNDERHEADS

TERCENTENARY EXTRAVAGANZA

AUTUMNAL PASTICHE

SERVES 8

INGREDIENTS

AUTUMNAL GARNISH

70g/2½oz currants

125ml/4fl oz port

140g/5oz toasted hazelnuts, halved (see page 22 for tips on toasting hazelnuts)

AUTUMN LEAF BISCUITS

225g/8oz unsalted butter

200g/7oz caster sugar

¼ teaspoon salt

6 size-3 egg whites

½ teaspoon pure vanilla essence

280g/10oz plain flour

2 tablespoons soft dark brown sugar

2 tablespoons warm water

WARM CINNAMON CUSTARD

250ml/8fl oz half cream

125ml/4fl oz whipping cream

2 size-3 egg yolks

3 tablespoons caster sugar

1 teaspoon cornflour

½ teaspoon ground cinnamon

LATE HARVEST SORBET

Late Harvest Sorbet (see page 68)

EQUIPMENT

Measuring jug, two 25 × 38cm/10 × 15in baking trays, paring knife, cutting board, measuring spoons, plastic container with lid, oak or maple leaf (leaf should be no larger than 11 × 16cm/4½ × 6½in), lightweight card, pencil, artist's scalpel, electric mixer with flat beater, rubber spatula, 1 litre/2 pint stainless steel bowl, baking parchment, palette knife, large flat plastic container with lid, 1.5 litre/2½ pint saucepan, whisk, two 3 litre/5 pint stainless steel bowls, instant-read thermometer, ice cream scoop

SOAK THE CURRANTS

Combine the currants and port in a plastic container with a tight-fitting lid. Allow to stand at room temperature for several hours or overnight.

PREPARE THE AUTUMN LEAF BISCUITS

Preheat the oven to 150°C/300°F/Gas 2.

Pick out a suitably shaped leaf, then make a template: using a pencil, trace an outline of the leaf on to a 13 × 18cm/5 × 7in piece of lightweight card; then cut along the outline of the leaf using an artist's scalpel or scissors (remove the leaf-shaped cutout). The outer piece of card with the leaf-shaped hole is the template.

To make the biscuit mixture, place the butter, caster sugar and salt in the bowl of an electric mixer fitted with a flat beater. Beat on low for 1 minute, then on medium for 1 minute. Scrape down the sides of the bowl and beat on high for 1 additional minute. Once again, scrape down the sides of the bowl.

Add the egg whites, one at a time, beating on high for 1 minute and scraping down the bowl after each addition. Add the vanilla essence and beat on medium for 30 seconds. Add the flour and beat on low for 15 seconds, then on medium for 10 seconds. Remove the bowl from the mixer and use a rubber spatula to finish mixing until smooth and thoroughly combined.

Transfer 125ml/4fl oz of the biscuit mixture to a 1 litre/2 pint bowl. Add the dark brown sugar and warm water. Use a rubber spatula to stir gently, until thoroughly combined. Form a piping cone with baking parchment. Transfer the mixture to the piping cone. Cut off a 3mm/⅛in tip from the cone. (This mixture will be used to create the 'veins' in the leaves.)

Line two 25 × 38cm/10 × 15in baking sheets with baking parchment.

Place the template on the parchment so that it touches one of the inside corners of the baking sheet. Place 1 level tablespoon of the plain biscuit mixture in the centre of the leaf outline. Use a palette knife to smear a thin coating of mixture to cover the inside of the template completely (carefully scrape away any excess mixture on the surface of the template).

Carefully lift the template away from the leaf-shaped biscuit. Repeat this procedure to form 3 more leaves, one at a time, in the 3 remaining corners of the baking sheet. Then repeat to form 4 more leaves on the second baking sheet. Pipe out 'veins' on each leaf-shaped biscuit using the paper piping cone filled with the darkened mixture. Bake both sheets on the centre shelf of the preheated oven for 6 to 8 minutes or until golden brown.

While the leaf biscuits are baking, cut 10 more pieces of baking parchment to fit the baking sheets.

Remove the biscuits from the oven. Work quickly, using a palette knife to lift the baked biscuits off the parchment, resting each biscuit against the outside edge of a dinner plate so that it bends in a naturalistic way as it cools. (This must be done quickly—otherwise the leaves will harden before they are shaped.)

Prepare the remaining leaves following the same procedure used with the first batch, baking 8 biscuits at a time on 2 baking sheets (line the baking sheets with new parchment for each batch of biscuits).

Once all the leaf biscuits have been baked and cooled, they can be stored in a tightly sealed plastic container at room temperature until needed (they will stay crisp for several days in a tightly sealed container at cool room temperature).

PREPARE THE WARM CINNAMON CUSTARD

Heat the half cream and whipping cream in a 1.5 litre/2½ pint saucepan over moderately high heat. Bring to the boil.

While the cream is heating, whisk the egg yolks, caster sugar, cornflour and cinnamon in a 3 litre/5 pint stainless steel bowl for 4 minutes or until slightly thickened and lemon-coloured. Pour the boiling cream into this mixture and stir gently to combine. Return to the saucepan and heat over moderate heat, stirring constantly, until the cream reaches a temperature of 82°C/180°F, 1 to 1½ minutes. Remove from the heat and pour into a stainless steel bowl.

The custard can be used immediately or cooled in an iced-water bath to a temperature of 5°C/40°F, about 15 minutes. Transfer the cooled custard to a tightly sealed plastic container. Refrigerate until ready to use, for up to 3 days. To use, heat the custard in a double boiler over moderate heat.

ARRANGE THE AUTUMNAL PASTICHE

Place 4 to 5 leaf biscuits in the centre of each plate. Place 3 small scoops of Late Harvest Sorbet in the centre of each grouping of leaf biscuits. Drizzle 3 tablespoons of Warm Cinnamon Custard over the sorbet. Sprinkle the port-soaked currants and the toasted hazelnuts over the sorbet on each plate and serve immediately.

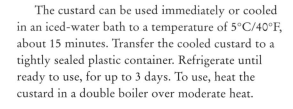

Using a pencil, trace an outline of the leaf onto 13 × 18cm/ 5 × 7in piece of lightweight cardboard.

Cut along the outline of the leaf, using a sharp artist's scalpel.

The completed template.

Use a palette knife to smear a thin coating of the batter to completely cover the inside of the template.

Carefully lift the template away from the leaf-shaped batter.

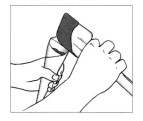

Transfer the darkened batter to the pastry cone.

Pipe out veins onto the leaf-shaped batter using the pastry bag filled with the darkened batter.

Working quickly, use a palette knife to lift the baked biscuits off the baking parchment, resting each biscuit against the outside edge of a dinner plate so that the biscuit bends in a naturalistic way as it cools.

CHERRY BOMB WITH CHERRIES AND BERRIES

SERVES 6

INGREDIENTS

BURNT ORANGE SNAP 'FIRECRACKERS'

Burnt Orange Snaps mixture (see page 136), uncooked

WHITE CHOCOLATE MOUSSE

115g/4oz white chocolate, broken into 15g/½oz pieces

500ml/16fl oz whipping cream

CHERRIES AND BERRIES

675g/1½lb fresh strawberries, stemmed

340g/12oz fresh blueberries, stemmed

50g/scant 2oz caster sugar

1 tablespoon fresh lemon juice

450g/1lb fresh cherries, stoned and cut in half (save 6 whole cherries with stalks for the firecracker fuses)

2 tablespoons orange liqueur

EQUIPMENT

Vegetable peeler, chef's knife, cutting board, measuring jug, measuring spoons, paring knife, electric mixer with flat beater and balloon whisk, rubber spatula, 2 baking sheets, baking parchment, palette knife, 18 to 20 × 4 to 5cm/7 to 8 × 1½ to 2in wooden dowel, double boiler, heat-resistant cling film, two 3 litre/5 pint stainless steel bowls, stiff wire whisk, food processor with metal blade, piping bag, medium straight nozzle, oval soup spoon

PREPARE THE BURNT ORANGE SNAP 'FIRECRACKERS'

Make the burnt orange snap mixture.

Preheat the oven to 180°C/350°F/Gas 4.

Line 2 baking sheets with baking parchment.

Portion 1 heaping tablespoon of the mixture in the centre of both parchment-lined baking sheets (do not spread the mixture—it will spread in the oven). Bake on the centre shelf of the pre-heated oven for 11 to 12 minutes or until uniformly golden brown in the centre and dark brown around the edges. Remove both baking sheets from the oven. Set one baking sheet aside. Immediately remove the parchment with the Burnt Orange Snap from the other baking sheet. Invert the snap (parchment side up) on to a clean flat surface. Peel the parchment from the snap using a palette knife to press down one edge of the snap while peeling away the paper. Avoid tearing the snap.

Lay an 18 to 20cm/7 to 8in long by 4 to 5cm/1½ to 2in diameter dowel (or similarly shaped object, such as a section of clean, new PVC pipe) centred horizontally at the edge of the snap. Roll the snap around the dowel to form a tubular-shaped firecracker (this must be done quickly or the snap will harden and break when rolled around the dowel). Once the snap has been completely rolled, push the dowel through the snap to remove it. Repeat this procedure with the remaining snap. (If the snap becomes too hard and brittle to roll, pop it back in the oven for 30 to 45 seconds.) Set the firecrackers aside to cool.

Bake the remaining 4 firecrackers, 2 at a time, following the same procedure used with the first 2 (use new parchment for each). Allow the rolled firecrackers to cool thoroughly before using.

MAKE THE WHITE CHOCOLATE MOUSSE

Heat 2.5cm/1in of water in the bottom half of a double boiler over moderate heat. Place the white chocolate in the top half of the double boiler. Tightly cover the top with heat-resistant cling film and allow to heat for 6 to 7 minutes. Remove from the heat and stir until smooth. Transfer the melted white chocolate to a 3 litre/5 pint stainless steel bowl. Set aside at room temperature until needed.

Place the cream in the well-chilled bowl of an electric mixer fitted with a well-chilled balloon whisk. Whip on high until stiff, about 30 seconds. Remove the bowl from the mixer. Transfer one third of the whipped cream to the bowl of white chocolate. Use a stiff hand-held wire whisk to whisk the cream and chocolate vigorously together. Add the remaining whipped cream to the combined chocolate and cream, and use a rubber spatula to fold together until smooth. Cover the bowl with cling film and refrigerate for at least 30 minutes before assembling the dessert.

PREPARE THE CHERRIES AND BERRIES

First place 340g/12oz whole strawberries, 85g/3oz blueberries, the sugar and lemon juice in the bowl of a food processor fitted with a metal blade. Process the berries until liquefied, about 30 seconds (this should yield 440ml/14fl oz of berry coulis). Transfer the coulis to a stainless steel bowl, cover with cling film and refrigerate until needed.

Cut the remaining strawberries into quarters. Place the quartered strawberries, the remaining blueberries and the cherry halves in a 3 litre/5 pint stainless steel bowl. Sprinkle the orange liqueur over the berries. Toss gently to combine. Cover with cling film and refrigerate until needed.

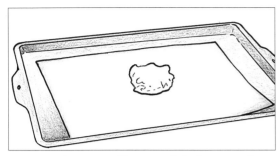

Portion 1 heaping tablespoon of the batter in the centre of the baking parchment–lined baking sheet.

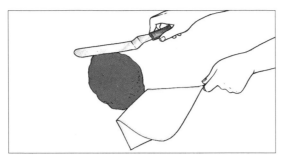

Peel the baking parchment from the snap, using a palette knife to press down one edge of the snap while peeling.

TO SERVE

Splatter 2 to 3 heaping tablespoons of berry coulis on each 25 to 30cm/10 to 12in diameter plate (if splattering a plate with coulis seems a bit odd, see The Chef's Touch for the 'What a Chunk of Chocolate' Ice Cream Terrine on page 86). Alternatively, you can simply ladle the coulis on to the centre of each plate.

Fill a piping bag fitted with a medium straight nozzle with half the mousse. Pipe a small mound of mousse on to the centre of each plate, evenly dividing the mousse among the 6 plates. Stand a 'firecracker' on its end in the centre of each mound of mousse. Use an oval soup spoon to fill each firecracker with about 3 tablespoons of the flavoured cherries and berries mixture, leaving about 1.5cm/½in of space from the top. Fill the piping bag with the remaining white chocolate mousse, then top the fruit in each 'firecracker' with an equal amount of the mousse. Place a whole cherry with stalk (the fuse) on top of the mousse on each 'firecracker'. Sprinkle the remaining cherries and berries (about 3 tablespoons per plate) around the base of each 'firecracker'. Serve immediately.

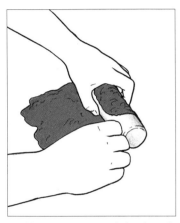

Roll the snap around the dowel to form a 'firecracker' shape.

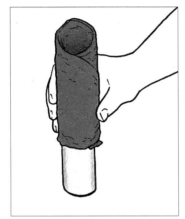

Once the snap has been completely rolled, push the dowel through the snap to remove.

Pipe a small mound of mousse onto the centre of each plate, evenly dividing the mousse among the six plates.

Use an oval soup spoon to fill each 'firecracker' with about 3 tablespoons of the flavoured cherries and berries mixture, leaving about 1cm/½ in of space from the top.

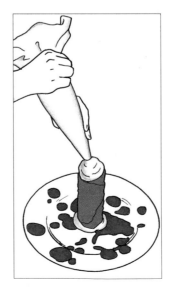

Fill the piping bag with the remaining mousse, then top the fruit in each 'firecracker' with an equal amount of the mousse.

WILD ORCHID
SERVES 8

INGREDIENTS

MACADAMIA NUT PETALS

225g/8oz unsalted butter

100g/3½oz caster sugar

125ml/4fl oz light corn syrup or liquid glucose

1 teaspoon pure vanilla essence

115g/4oz toasted macadamia nuts, finely chopped

175g/6oz plain flour

COCONUT CREAM

450g/1lb cream cheese, softened

225g/8oz fresh coconut meat, finely chopped

4 tablespoons coconut liquid

6 tablespoons icing sugar

MANGO COULIS

2 ripe medium mangoes, peeled, stoned and
 cut into large chunks

100g/3½oz caster sugar

125ml/4fl oz water

2 tablespoons fresh lemon juice

125ml/4fl oz fresh orange juice

2 tablespoons dark rum

GARNISH

4 whole kiwi fruit, peeled, halved lengthwise and
 each cut into 6 slices

8 whole strawberries, stemmed and quartered

115g/4oz toasted macadamia nuts, quartered

EQUIPMENT

Measuring jug, measuring spoons, two 23 × 33cm/
9 × 13in baking sheets, food processor with metal
blade, chef's knife, cutting board, baking
parchment, electric mixer with flat beater, rubber
spatula, palette knife, two 20 to 25cm/8 to 10in
long by 4.5cm/1¾in diameter wooden dowels, flat
plastic container with lid, 2 litre/3 pint stainless
steel bowl, cling film, 3 litre/5 pint saucepan,
3 litre/5 pint stainless steel bowl, 5 litre/8 pint
stainless steel bowl, instant-read thermometer,
piping bag, medium straight nozzle

PREPARE THE MACADAMIA NUT PETALS

Preheat the oven to 170°C/325°F/Gas 3.

Line 2 baking sheets with baking parchment.
Place the butter, caster sugar and corn syrup in the
bowl of an electric mixer fitted with a flat beater.
Beat on medium for 2 minutes. Scrape down the
sides of the bowl. Beat on medium for an additional 2 minutes. Scrape down the sides of the
bowl. Add the vanilla essence and beat on high for
30 seconds. Add the chopped macadamia nuts and
beat on high for 30 seconds. Once more, scrape
down the sides of the bowl. Add the flour and beat
on low for 30 seconds. Remove the bowl from the
mixer and use a rubber spatula to finish mixing
until smooth and thoroughly combined.

Portion 4 level *tablespoons* of mixture, evenly
spaced, on to each of the 2 parchment-lined baking
sheets (no need to spread the mixture—it will do so
on its own). Bake both sheets on the centre shelf
of the preheated oven for 12 minutes or until the
petals are golden brown around the edges. Remove
both baking sheets from the oven. Use a palette
knife immediately to remove the petals, one at a
time, from the baking sheets and drape each over
one of the wooden dowels (if the petals are so delicate that they tear, wait a few seconds before
removing them from the parchment). Allow the
petals to cool on the dowels for about 2 to 3 minutes. Set the petals aside until needed.

Prepare 2 more batches of petals following the
same procedure used with the first batch, making
8 petals at a time on 2 baking sheets, until 24 petals
have been baked. (Line the baking sheets with new
parchment for each batch of petals you make.)

Next, prepare smaller petals. Portion 6 level *teaspoons* of mixture, evenly spaced, on to each of 2
parchment-lined baking sheets. Bake both sheets on

the centre shelf of the preheated oven for 7 to 8 minutes or until the petals are golden brown around the edges. Remove both baking sheets from the oven. Immediately use a palette knife to remove the petals, one at a time, from the baking sheets, draping each over the wooden dowel.

Allow the petals to cool on the dowels for about 2 to 3 minutes. Set the petals aside until needed.

Prepare one more batch of small petals following the same procedure used with the first batch, baking 12 petals on 2 baking sheets. (Line the baking sheets with new parchment for the last batch of petals.)

Once all the petals have been baked and cooled, they can be stored in a tightly sealed plastic container at cool room temperature. They will stay crisp for several days.

MAKE THE COCONUT CREAM

Place the softened cream cheese, chopped coconut and coconut liquid in the bowl of an electric mixer fitted with a flat beater. Beat on medium for 3 minutes. Scrape down the sides of the bowl. Sift in the icing sugar and beat on low for 1 minute. Scrape down the sides of the bowl. Beat on medium for an additional 2 minutes or until smooth. Remove the bowl from the mixer. Transfer the coconut cream to a stainless steel bowl. Cover with cling film and refrigerate for 1 hour before using.

PREPARE THE MANGO COULIS

Heat the mango chunks, caster sugar, water and lemon juice in a 3 litre/5 pint saucepan over moderately high heat. When hot, stir to dissolve the sugar. Bring to the boil, then adjust the heat and allow the mixture to simmer for 15 minutes or until thick. Remove the mixture from the heat. Cool in an iced-water bath to a temperature of 5 to 7°C/40 to 45°F, about 20 minutes.

Transfer the cold mango mixture to the bowl of a food processor fitted with a metal blade. Add the orange juice and rum and process until smooth, about 1 minute (this should yield about 440ml/14fl oz of coulis). Transfer the coulis to a stainless steel bowl, cover with cling film, and refrigerate until needed.

ASSEMBLE THE WILD ORCHIDS

Portion 2 to 3 tablespoons mango coulis on to each dessert plate.

Fill a piping bag, fitted with a medium straight nozzle, with the coconut cream.

Arrange 3 of the larger petals, like a propeller, in the centre of each plate (the curved edges of the petals should be facing up). Place a slice of kiwi fruit on the coulis in between the petals (3 slices of kiwi per plate). Pipe approximately 1½ tablespoons of coconut cream in the centre of the petals. Then pipe approximately 1½ tablespoons of coconut cream into each open petal (the coconut cream is very rich and the recipe yield is very exact, so make sure to use the amount suggested).

Arrange 3 small petals around the mound of coconut cream in the centre of each plate. The curved edges of the petals should be facing towards the centre. Arrange 4 strawberry quarters around the inside of the small petals on each plate. Finish each wild orchid by sprinkling a few quartered macadamia nuts over it. Serve immediately.

Using a palette knife, immediately remove the petals, one at a time, from the baking sheet.

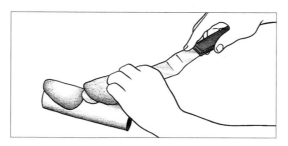

Drape each petal over a wooden dowel and allow to cool, about 2 to 3 minutes.

CHOCOLATE MADONNA

SERVES 6

INGREDIENTS

CHOCOLATE BUSTIERS

115g/4oz soft light brown sugar

115g/4oz unsalted butter

85g/3oz dark corn syrup or golden syrup

225g/8oz bittersweet chocolate, cut into 15g/½oz pieces

80g/scant 3oz plain flour

115g/4oz white chocolate, cut into 15g/½oz pieces

RED RASPBERRY MOUNDS

340g/12oz fresh red raspberries

50g/scant 2oz caster sugar

2 tablespoons raspberry liqueur

750ml/1¼ pint whipping cream

RED RASPBERRY SAUCE

Red Raspberry Sauce (see page 130)

EQUIPMENT

Measuring jug, measuring spoons, 3 litre/5 pint saucepan, whisk, rubber spatula, three 25 × 38cm/ 10 × 15in baking trays, baking parchment, 2 large (about 16cm/6½in in length) cream horn moulds, double boiler, heat-resistant cling film, cooling rack, oval soup spoon, electric mixer with balloon whisk, 3 litre/5 pint stainless steel bowl

PREPARE THE CHOCOLATE BUSTIERS

Preheat the oven to 170°C/325°F/Gas 3.

Heat the light brown sugar, butter and dark corn syrup in a 3 litre/5 pint saucepan over moderate heat. Bring to the boil, stirring frequently with a whisk. Remove the pan from the heat and add one piece of the bittersweet chocolate. Stir with a rubber spatula until the chocolate has melted and blended into the mixture. Add the flour and stir the mixture for several minutes or until the mixture is thoroughly combined.

Line 2 baking sheets with baking parchment.

Portion 1 slightly heaping tablespoon (about 30g/1oz) of mixture in the centre of each of the parchment-lined baking sheets (do not spread the mixture—it will spread in the oven).

Bake in the centre of the preheated oven for 7 to 8 minutes or until evenly browned. Remove both baking sheets from the oven. Set 1 baking sheet aside in a warm place (on top of the stove). Immediately remove the parchment from the baked biscuit on the other baking sheet. Invert the now flat (but soon to be voluptuous) baked bustier biscuit (parchment side up) on to a clean flat surface. Peel the parchment from the baked biscuit (this will be quite easy, as the ample butter in the mixture will prevent it from sticking to the paper). Place a cream horn mould on its side directly on the edge of the baked biscuit at the narrowest point. Roll the baked biscuit around the mould to form a pointed cone (this must be done quickly or the baked biscuit will harden and break while being rolled around the metal mould). Allow the cone to cool to room temperature before removing the mould. Repeat this procedure with the remaining baked biscuit (if the biscuit has become hard and brittle, pop it back in the oven for 30 to 45 seconds—this will make the biscuit pliable again).

Bake the remaining 10 biscuits, 2 at a time, following the same procedure used with the first 2 (use new parchment for each). Shape the cones, and allow them all to cool thoroughly before proceeding.

ADORN THE CONES WITH CHOCOLATE

Heat 2.5cm/1in of water in the bottom half of a double boiler over moderate heat. Place the remaining bittersweet chocolate in the top half. Tightly cover the top with heat-resistant cling film. Allow to heat for 8 to 9 minutes. Remove from the heat and stir until smooth.

Place a cooling rack on a baking tray. Put 1 cone seam side down on the cooling rack. Using an oval soup spoon, drizzle thin and separate parallel lines (think stripes) of chocolate across the width of the cone, starting at the tip and working towards the open end.

Move the decorated cone, seam side down, on to a baking sheet lined with parchment. Repeat this procedure with the remaining cones. Use 2 baking sheets so that the decorated cones are not touching each other. When all the cones have received their dark chocolate stripes, place them in the refrigerator while preparing the white chocolate.

Heat 2.5cm/1in of water in the bottom half of a double boiler over moderate heat. Place the white chocolate in the top half of the double boiler. Tightly cover the top with heat-resistant cling film. Heat for 4 minutes. Remove from the heat and stir until smooth. Remove the cones from the refrigerator. Repeat the decorating procedure used with the dark chocolate, making the white chocolate lines parallel to the dark (this will create a zebra stripe effect). Refrigerate the cones until needed.

PREPARE THE RED RASPBERRY MOUNDS

Place 170g/6oz of raspberries, the caster sugar and the raspberry liqueur in the well-chilled bowl of an electric mixer fitted with a well-chilled balloon whisk. Whisk on low for 30 seconds. Add the cream and whisk on high until stiff, about 1 minute. Remove 12 whole red raspberries from the remaining raspberries and refrigerate until needed (as garnish). Fold the remaining whole berries into the whipped cream. Refrigerate until needed.

ASSEMBLE THE MADONNA

Spoon 3 to 4 tablespoons of Red Raspberry Sauce on to each of 6 dessert plates. Form 2 red raspberry mounds in the centre of each plate, 1 heaping tablespoon of the red raspberry cream mixture per mound. Spoon 2 tablespoons of the cream mixture into a cone. Place the cone into a mound of cream, tip side up. Repeat with the remaining 11 cones, placing each cone into its own mound of cream. Crown the tip of each cone with a whole red raspberry. Serve immediately.

THE CHEF'S TOUCH

Practice makes perfect on the cones, so don't become discouraged with your first attempt. You may want to double the batch for insurance.

The uncooked cone mixture will become firmer as time goes by. To compensate, slightly increase the baking time from the first batch to the last.

The decorated cones will stay crisp in the refrigerator for a couple of days. You can also freeze them in a tightly sealed plastic container for a week or two.

Cream horn moulds can be found in kitchenware shops.

We use Chambord liqueur at the Trellis for the raspberry mounds. The smooth raspberry flavour is incomparable, although in a pinch you can use raspberry schnapps.

Save a splash of the Chambord for a tall slender flute of Champagne to accompany this exotic dessert.

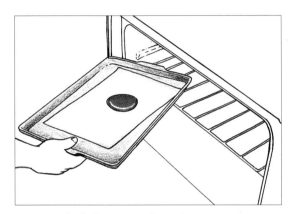

Remove the baking trays from the oven.

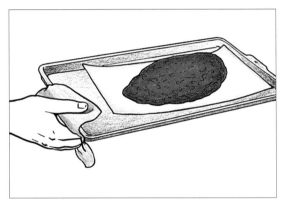

Set one baking tray aside in a warm place (such as on top of the stove).

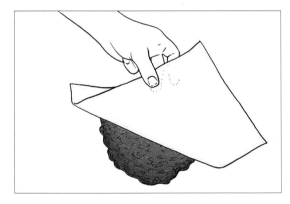

Immediately remove the baking parchment from the baked biscuit on the baking sheet.

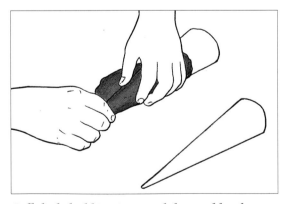

Roll the baked biscuit around the mould to form a pointed cone.

CHOCOLATE EXQUISITE PAIN

SERVES 10

INGREDIENTS

CHOCOLATE PASTRY

175g/6oz plain flour

1 tablespoon caster sugar

¼ teaspoon unsweetened cocoa powder

¼ teaspoon salt

55g/2oz chilled unsalted butter, cut into 4 equal pieces

6 tablespoons iced water

INTRIGUING INTERIOR

170g/6oz bittersweet chocolate, cut into 15g/½oz pieces

115g/4oz unsalted butter

3 size-3 eggs

100g/3½oz caster sugar

½ teaspoon salt

½ teaspoon pure vanilla essence

GLAZE

125ml/4fl oz whipping cream

30g/1oz unsalted butter

115g/4oz bittersweet chocolate, cut into 15g/½oz pieces

SHARDS

225g/8oz bittersweet chocolate, chopped into 5mm/¼in pieces

BITTER MOUSSE

115g/4oz bittersweet chocolate, cut into 15g/½oz pieces

115g/4oz unsweetened chocolate, cut into 15g/½oz pieces

375ml/12fl oz whipping cream

2 tablespoons crème de cacao (chocolate liqueur)

2 size-3 egg whites

EQUIPMENT

Measuring jug, measuring spoons, electric mixer with flat beater and balloon whisk, heat-resistant cling film, baking parchment, rolling pin, 25 × 38cm/10 × 15in baking sheet, 24 × 2cm/9½ × ¾in round loose-based tart tin, chef's knife, double boiler, rubber spatula, wooden cocktail stick, 1.5 litre/2½ pint saucepan, two 3 litre/5 pint stainless steel bowls, instant-read thermometer, palette knife, cutting board, whisk, serrated slicer

PREPARE THE CHOCOLATE PASTRY

Place 140g/5oz flour, the caster sugar, cocoa and salt in the bowl of an electric mixer fitted with a flat beater. Mix on low for 15 seconds to combine the ingredients. Add the chilled butter and mix on low for 2 minutes or until the butter is 'rubbed' into the flour and the mixture develops a coarse, mealy texture. Add the iced water and continue to mix on low until the dough comes together, about 30 seconds. Remove the dough from the mixer and form it into a smooth round ball. Wrap in cling film and refrigerate for at least 1 hour.

After the dough has relaxed in the refrigerator for 1 hour, transfer it to a clean, dry lightly floured sheet of baking parchment (greaseproof paper will work too). Roll out the dough (using the remaining flour as necessary to prevent the dough from sticking) into a round about 30cm/12in in diameter and 3mm/⅛in thick. Place the rolled dough (leave it on the parchment) on a baking sheet (the baking sheet is for convenience and keeps the dough flat) and refrigerate for 10 to 15 minutes. Remove the parchment with the dough from the baking sheet. Invert the rolled dough into the tart tin. Carefully remove the parchment and gently press the dough on to the bottom and sides of the tin. Cut away the excess dough, leaving it flush with the top edge of the tin. Refrigerate for at least 30 minutes or until needed.

CREATE THE INTRIGUING INTERIOR

Preheat the oven to 170°C/325°F/Gas 3.

Heat 2.5cm/1in of water in the bottom half of a double boiler over moderate heat. Place the bittersweet chocolate and butter in the top half. Tightly cover the top with heat-resistant cling film. Allow to heat for 8 to 10 minutes. Remove from the heat and stir until smooth. Set aside at room temperature until needed.

Place the eggs, sugar, salt and vanilla essence in the bowl of an electric mixer fitted with a flat beater. Beat on high for 10 minutes or until thickened and velvety smooth. Add the melted chocolate mixture and beat on medium until combined, about 1 minute. Remove the bowl from the mixer and use a rubber spatula to finish mixing until smooth and thoroughly combined.

Remove the tart case from the refrigerator. Pour the filling mixture into the tart case. Place the tart on a baking sheet and bake on the centre shelf of the preheated oven for about 23 to 25 minutes or until a wooden cocktail stick inserted in the centre comes out clean. Remove the tart from the oven and allow to cool to room temperature for 30 minutes. Cover the tart with cling film and refrigerate for 30 minutes.

MAKE THE GLAZE

Heat the cream and butter in a 1.5 litre/2½ pint saucepan over moderately high heat. Bring to the boil. Place the bittersweet chocolate in a 3 litre/ 5 pint stainless steel bowl and pour the boiling cream over the chocolate. Allow to stand for 5 minutes, then stir until smooth.

Remove the tart from the refrigerator and remove the cling film. Pour the glaze over the top of the baked filling (the filling will flow towards the edges on its own). Place the tart, uncovered, in the freezer for 30 minutes, or refrigerate for at least 1 hour to set the glaze (once the glaze is firm the tart should be kept refrigerated while preparing the shards and the mousse).

PREPARE THE SHARDS

Line a 25 × 38cm/10 × 15in baking sheet with a sheet of baking parchment.

Heat 2.5cm/1in of water in the bottom half of a double boiler over moderate heat. Place the bitter-sweet chocolate in the top half. Heat the chocolate uncovered, stirring constantly, until it has melted or about 3 minutes. Transfer the melted chocolate to a stainless steel bowl and continue to stir until the temperature of the chocolate is reduced to 32°C/90°F.

Pour the chocolate on to the parchment-lined baking sheet. Use a palette knife to spread the chocolate evenly over the surface of the parchment, to within 5mm/¼in of the edges. Place the baking sheet in the refrigerator until the chocolate has hardened, about 10 minutes. Remove the hardened chocolate from the refrigerator. Invert the chocolate (parchment side up) on to a cutting board. Peel the parchment from the chocolate. Use a chef's knife to cut the chocolate rectangle in half lengthwise. Cut each half, widthwise, into thin, uneven strips (shards) about 3 to 5mm/⅛ to ¼in wide (this should be done quickly—otherwise, the chocolate may soften, especially if the ambient room temperature is above 25°C/78°F).

Transfer the shards to a baking sheet, then tightly wrap the baking sheet with cling film. Place in the freezer until ready to use.

PREPARE THE BITTER MOUSSE

Heat 2.5cm/1in of water in the bottom half of a double boiler over moderate heat. Place the bitter-sweet chocolate and unsweetened chocolate in the top half. Tightly cover the top with heat-resistant cling film. Allow to heat for 8 to 10 minutes. Remove from the heat and stir until smooth. Set aside until needed.

Place the cream and the crème de cacao in the well-chilled bowl of an electric mixer fitted with a well-chilled balloon whisk. Whip on high until stiff peaks form, about 1 minute. Set aside for a few moments.

Whisk the egg whites in a 3 litre/5 pint stainless steel bowl until stiff peaks form or about 2 minutes. Use a rubber spatula to fold half of the whisked egg whites into the melted chocolate. Then place the whipped cream and the remaining egg whites on top of the mixture and use a rubber spatula to fold together until smooth and completely combined.

Remove the tart from the refrigerator. Turn all the mousse on to the glazed tart. Use a palette knife to spread the mousse over the surface of the tart to the edges, creating a dome-shaped layer of mousse. Refrigerate for 30 minutes before cutting and serving.

TO SERVE

Heat the blade of the slicer under hot running water and wipe the blade dry before cutting each slice. Place a piece of tart in the centre of each serving plate. For the *coup de grace*, sprinkle an equal amount of chocolate shards over the top of each piece of tart. Serve immediately.

THE CHEF'S TOUCH

This remarkable creation is from the Marquis de Sade school of desserts. Here, chocolate is taken to the limits of indulgence.

To spread out the preparation of Chocolate Exquisite Pain, the Chocolate Pastry can be prepared in advance and kept frozen in the tart tin several days or even a couple of weeks before being baked (completely thaw the dough in the refrigerator before baking).

The chocolate shards can be kept frozen for several days before using.

After assembly, you can keep the dessert refrigerated (minus the shards—keep them in the freezer) for a couple of days before serving.

Depending on your threshold for 'pain', this dessert can be cut into as many as twenty slices. However, if you find the chocolate elements—dense, moist, rich, textural, voluptuous—as compelling as I do, you may opt for fewer but more intense slashes.

For chocolate-induced delirium, I suggest accompanying Chocolate Exquisite Pain with a glass of your favourite cocoa-flavoured liqueur.

CHOCOLATE RESURRECTION

SERVES 4

INGREDIENTS

GOLDEN CHALICES

1 teaspoon vegetable oil

200g/7oz caster sugar

⅛ teaspoon fresh lemon juice

RESURRECTION CAKES

250g/9oz unsalted butter (30g/1oz melted)

170g/6oz bittersweet chocolate, cut into
    15g/½oz pieces

3 size-3 eggs

3 size-3 egg yolks

70g/2½oz caster sugar

1 teaspoon pure vanilla essence

50g/scant 2oz plain flour

¼ teaspoon salt

ESPRESSO KAHLUA CREAM SAUCE

Espresso Kahlua Cream Sauce (see page 131), warm

RED RASPBERRY OFFERING

340g/12oz fresh red raspberries

EQUIPMENT

Measuring spoons, measuring jug, small non-stick pan, pastry brush, 4 smooth-sided individual tartlet moulds, each 11cm/4½in diameter and 2.5cm/1in deep, 3 litre/5 pint saucepan, whisk, baking parchment, oval soup spoon, flat plastic container with lid, 4 individual soufflé dishes, each about 250ml/8fl oz capacity, double boiler, heat-resistant cling film, rubber spatula, electric mixer with flat beater, baking sheet

MAKE THE GOLDEN CHALICES

Lightly coat the insides of the tartlet moulds with vegetable oil.

Place the sugar and lemon juice in a 3 litre/5 pint saucepan. Stir with a whisk to combine (the sugar will resemble moist sand). Caramelise the sugar by heating for 4½ minutes over moderately high heat, stirring constantly with a wire whisk to break up any lumps (the sugar will first turn clear as it liquefies, then light brown as it caramelises). Remove the saucepan from the heat. Allow the caramelised sugar to stand at room temperature for about 1 minute. Place the tartlet moulds 5 to 7.5cm/2 to 3in apart on a large piece of baking parchment. Dip an oval soup spoon into the caramelised sugar and drizzle the hot sugar in a thin stream on to the inside of a tartlet mould, creating a spider web–like pattern. Use 5 to 6 spoonfuls of caramelised sugar to create a golden chalice. Repeat this procedure with the 3 remaining tartlet moulds. Allow the caramelised sugar to harden in the moulds. Use your fingers to break away any sugar that has hardened on the top edge of the moulds.

Remove the chalices from the moulds, one at a time, by holding a mould in one hand and turning the chalice out into the other hand. The chalices are delicate, so handle them gently. After removing all the chalices from the moulds, store them in a tightly sealed plastic container at cool room temperature.

PREPARE THE RESURRECTION CAKES

Preheat the oven to 200°C/400°F/Gas 6.

Lightly coat the inside of each soufflé dish with melted butter.

Heat 2.5cm/1in of water in the bottom half of a double boiler over moderate heat. Place the remaining 225g/8oz of butter and the chocolate in the top half of the double boiler. Tightly cover the top with heat-resistant cling film. Allow to heat for 8 to 10 minutes. Remove from the heat and stir until smooth. Set aside at room temperature until needed.

Place the eggs, egg yolks and sugar in the bowl of an electric mixer fitted with a flat beater. Beat on high until slightly thickened, about 4 minutes. Scrape down the sides of the bowl. Add the vanilla essence and beat on high for 30 seconds. Add the melted chocolate and butter, and beat on medium for 30 seconds. Add the flour and salt and beat on medium for 30 seconds. Remove the bowl from the mixer and use a rubber spatula to finish mixing until smooth and thoroughly combined.

Evenly divide the resurrection mixture among the prepared soufflé dishes. Place the soufflé dishes on a baking sheet on the centre shelf of the preheated oven and bake for 14 to 15 minutes. Remove from the oven and allow the Resurrection Cakes to cool at room temperature in the soufflé dishes for 3 to 4 minutes (at this point the cakes will be cool enough to handle—any longer and they will continue to cook, which would eliminate the delectable liquid centre).

TO SERVE

Turn out the cakes on to a clean sheet of baking parchment (if the cakes do not release from the dishes, use a thin-bladed paring knife to cut around the outside edge of the cakes).

Use a spatula to place a still-warm Resurrection Cake (upside down) in the centre of each plate. Spoon 3 to 4 tablespoons of Espresso Kahlua Cream Sauce directly over each cake, allowing the sauce to flow over the cakes on to the plates. Crown each cake with a golden chalice. Equally divide the red raspberries into the chalices. Serve immediately.

The resurrection cake is a dichotomy of textures: soft and moist on the outer edges and liquid in the centre. Serve it only minutes from the time it is removed from the oven—otherwise the mixture will continue to bake to the centre, denying you the surprising liquid chocolate nectar.

If the preparation of this dessert seems formidable, consider the following suggestions. First, the Golden Chalices can be prepared several days in advance. Keep the chalices in the tartlet moulds after they have cooled, and individually wrap each one. Place them in a tightly sealed plastic container in the freezer until a few minutes before using. You can prepare the Espresso Kahlua Cream Sauce the day before serving the dessert. The sauce can be served cold, but is better slightly warm (heat in a double boiler to the desired temperature).

Here's a tip to save you quite a bit of cleaning time and elbow grease. After preparing the Golden Chalices, run hot tap water into the saucepan used to caramelise the sugar and heat over moderate heat until the water begins to boil. Lower the heat and allow to simmer until all the hardened caramelised sugar has been dissolved.

Although red raspberries are my first choice to fill the Golden Chalices, other offerings may be considered, such as an assortment of berries. If you are feeling decadent, I would suggest Double Cappuccino Ice Cream (see page 77, as well as your cardiologist, before making this decision).

When last encountered, the Chocolate Resurrection was accompanied by a glass of Bouzy Comtesse Marie de France 1985 vintage Champagne.

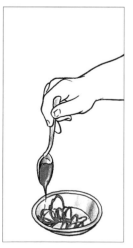

Create a spider web–like pattern with the hot sugar: dip an oval spoon into the caramelised sugar and drizzle in a thin stream onto the inside of a tartlet mould.

Use 5 to 6 spoonfuls of caramelised sugar to create a Golden Chalice.

PILLAR OF CHOCOLATE WITH COCOA THUNDERHEADS

SERVES 8

INGREDIENTS

DOUBLE CAPPUCCINO ICE CREAM

Double Cappuccino Ice Cream (see page 77)

CHOCOLATE CAKE

250g/9oz unsalted butter (30g/1oz melted)
225g/8oz bittersweet chocolate, cut into
    15g/½oz pieces
6 size-3 egg yolks
150g/5½oz caster sugar
10 size-3 egg whites

GANACHE

375ml/12fl oz whipping cream
1 tablespoon caster sugar
15g/½oz unsalted butter
450g/1lb bittersweet chocolate, cut into
    15g/½oz pieces
280g/10oz toasted flaked almonds

COCOA THUNDERHEADS

750ml/1¼ pints whipping cream
70g/2½oz caster sugar
2 tablespoons unsweetened cocoa powder

EQUIPMENT

Measuring jug, measuring spoon, baking sheet, small non-stick pan, pastry brush, three 25 × 38cm/ 10 × 15in baking trays, baking parchment, double boiler, heat-resistant cling film, whisk, electric mixer with flat beater and balloon whisk, rubber spatula, 5 litre/8 pint stainless steel bowl, paring knife, 3 litre/5 pint stainless steel bowl, food processor with metal blade, 1 litre/2 pint stainless steel bowl, palette knife, cutting board, serrated knife, serrated slicer, cooling rack

PREPARE THE DOUBLE CAPPUCCINO ICE CREAM

Make the ice cream, then place in the freezer for at least 2 hours before assembling the pillars.

PREPARE THE CHOCOLATE CAKE

Preheat the oven to 170°C/325°F/Gas 3.

Lightly coat the bottom and sides of two 25 × 38cm/10 × 15in baking trays with melted butter. Line each sheet with baking parchment, then lightly coat the parchment with more melted butter. Set aside.

Heat 2.5cm/1in of water in the bottom half of a double boiler over moderate heat. Place the remaining 225g/8oz butter and the bittersweet chocolate in the top half of the double boiler. Tightly cover the top with heat-resistant cling film. Allow to heat for 10 to 12 minutes. Remove from heat, stir until smooth and set aside at room temperature until needed.

Place the egg yolks and sugar in the bowl of an electric mixer fitted with a flat beater. Beat on high until slightly thickened and lemon-coloured, about 4 minutes. Scrape down the sides of the bowl and beat on high for 2 additional minutes.

While the egg yolks are beating, whisk the egg whites in a 5 litre/8 pint stainless steel bowl until stiff but not dry, about 5 to 6 minutes.

Using a rubber spatula, fold the melted chocolate mixture into the beaten egg yolk mixture. Add one quarter of the beaten egg whites and stir to incorporate, then gently fold in the remaining egg whites.

Divide the mixture between the prepared baking trays, spreading evenly. Bake on the centre shelf in the preheated oven for about 12 minutes or until the tops of the cake are dry to the touch (when touched prior to that, the cakes will leave you with sticky fingers). Remove the cakes from the oven and cool in the baking trays for 5 minutes.

Turn out the cakes on to 2 clean sheets of parchment cut to fit the insides of the baking trays. (If the cakes adhere to the sides of the baking trays, use a sharp paring knife to cut along the inside edges of the trays to free the cakes.) Remove the parchment from the base of each cake. Wash and dry the baking trays. Slide the cake layers with the clean sheets of parchment on the bottom back into the baking trays and place them in the freezer while preparing the ganache.

PREPARE THE GANACHE

Heat the cream, caster sugar and butter in a 3 litre/ 5 pint saucepan over moderately high heat. When hot, stir to dissolve the sugar. Bring to the boil. Place the bittersweet chocolate in a 3 litre/5 pint stainless steel bowl. Pour the boiling cream over the chocolate and allow to stand for 5 minutes. Stir until smooth.

Process the almonds in the bowl of a food processor fitted with a metal blade until finely ground or about 20 seconds.

In a small bowl, combine one third of the ground almonds with 250ml/8fl oz of chocolate ganache. Keep the chocolate almond ganache and the remaining plain chocolate ganache at room temperature until needed.

BEGIN ASSEMBLING
THE PILLARS

Remove the cakes from the freezer. Evenly divide the chocolate almond ganache between the cakes. Spread the ganache evenly to within 3mm/⅛in of the edges of each cake. Return the cakes to the freezer for 30 minutes.

Remove one cake layer from the freezer. Spoon all of the ice cream on to the top of the cake layer. Use a palette knife to spread the ice cream evenly to the edges of the cake. Remove the other cake layer from the freezer and invert it on to the ice cream, pressing gently with your hands to even the layer. Place in the freezer for 30 minutes.

Remove the cake from the freezer. Invert it on to a cutting board. Remove the parchment. Using a very sharp serrated knife, cut away the uneven edges of the cake so that it will measure 23 × 30cm/ 9 × 12in. Use a serrated slicer to cut the cake across into 8 pillars, each 4cm/1½in wide. Place the pillars on the baking sheet and return to the freezer for 30 minutes.

Place a cooling rack on a baking tray. Warm the plain chocolate ganache over hot water until it is smooth and flowing. Remove one of the cake pillars from the freezer and place lengthwise on the cooling rack. Spoon 2 tablespoons of ganache over the top of the pillar. Use a palette knife to spread the ganache evenly over the top and sides of the pillar. Return the coated pillar to the freezer, placing it on the baking sheet plain side down. Repeat the coating step with the remaining 7 pillars, coating them and returning them to the freezer one at a time. (To prevent the coated pillars from touching each other, place them on 2 baking sheets in the freezer.)

Spread the remaining ground almonds on a clean baking tray. One at a time, roll the pillars in the ground almonds, coating them on all 4 long sides. Place the coated pillars on a clean baking sheet, cover with cling film, and return to the freezer for at least 2 hours before serving the dessert.

PREPARE THE COCOA
THUNDERHEADS

Place the cream, sugar and cocoa in the well-chilled bowl of an electric mixer fitted with a well-chilled balloon whisk. Whip on high until stiff, about 1 minute.

TO SERVE

Spoon 3 tablespoons of billowy Cocoa Thunderheads on to each of the dessert plates. Remove the pillars from the freezer. Trim about 3mm/⅛in from each end to form a flat surface. Use a serrated slicer to cut each pillar in half diagonally (heat the blade of the slicer under hot running water and wipe the blade dry before making each slice). Stand 2 pillar halves, flat end down, in the Cocoa Thunderheads. Serve immediately.

Use a serrated slicer to cut each pillar in half diagonally.

Stand the pillar halves, flat end down, into the Cocoa Thunderheads.

TERCENTENARY EXTRAVAGANZA

SERVES 8

INGREDIENTS

WILLIAM'S GLORIFIED FRUIT

1 litre/1⅔ pints cold water
125ml/4fl oz plus 1 tablespoon fresh lemon juice
2 Granny Smith apples
2 Red Delicious apples
2 pears
340g/12oz clear honey
250ml/8fl oz port
70g/2½oz currants

MARY'S HONEY VANILLA CAKES

185g/6½oz unsalted butter (15g/½oz melted)
210g/7½oz plain flour
1 teaspoon bicarbonate of soda
½ teaspoon salt
1 vanilla pod
125ml/4fl oz whipping cream
170g/6oz clear honey
2 size-3 eggs
100g/3½oz toasted flaked almonds

THIRD CENTURY ALMOND MORTAR BOARDS

115g/4oz unsalted butter
115g/4oz soft light brown sugar
¼ teaspoon salt
2 size-3 egg whites
¼ teaspoon almond essence
100g/3½oz toasted flaked almonds, finely chopped
105g/3½oz plain flour

HONEY VANILLA CREAM

500ml/16fl oz whipping cream
170g/6oz clear honey
1 teaspoon pure vanilla essence

EQUIPMENT

Measuring jug, measuring spoons, small non-stick pan, two 23 × 33cm/9 × 13in baking trays, food processor with metal blade, 3 litre/5 pint stainless steel bowl, paring knife, chef's knife, cutting board, 3 litre/5 pint saucepan, whisk, colander, rubber spatula, cling film, small bowl, 8 straight-sided tartlet moulds, each 11cm-/4½in-diameter and 2.5cm/1in deep, pastry brush, sieve, greaseproof paper, 1.5 litre-/2½ pint-saucepan, electric mixer with flat beater and balloon whisk, wooden cocktail stick, baking parchment, palette knife, pizza cutter, double boiler

PREPARE WILLIAM'S GLORIFIED FRUIT

In a 3 litre/5 pint stainless steel bowl, acidulate the water with 1 tablespoon lemon juice.

Peel, core and quarter the apples and pears and chop, one at a time, into 5mm/¼in pieces, placing the pieces in the acidulated water as each individual fruit is chopped (this will prevent the fruit from discolouring). Set aside at room temperature while preparing the honey and port syrup.

Heat the honey, port and the remaining lemon juice in a 3 litre/5 pint saucepan over moderately high heat. Bring the mixture to the boil, stirring frequently with a whisk to dissolve the honey, then adjust the heat to moderate and continue to boil for 15 minutes. Remove the syrup from the heat.

Thoroughly drain the chopped fruit in a colander. Add the fruit to the hot syrup and stir with a rubber spatula to combine. Add the currants and stir to combine. Allow the fruit to steep in the syrup for 1 hour. Strain the syrup from the fruit into a 3 litre/5 pint saucepan. Transfer the fruit to a 3 litre/5 pint stainless steel bowl or other appropriately sized non-reactive container, cover with cling film, and refrigerate until needed. Heat the syrup to the boil over moderately high heat, and boil for 15 minutes. Cool the syrup in an iced-water bath to a temperature of 5 to 7°C/40 to 45°F, about 15 minutes. Refrigerate the syrup until needed.

PREPARE MARY'S HONEY VANILLA CAKES

Preheat the oven to 170°C/325°F/Gas 3.

Lightly coat the insides of the tartlet moulds with the melted butter.

Combine together in a sieve the flour, bicarbonate of soda and salt. Sift on to greaseproof paper and set aside.

Use a sharp paring knife to split the vanilla pod in half lengthwise. Heat the cream and the split vanilla pod in a 1.5 litre/2½ pint saucepan over moderately high heat. Bring to the boil. Remove from the heat and allow to cool at room temperature for 30 minutes. Remove the vanilla pod halves from the cream. Using the back of a paring knife, scrape the tiny seeds from each half, then discard the halves. Add the seeds to the cream and whisk to disperse. Set aside until needed.

Place the remaining 170g/6oz butter and the honey in the bowl of an electric mixer fitted with a flat beater. Beat on medium for 2 minutes. Scrape down the sides of the bowl. Increase the speed to high and beat for an additional 2 minutes. Scrape down the sides of the bowl. Add the eggs, one at a time, beating on medium for 30 seconds and scraping down the bowl after each addition. Increase the speed to high and beat for 1 minute. Scrape down the sides of the bowl. Add the sifted dry ingredients and combine on low for 15 seconds. Add the vanilla-infused cream and beat on medium for 30 seconds. Remove the bowl from the mixer and use a rubber spatula to finish mixing until smooth and thoroughly combined (all of the mixing and scraping down creates a velvety smooth and ethereal mixture.)

Evenly divide the cake mixture among the prepared tartlet moulds (about 4 heaping tablespoons per mould). Sprinkle an equal amount of flaked almonds over the mixture in each tartlet mould. Divide the moulds on to 2 baking sheets and bake on the centre shelf of a preheated oven for 15 to 16 minutes or until a wooden cocktail stick inserted in the centre comes out clean. Remove the baked cakes from the oven and allow to cool in the moulds at room temperature for 15 minutes. Remove the cakes from the moulds, one at a time, by holding a mould in one hand and turning the cake upside down into the other hand. Place the cakes right side up on a large piece of baking parchment or greaseproof paper. Set aside at room temperature until needed, or up to 2 hours. (For longer storage, the thoroughly cooled cakes can be placed in a tightly sealed plastic container and kept at room temperature for two to three days.)

PREPARE THE THIRD CENTURY ALMOND MORTAR BOARDS

With a pencil, trace an 18 × 28cm/7 × 11in rectangle on each of 4 sheets of baking parchment (each one cut to fit a baking sheet).

Place the unsalted butter, light brown sugar and salt in the bowl of an electric mixer fitted with a flat beater. Beat on medium for 2 minutes. Scrape down the sides of the bowl. Add the egg whites, one at a time, while mixing on high for 10 seconds and scraping down the bowl after each addition. Add the almond essence and beat on high for 10 seconds. Add the chopped almonds and beat on high for 10 seconds. Scrape down the sides of the bowl. Add the flour and combine on low for 15 seconds. Remove the bowl from the mixer and use a rubber spatula to finish mixing until smooth and thoroughly combined.

Place a sheet of baking parchment, with the pencilled mark down, on each of 2 baking sheets. Place 125ml/4fl oz mixture in the centre of each rectangle. Use a palette knife to smear a uniformly thin coating of batter to cover the inside of each rectangle completely. Bake both sheets on the centre shelf of the preheated oven for 6½ to 7 minutes or until most of the surface of the baked rectangle is a light golden brown. Remove both baking sheets from the oven. Set one baking sheet aside. Immediately remove the parchment with the baked rectangle from the other baking sheet to a cutting board.

Use a pizza cutter to cut the rectangle into 6 square pieces (cut the rectangle in half lengthwise, then make 2 cuts across the width of the rectangle at about 10cm/4in intervals). Repeat this procedure with the remaining rectangle (it is essential that the rectangles are cut within seconds of being removed from the oven—otherwise they will harden, become brittle and break apart during the cut-

ting). Bake the next 2 rectangles following the same procedure (use new parchment for each). Allow the almond mortar boards to cool for 30 minutes before using.

MAKE THE HONEY VANILLA CREAM

Place the cream, honey and vanilla essence in the well-chilled bowl of an electric mixer fitted with a well-chilled balloon whisk. Whip on medium for 15 seconds. Scrape down the sides and bottom of the bowl (this will release any honey that may be sticking to the bowl). Now whip the cream on high until stiff, about 1 minute. Refrigerate the honey vanilla cream until needed.

TO SERVE

Heat 2.5cm/1in of water in the bottom half of a double boiler over moderate heat. Place the glorified fruit in the top half. Heat, gently stirring with a rubber spatula, for about 6 minutes or until warm throughout.

Portion 4 tablespoons of the fruit on to each of the dessert plates, spreading the fruit evenly over the surface of the plates. Drizzle 2 level tablespoons of the syrup over the fruit on each plate. Place a Honey Vanilla Cake on the fruit in the centre of each plate. Portion 1 heaping tablespoon of Honey Vanilla Cream on to each cake. Top each mound of cream with an Almond Mortar Board. Continue alternating the Honey Vanilla Cream and the Almond Mortar Boards on each plate, finishing each extravaganza with a mortar board on top (3 mortar boards per extravaganza, one for every hundred years). For the final touch, drizzle ½ tablespoon of syrup on to each of the top mortar boards. Serve immediately.

Use a palette knife to smear a uniformly thin coating of batter to completely cover the inside of the rectangle.

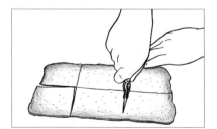

Use a pizza cutter to cut the rectangle into 6 square pieces.

CHAPTER SIX

SWEET NOTHINGS

'My tongue is smiling.'

—Abigail Trillin

DOUBLE CHOCOLATE SAUCE

RED RASPBERRY SAUCE

CHOCOLATE BOURBON SAUCE

ESPRESSO KAHLUA CREAM SAUCE

SAMBUCA ALMOND BISCOTTI

CITRUS SHORTBREAD BISCUITS

CHOCOLATE CINNAMON TIGER BISCUITS

BURNT ORANGE SNAPS

CHOCOLATE VALENCIENNES

WHITE CHOCOLATE LULLABY

DOUBLE CHOCOLATE SAUCE

YIELDS ABOUT 800ML/1 1/3 PINTS

INGREDIENTS

115g/4oz bittersweet chocolate, cut into 15g/1/2oz pieces

115g/4oz unsweetened chocolate, cut into 15g/1/2oz pieces

500ml/16fl oz whipping cream

100g/3 1/2oz caster sugar

20g/2/3oz unsweetened cocoa powder, sifted

2 tablespoons dark crème de cacao (chocolate liqueur)

1 teaspoon pure vanilla essence

EQUIPMENT

Measuring jug, measuring spoons, sieve, 3 litre/5 pint stainless steel bowl, 3 litre/5 pint saucepan, whisk, 5 litre/8 pint stainless steel bowl, instant-read thermometer, plastic container with lid

MAKE THE DOUBLE CHOCOLATE SAUCE

Place both the bittersweet and unsweetened chocolate in a 3 litre/5 pint stainless steel bowl.

Heat the cream and sugar in a 3 litre/5 pint saucepan over moderately high heat. When hot, stir to dissolve the sugar. Bring to the boil. Remove from the heat and add the sifted cocoa, whisking until smooth. Add the dark crème de cacao and the vanilla essence, stirring to incorporate. Pour the hot cream mixture over the chocolate and allow to stand for 5 minutes. Whisk vigorously until smooth.

Cool the Double Chocolate Sauce in an iced-water bath to a temperature of 5 to 7°C/40 to 45°F, about 15 minutes. Transfer to a plastic container, cover tightly and refrigerate for up to 5 days. Before serving, warm the sauce in a double boiler. Serve warm or at room temperature.

THE CHEF'S TOUCH

One could make a case for labelling this confection 'quadruple chocolate' sauce instead of 'double chocolate'. Although the two primary ingredients are bittersweet and unsweetened chocolate, the sauce also boasts additional chocolate in the form of cocoa and crème de cacao. But why nitpick—this doubly delicious sauce can be harmoniously paired with an infinite variety of desserts, not the least of which is For Chocolate Lovers Only (see page 21).

RED RASPBERRY SAUCE

YIELDS 500ML/16FL OZ

INGREDIENTS

675g/1 1/2lb fresh red raspberries

2 tablespoons caster sugar

1 teaspoon fresh lemon juice

2 tablespoons raspberry liqueur

EQUIPMENT

Measuring spoons, 3 litre/5 pint saucepan, kitchen spoon, medium sieve, 3 litre/5 pint stainless steel bowl, cling film

PREPARE THE RED RASPBERRY SAUCE

Heat 340g/12oz raspberries, the sugar and lemon juice in a 3 litre/5 pint saucepan over moderate heat. As the mixture heats, the sugar will dissolve and the raspberries will liquefy. Bring to the boil, then adjust the heat and allow the mixture to simmer for 5 minutes, stirring frequently. Remove the mixture from the heat and pass through a medium sieve into a stainless steel bowl. Discard the seeds. Immediately add the remaining 335g/12oz raspberries and the raspberry liqueur and stir to combine.

Cool in an iced-water bath to a temperature of 5 to 7°C/40 to 45°F, about 20 minutes. Cover with cling film and keep refrigerated for up to 3 days.

THE CHEF'S TOUCH

This remarkably uncomplicated and delightful Red Raspberry Sauce is at its best when fresh raspberries are in season (at other times of the year, imported berries would make this an expensive treat).

If the subtle flavour of the suggested amount of raspberry liqueur is too much of a palate teaser, consider doubling the quantity or adding a shooter of raspberry-flavoured brandy (of course, you can also omit the spirits altogether).

CHOCOLATE BOURBON SAUCE

YIELDS ABOUT 750ML/1¼ PINTS

INGREDIENTS

170g/6oz bittersweet chocolate, cut into
   15g/½oz pieces
115g/4oz unsweetened chocolate, cut into
   15g/½oz pieces
500ml/16fl oz whipping cream
150g/5½oz caster sugar
¼ teaspoon salt
125ml/4fl oz sour mash bourbon whiskey
1 teaspoon pure vanilla essence

EQUIPMENT

Measuring jug, measuring spoons, 3 litre/5 pint
stainless steel bowl, 3 litre/5 pint saucepan, whisk,
5 litre/8 pint stainless steel bowl, instant-read
thermometer, plastic container with lid

PREPARE THE CHOCOLATE BOURBON SAUCE

Place both the bittersweet chocolate and unsweetened chocolate in a 3 litre/5 pint stainless steel bowl.

Heat the cream, sugar and salt in a 3 litre/5 pint saucepan over moderately high heat. When hot, stir to dissolve the sugar. Bring to the boil. Remove from the heat and immediately pour over the chocolate. Allow to stand for 5 minutes. Add the bourbon whiskey and vanilla essence. Whisk vigorously until smooth.

Cool the Chocolate Bourbon Sauce in an iced-water bath to a temperature of 5 to 7°C/40 to 45°F, about 15 minutes. Transfer to a plastic container. Cover tightly and refrigerate until ready to use. The sauce can be kept refrigerated for up to 3 days. Before serving, warm the sauce in a double boiler. Serve warm.

> **THE CHEF'S TOUCH**
> *Obviously not for the abstemious, the Chocolate Bourbon Sauce comes loaded with gratifying flavour. Designed to accompany the Chocolate Pecan Bourbon Bash (see page 34), this consort to confectionery pleasure will have you dipping your beak to satisfaction, especially if you are wise enough to choose a designated driver.*
>
> *This sauce should be heated in a double boiler before serving (when cool, it is too thick to pour).*

ESPRESSO KAHLUA CREAM SAUCE

YIELDS 440ML/¾ PINT

INGREDIENTS

500ml/16fl oz whipping cream
15g/½oz espresso beans, freshly ground
50g/scant 2oz caster sugar
4 tablespoons Kahlua

EQUIPMENT

Measuring jug, coffee grinder, 3 litre/5 pint
saucepan, whisk, 3 litre/5 pint stainless steel bowl,
medium sieve, muslin

MAKE THE ESPRESSO KAHLUA CREAM SAUCE

Heat the cream, ground espresso beans and sugar in a 3 litre/5 pint saucepan over moderately high heat. Bring the mixture to the boil. Adjust the heat and allow to simmer for 20 minutes, stirring gently but frequently with a whisk (to prevent the cream from boiling over the sides of the saucepan), until the mixture becomes dark and slightly thickened. Remove from the heat and strain through several layers of muslin into a stainless steel bowl. Add the Kahlua and stir to combine. Serve warm immediately or keep warm in a double boiler, over low heat, for up to 2 hours.

> **THE CHEF'S TOUCH**
> *The viscosity of the Espresso Kahlua Cream Sauce will change dramatically if reheated (it will lose texture and become quite thin, albeit still delicious). For this reason, I recommend preparing the sauce as close to serving time as possible.*
>
> *If Kahlua is not on your shelf, another coffee liqueur can be used.*

SAMBUCA ALMOND BISCOTTI

YIELDS 24 BISCOTTI

INGREDIENTS

280g/10oz shelled whole almonds

280g/10oz plain flour, plus more for shaping

1½ teaspoons baking powder

½ teaspoon salt

150g/5½oz caster sugar

115g/4oz unsalted butter

2 size-3 eggs

2 tablespoons Sambuca

EQUIPMENT

Measuring jug, measuring spoons, 2 baking sheets, chef's knife, cutting board, sieve, greaseproof paper, electric mixer with flat beater, rubber spatula, baking parchment, serrated slicer, cooling rack, plastic container with lid

MAKE THE BISCOTTI

Preheat the oven to 170°C/325°F/Gas 3.

Toast the whole almonds on a baking sheet in the preheated oven for about 15 minutes or until they turn from cinnamon-coloured to chestnut-coloured. Remove from the oven and allow to cool to room temperature. Use a chef's knife to cut the almonds in half widthwise. Set aside until needed.

Combine together in a sieve the flour, baking powder and salt. Sift on to greaseproof paper and set aside.

Place the sugar and butter in the bowl of an electric mixer fitted with a flat beater. Beat on medium for 2 minutes. Use a rubber spatula to scrape down the sides of the bowl, then beat on medium for an additional 2 minutes. Scrape down the sides of the bowl, then beat on high for 2 minutes. Add the eggs, one at a time, while beating on medium for 1 minute, stopping to scrape down the bowl after incorporating each addition. Operate the mixer on low while gradually adding the sifted dry ingredients. Once all the dry ingredients have been incorporated, about 30 seconds, turn off the mixer and add the almond pieces and the Sambuca and mix on low for 20 seconds.

Remove the bowl from the mixer and use a rubber spatula to finish mixing until thoroughly combined.

Transfer the biscotti dough to a clean, dry, lightly floured work surface. Divide the dough into two equal portions, and shape each into a log 20cm/8in long, 6cm/2½in wide and 3cm/1¼in high (using a little more flour as necessary to prevent sticking). Carefully place the two logs, about 5cm/2in apart, on a baking sheet that has been lined with baking parchment. Bake the biscotti logs on the centre shelf of the preheated oven for 35 minutes or until lightly browned and firm to the touch. Remove the logs from the oven and reduce the oven temperature to 140°C/275°F/Gas 1. Allow the logs to cool for about 15 minutes at room temperature before handling.

Place the biscotti logs on a cutting board. Using a very sharp serrated slicer, trim the rounded ends from each log. Cut each biscotti log into 1.5cm/½in diagonal slices (12 slices per log). Divide the slices between 2 baking sheets lined with baking parchment.

Bake the biscotti slices in the centre of the preheated oven for 30 minutes or until crisp and evenly browned. Transfer the biscotti to a cooling rack to cool thoroughly before storing in a sealed plastic container.

THE CHEF'S TOUCH

At Ristorante Giannino in Milan, I modified the pleasurable ritual of dipping an almond biscotti into a glass of sweet wine. My palate was searching for a more intense postprandial than the requisite Vin Santo, so I requested a medium-sized, bowl-shaped wine glass with a double measure of Sambuca. Una delizioza armonia di gusti!

If you are more temperate than I, enjoy the biscotti with a steaming cup of cappuccino.

Be certain to store the biscotti in a tightly sealed plastic container as soon as they have cooled to room temperature. They will stay crisp and delicious stored this way for several days.

For an extra measure of decadence, try drizzling both white and dark chocolate over the baked biscotti. This indulgence requires 30g/1oz each of chopped bittersweet chocolate and white chocolate. First heat 2.5cm/1in of water in the top half of a double boiler over moderate heat. Melt the bittersweet chocolate in the top half of the double boiler while stirring constantly with a rubber spatula. Immediately remove the melted chocolate and transfer it to a small bowl. Using a teaspoon, drizzle a thin stream of melted chocolate in diagonal zigzags across the width of the biscotti. Then do the same with the white chocolate. Store the chocolate-striped biscotti in a cool place.

CITRUS SHORTBREAD BISCUITS

YIELDS 12 BISCUITS

INGREDIENTS

115g/4oz unsalted butter

5 tablespoons caster sugar

1 teaspoon finely chopped lemon zest

1 teaspoon finely chopped orange zest

1 teaspoon orange liqueur

140g/5oz plain flour

¼ teaspoon salt

EQUIPMENT

Measuring jug, measuring spoons, vegetable peeler, chef's knife, cutting board, electric mixer with flat beater, rubber spatula, cling film, two 23 × 33cm/ 9 × 13in non-stick baking sheets, plastic container with lid

THE CHEF'S TOUCH

Not only does this recipe yield exactly the amount of biscuit crumbs needed to prepare the Lemon and Blueberry Cheesecake Crust (see page 23), it is also perfect for the crust for My Cherry Clafouti (see page 51). If you fall in love with these little beauties, I suggest doubling the recipe.

Although only a modicum of butter is used for these biscuits, the overall impression on the palate is in fact buttery. That and the undertones of citrus make these biscuits reminiscent of a favourite chardonnay.

Use a sharp vegetable peeler to zest the citrus fruit. Be careful to remove only the coloured zest and not the bitter pith that lies directly beneath. After removing the coloured zest with a vegetable peeler, cut it into thin strips with a very sharp chef's knife. Finely chop the thin strips with the chef's knife.

For most people, a cool glass of lemonade would be the perfect accompaniment for the Citrus Shortbread. My preference after dinner, however, would be a more gratifying dry sherry or a madeira.

MAKE THE BISCUITS

Preheat the oven to 170°C/325°F/Gas 3.

Place the butter and sugar in the bowl of an electric mixer fitted with a flat beater. Beat on medium for 2 minutes. Scrape down the sides of the bowl. Beat on high for 3 minutes, until the mixture is light (but not fluffy). Add the chopped lemon and orange zests and the orange liqueur. Beat on high for 30 seconds. Operate the mixer on low while gradually adding the flour and salt, and mix for 1 minute. Remove the bowl from the mixer and use a rubber spatula to finish mixing until thoroughly combined.

Wrap the dough in cling film. Roll the dough on a flat surface to form a cylinder that is 15cm/6in long and 4cm/1½in in diameter. Place the dough in the refrigerator to chill for 1½ hours.

Remove the dough from the refrigerator and discard the cling film. Cut the cylinder of dough into 12 slices, each 1.5cm/½in thick. Divide the slices between 2 baking sheets. Place the baking sheets on the centre shelf in the preheated oven and bake for 16 to 18 minutes or until lightly browned around the edges. Halfway through the baking time, rotate each baking sheet 180°. Remove the biscuits from the oven and cool to room temperature on the baking sheets, about 20 minutes. The cooled biscuits can be stored in a tightly sealed plastic container for several days at room temperature, or for several weeks in the freezer.

CHOCOLATE CINNAMON TIGER BISCUITS

YIELDS 12 BISCUITS

INGREDIENTS

CINNAMON STRIPES

210g/7½oz plain flour
½ teaspoon ground cinnamon
½ teaspoon bicarbonate of soda
½ teaspoon salt
225g/8oz soft light brown sugar
115g/4oz unsalted butter, cut into 8 equal pieces
2 size-3 eggs
½ teaspoon pure vanilla essence
115g/4oz toasted pecans, chopped

CHOCOLATE STRIPES

140g/5oz bittersweet chocolate, cut into
    15g/½oz pieces
55g/2oz unsweetened chocolate, cut into
    15g/½oz pieces
105g/3½oz plain flour
20g/⅔oz unsweetened cocoa powder
½ teaspoon bicarbonate of soda
½ teaspoon salt
170g/6oz soft light brown sugar
115g/4oz unsalted butter, cut into 8 equal pieces
1 size-3 egg
½ teaspoon pure vanilla essence
200g/7oz plain chocolate chips

EQUIPMENT

Measuring jug, measuring spoons, sieve,
greaseproof paper, electric mixer with flat beater,
rubber spatula, 3 litre/5 pint stainless steel bowl,
double boiler, heat-resistant cling film, whisk,
3 non-stick baking sheets, flexible fish slice, cooling
rack, plastic container with lid

FIRST MAKE THE CINNAMON STRIPES DOUGH

Preheat the oven to 170°C/325°F/Gas 3.

Sift together the flour, cinnamon, bicarbonate of soda and salt on to greaseproof paper. Set aside.

Place the light brown sugar and pieces of butter in the bowl of an electric mixer fitted with a flat beater. Beat on medium for 1 minute. Scrape down the sides of the bowl and beat on high for an additional 30 seconds. Scrape down the bowl. Add the eggs, one at a time, while beating on medium, stopping to scrape down the sides of the bowl after incorporating each addition. Add the vanilla essence and beat on medium for 30 seconds. Add the sifted dry ingredients and mix on low until thoroughly combined, about 30 seconds. Scrape down the bowl. Add the chopped pecans and mix on medium for 15 seconds. Remove the bowl from the mixer and use a rubber spatula to finish mixing until thoroughly combined. Transfer the Cinnamon Stripes Dough to a separate container and set aside.

MAKE THE CHOCOLATE STRIPES DOUGH

Heat 2.5cm/1in of water in the bottom half of a double boiler over moderate heat. Place the bittersweet and unsweetened chocolate in the top half of the double boiler. Tightly cover the top with heat-resistant cling film and allow to heat for 7 to 8 minutes. Remove from the heat and stir until smooth. To keep out of trouble while the chocolate is heating, sift together the flour, cocoa, bicarbonate of soda and salt on to greaseproof paper. Set aside.

Place the light brown sugar and pieces of butter in the bowl of an electric mixer fitted with a flat beater. Beat on medium for 1 minute. Scrape down the sides of the bowl and beat on high for an additional 30 seconds. Scrape down the bowl. Add the egg and beat on medium until thoroughly incorporated, about 1 minute. Scrape down the bowl and continue to beat on medium for an additional 30 seconds. Add the vanilla essence and beat on medium for 30 seconds. Add the melted chocolate and mix on low for 10 seconds. Add the sifted dry ingredients and the chocolate chips and mix on low for 30 seconds. Remove the bowl from the mixer and use a rubber spatula to finish mixing until thoroughly combined.

BAKE THE TIGER BISCUITS

On each of 3 non-stick baking sheets, portion 4 biscuits per sheet. For each biscuit, drop 2 slightly heaping tablespoons of chocolate stripe dough directly on top of 2 slightly heaping tablespoons of cinnamon stripe dough. Place the baking sheets on the top and centre shelves of the preheated oven and bake for 20 to 24 minutes, rotating the sheets from top to centre halfway through the baking time. Remove the biscuits from the oven, then allow to cool for 5 to 6 minutes on the baking sheets. Transfer the biscuits to a cooling rack and cool thoroughly before storing in a sealed plastic container.

THE CHEF'S TOUCH

You can hold that tiger down by preparing smaller biscuits. (A level tablespoon of each dough per biscuit will yield some 2 dozen equally delicious, kitten-sized biscuits.) Baking time is 14 to 16 minutes.

Enhance the flavour of the pecans by toasting them in a 170°C/325°F/Gas 3 oven for 10 to 12 minutes. This also eliminates any moisture the nuts may have acquired through improper storage.

These tigers are made for walking. Give them to a friend, take them on a picnic, pack them in a lunch box. Whatever the destination, tiger biscuits will like the trip and be as, if not more, delicious several days (or miles) down the road. Of course, these biscuits are also the perfect snack after school (or work), especially when washed down with a smooth chocolate milk shake. In fact, this combination is guaranteed to please both big and little kids.

BURNT ORANGE SNAPS
YIELDS ABOUT 12 SNAPS

INGREDIENTS

1 medium orange
115g/4oz unsalted butter
150g/5½oz caster sugar
1 tablespoon orange liqueur
½ teaspoon salt
50g/scant 2oz plain flour

EQUIPMENT

Measuring jug, measuring spoons, vegetable peeler, chef's knife, cutting board, electric mixer with flat beater, rubber spatula, two 25 × 38cm/10 × 15in baking sheets, baking parchment, small metal spatula, 4 chopsticks, paper towels, plastic container with lid

PREPARE THE BURNT ORANGE SNAPS

Preheat the oven to 180°C/350°F/Gas 4.

Zest the orange by peeling the coloured skin from a whole orange using a vegetable peeler. Remove the zest in long 2.5cm/1in wide strips, being careful to remove only the coloured zest and not the bitter white pith that lies beneath. Use a very sharp chef's knife to cut the peeled zest widthwise into very thin strips (as you do this, savour the aroma of the citrus oils being released from the zest).

Place the butter, sugar, orange zest, orange liqueur and salt in the bowl of an electric mixer fitted with a flat beater. Beat on medium for 2 minutes (if you enjoyed the aroma of the orange zest, you will swoon over the fragrance now coming from the mixing bowl). Scrape down the sides of the bowl, then beat on medium for 1 additional minute. Scrape down the sides of the bowl. Beat on high for 1 minute. Add the flour and mix on low for 15 seconds. Scrape down the sides of the bowl.

Increase the mixer speed to medium and beat for 30 seconds. Remove the bowl from the mixer. Use a rubber spatula to finish mixing until thoroughly combined.

Line 2 baking sheets with baking parchment.

Portion 2 snaps per baking sheet by dropping 1 heaping teaspoon of mixture for each snap (do not spread the mixture). Allow plenty of space between each portion of mixture since it spreads on its own during baking. Bake on the centre shelf of the preheated oven for 10 minutes or until uniformly golden brown in the centre and dark brown around the edges. Remove both baking sheets from the oven. Set one baking sheet aside. Immediately remove the parchment with the snaps from the other baking sheet. Invert the snaps (parchment side up) on to a clean flat surface. Peel the parchment

from the snaps, using a small spatula if necessary. Roll each snap into a cigar-shaped cylinder around a chopstick, then place on a paper towel.

Allow the snaps to cool on the paper towels for 5 minutes before removing the chopsticks. Moving quickly, repeat this procedure with the remaining 2 snaps (if the snaps become too hard and brittle to roll, return them to the oven for 10 to 15 seconds).

Portion the remaining snaps on to new sheets of parchment, and use the same procedure and baking time until all the mixture has been used. Allow all the baked snaps to cool thoroughly before storing them in a sealed plastic container at room temperature (the snaps will stay crisp stored in this manner for several days).

> ## THE CHEF'S TOUCH
> *This biscuit is a marvel of taste and texture. They are best if baked the day before serving. You will be rewarded with a generously aromatic and sweet citrus biscuit that literally melts in your mouth.*
>
> *Remember to work quickly once the snaps have been removed from the oven. If preparing two baking sheets at a time (two snaps per baking sheet) seems daunting, then only prepare one baking sheet at a time.*
>
> *Enjoy the snaps with a bowl of Double Cappuccino Ice Cream (see page 77) or, if it is a frosty day out there, a steaming hot cup of cappuccino might suit your fancy.*

CHOCOLATE VALENCIENNES

YIELDS ABOUT 42 BISCUITS

INGREDIENTS

4 rounded tablespoons soft light brown sugar

50g/scant 2oz caster sugar

4 tablespoons water

55g/2oz unsalted butter

115g/4oz bittersweet chocolate, cut into
  15g/½oz pieces

55g/2oz plain flour, sifted

EQUIPMENT

Measuring jug, measuring spoons, sieve, 3 litre/
5 pint saucepan, whisk, 3 litre/5 pint stainless steel
bowl, two 25 × 38cm/10 × 15in non-stick baking
sheets, metal spatula, paper towels

MAKE THE VALENCIENNES

Preheat the oven to 170°C/325°F/Gas 3.

Heat the light brown sugar, caster sugar, water
and butter in a 3 litre/5 pint saucepan over moderately high heat. When hot, stir to dissolve the sugar.
Bring to the boil. Place the chocolate in a stainless
steel bowl. Pour the boiling liquid over the chocolate
and allow to stand for 5 minutes. Stir until smooth.
Add the sifted plain flour and stir until smooth.

Portion 6 biscuits per non-stick baking sheet by
dropping 1 teaspoon of mixture per biscuit on to
each of the 2 baking sheets. Since the mixture
spreads quite a bit during baking, portion only
6 biscuits per baking sheet. Bake the biscuits, one
baking sheet at a time, on the centre shelf of the
preheated oven (have the second baking sheet with
the 6 teaspoons of mixture ready to place in the
oven as soon as the first batch is removed). Bake
for 6½ to 7½ minutes. Remove the biscuits from
the oven and allow to cool until crisp, about 3 minutes. Transfer the crisp biscuits to paper towels to
cool completely. Continue this procedure until all
of the biscuits have been baked. Serve immediately
or store the biscuits in a tightly sealed plastic container at room temperature for up to 3 days.

THE CHEF'S TOUCH

*Former pastry chef Andrew O'Connell devel-
oped this lace-like chocolate biscuit for a lunch
the Trellis prepared for 350 members of the
American Institute of Wine and Food at their
first national conference on gastronomy in Santa
Barbara, California, in January 1985. The biscuits accompanied a white grape and currant
sorbet that Andrew made in Williamsburg and
transported in dry ice to the lunch site at the Biltmore Hotel. After Andrew baked more than five
hundred biscuits in the Biltmore's pastry shop, a
housekeeper remarked that the biscuits reminded
her of Valenciennes (a type of lace). I wasted no
time in appropriating the name for our biscuit.*

*If non-stick baking sheets are not avail-
able, line your baking sheets with baking
parchment or aluminium foil (both will work
well). Do not under any circumstances butter
or grease the baking sheets. There is an ample
amount of butter in the recipe; any additional butter will make the biscuits greasy
and unpleasant to handle.*

*Room temperature will vary from kitchen
to kitchen. If your kitchen is cool, you can
keep the biscuit mixture warm during the
baking process by placing the bowl of mixture over a 3 litre/5 pint saucepan containing
2.5cm/1in of heated (not boiling) water. Try
to keep the mixture at a temperature of 43
to 49°C/110 to 120°F (an instant-read thermometer comes in handy) so that it has a
smooth, but not watery, consistency. (You can
also place the bowl of mixture on top of your
warm oven with similar results.)*

*I suggest that you avoid distractions dur-
ing the baking of the Valenciennes since they
are gossamer thin and will quickly overbake.*

*Chocolate Valenciennes can be an elegant
finale to an evening of dining, especially if
they are enjoyed with a steaming cup of your
favourite tea or coffee.*

WHITE CHOCOLATE LULLABY

SERVES 2

INGREDIENTS

750ml/1¼ pints White Chocolate Ice Cream (see page 86)

125ml/4fl oz brandy

4 tablespoons dark crème de cacao (chocolate liqueur)

4 tablespoons Frangelico

¼ teaspoon unsweetened cocoa powder

EQUIPMENT

Measuring jug, measuring spoons, blender

MAKE THE WHITE CHOCOLATE LULLABIES

First place the White Chocolate Ice Cream in the blender. Add the brandy, dark crème de cacao and Frangelico. Blend until smooth. Pour the blended drink into tall glasses and garnish with cocoa. Enjoy, and sweet dreams!

THE CHEF'S TOUCH

The name for this delightful frozen concoction was inspired by 'Golden Slumbers', from the Beatles' Abbey Road *album (Apple Records).*

To make four lullaby drinks at once, double the ingredients and use a food processor fitted with a metal blade. Process all the ingredients until smooth. (Incidentally, the recipe for the White Chocolate Ice Cream makes 1.5 litres/2½ pints of ice cream—exactly what you need for four drinks.)

If time does not permit the preparation of the White Chocolate Ice Cream ('pretty darling, do not cry'), purchase top-quality vanilla ice cream and use that instead.

TECHNIQUES AND EQUIPMENT

In this section, I want to give you the tricks of the trade that will bring kudos to you, the dessert maker.

You will notice that each recipe in *Desserts To Die For* has a section called 'The Chef's Touch,' where you will find anecdotes and helpful information regarding techniques, equipment, handling and storage for that particular confection. Then why do you need an additional section dealing with more information? My feeling is that a dessert maker can never be overly informed, and the more you know about chilling, melting, slicing, sifting and whipping, the more luscious your desserts will be.

The following information is pertinent for creating all desserts, especially *Desserts To Die For*.

TECHNIQUES

CHILLING OUT

Be sure to follow instructions about refrigerating or freezing a cake or dessert component for a specific period of time. In most instances, the chilling firms the dessert to the consistency needed for successful assembly. If the time specified is cut short, the results could be a very messy—although perhaps still delicious—dessert.

It is important to note that the designated length of time for 'chilling out' is planned for spaces that are not unusually crowded. If you need to lean an armoire against your refrigerator door to keep it closed, the airflow inside the refrigerator will be restricted and it will take much longer for the dessert to cool or freeze properly.

COOLING IN AN ICED-WATER BATH

The fastest and most effective way to cool sauces and other liquids is to place the container holding the food in another, larger container that is partially filled with ice and water. Stir the food frequently to cool it as quickly as possible. A large container or cooking pan can be cooled in a kitchen sink partially filled with water and ice.

The purpose of quickly chilling foods is to inhibit bacteria. Consequently, these foods are less likely to spoil as quickly as foods that were incorrectly handled.

CARAMELISING SUGAR

Caramelising sugar is like spinning flax into gold.

Turning a saucepan of caster sugar into a smooth and lustrous liquid requires some attention. The best advice when caramelising sugar is to concentrate on that task, and don't get involved with anything but the constant stirring of the sugar as it turns to liquid. As the liquid sugar heats, it picks up colour (and flavour) very quickly, so keep a very watchful eye. Also, be very careful in handling this molten sugar, as it is very hot and will cause a serious burn if it comes into contact with the skin.

CUTTING UP

I suggesting using a 25 to 30cm/10 to 12in serrated slicer when cutting cakes and other solid desserts into portions. Always place the dessert to be cut on a solid surface, such as a clean cutting board. For professional-looking portions with clean lines and even cuts, heat the blade of the slicer under hot running water and wipe the blade dry before making each slice.

A word on 'to die for' portion sizes: the recommended portions in each recipe create the most opulent and visually decadent desserts possible. For instance, most cakes serve 10 to 12 portions so that when cut, each slice will tower straight up, offering an orgy for the eye before the pleasure is consummated on the palate. Many more portions could potentially be cut from most cakes if you prefer a more discreet, but still delicious, confectionery rendezvous.

HANDLING EGGS

'Prudence' is the word that comes to mind when discussing how to handle eggs. Government information has made us aware of the unhealthy and often serious results from consuming raw eggs. Obviously, the danger of salmonella is present in the handling of many foods derived from animals.

Many risks can be mitigated by proper handling, which in the case of eggs means that they should be refrigerated until utilised. I also don't believe in storing separated eggs for more than 2 or 3 days under refrigeration, and I advise against freezing separated eggs. If you have concerns regarding the use of raw or lightly cooked eggs, see the last page of every issue of *Chocolatier* magazine, which always contains some good instructions on this subject.

In several of the recipes in *Desserts To Die For*, egg yolks are combined with cream to make a custard. I emphasise the necessity of continuously whisking the egg yolks (to ensure a smooth custard) while waiting for the cream to boil. When the boiling cream is added to the eggs and returned to the heat, it is essential to bring the mixture to a temperature of 85°C/185°F to cook the eggs and inhibit the growth of bacteria.

Also, immediately remove the custard from the heat source once it reaches 85°C/185°F. Otherwise, the custard may separate.

Finally, cool the custard quickly in an iced-water bath to guard against the introduction of bacteria.

MELTING CHOCOLATE

Of all the recommended methods for melting chocolate (including using the microwave and such idiosyncratic ways as using a hair dryer), I find that slowly heating chocolate in a double boiler is the most foolproof. Overheating chocolate will cause it to do some weird things, including something called seizing. Seizing occurs when melted chocolate stiffens and separates like spoiled curd cheese (this sad situation can also occur if small amounts of liquid, such as water, inadvertently come into contact with melting or melted chocolate). Additionally, chocolate will scorch and have an unpleasant taste if heated too intensely over a direct heat source. Use a double boiler (see page 140) and melt the chocolate slowly—the reward will be a glistening pool of ecstasy.

SIFTING DRY INGREDIENTS

Certain mixtures call for sifting the flour or the dry ingredients. Fundamentally, sifting serves to aerate the mixture, thereby promoting the incorporation of the dry ingredients into the liquids. Also, sifting eliminates any foreign objects or lumps from flour or other dry ingredients and evenly distributes dry raising agents (such as bicarbonate of soda) and seasonings (such as ground cinnamon). It is a good idea to sift the dry ingredients on to a large piece of greaseproof paper or baking parchment (the paper facilitates carrying the sifted ingredients, and because it can be folded, it also makes adding the ingredients to a mixing bowl a cinch). Make certain the paper is large enough to hold all the ingredients once you pick it up. Once sifted, flour becomes quite light, so be careful to sneeze away from your sifted ingredients.

TOASTING NUTS

'Nuts,' you say...peanuts, hazelnuts, almonds, walnuts, pecans and even precious macadamia nuts. Twenty-three of the recipes in *Desserts To Die For* list one of these nuts as a crunchy component. In every recipe, I suggest toasting the nuts before adding them. Although most of the nuts you purchase have been roasted, additional toasting brings out the flavour. Furthermore, nuts can acquire moisture during the time they have been stored, so the suggested toasting will help to dissipate that moisture.

Unsalted nuts are the preferred choice for baking.

HAZELNUTS

If you are unable to purchase skinned hazelnuts, you can skin them yourself. First, toast the nuts on a baking sheet at 170°C/325°F/Gas 3 for 18 to 20 minutes (be certain not to overtoast the nuts as they have a tendency to become bitter). Remove the toasted nuts from the oven and immediately cover with a damp 100% cotton tea towel. Invert another baking sheet over the first one to hold in the steam (this makes the nuts easier to skin). After 5 minutes, remove the skins from the nuts by placing them, a few at a time, inside a folded dry tea towel and rubbing vigorously. If skinned

hazelnuts are purchased, toast at 170°C/325°F/Gas 3 for 10 to 12 minutes, then allow the nuts to cool before using.

WHIPPING CREAM

The whipping cream we use at the Trellis is a fresh cream with a 40% butterfat content. If you prefer, you can substitute double cream (with a minimum butterfat content of 48%) for whipping cream in *Desserts to Die For*. However, I am confident that you will be more than pleased with the results using whipping cream, and you can persuade yourself that the dessert is a little bit more 'healthy' too!

I always recommend whipping the cream with well-chilled equipment. getting the equipment as cold as possible—in the freezer or with iced-water (be sure to wipe dry before using)—will ensure that the cream whips quickly and voluminously.

EQUIPMENT

BAKING SHEETS AND CAKE TINS

I believe a cookery book author should use the same equipment typically found in the home kitchen. Accordingly, all of the baking sheets and cake tins used for testing *Desserts To Die For* were purchased either in a kitchenware shop or at the supermarket. I suggest purchasing the best-quality, heaviest-gauge steel baking sheets and tins you can find. Purchase baking sheets with sides (sides give the sheets extra rigidity, which hopefully will keep them from warping in the oven). If you don't mind the extra cost, you can purchase double gauge aluminium tins and sheets from a specialist supplier; baking times will be a wee bit longer with this equipment, but you will have something to leave to your grandchildren.

COOLING RACK

Most baked items should be cooled to room temperature upon removal from the oven, before slicing or being used as a component in a dessert. In most situations, cooling is most efficient when the bake item is placed on a cooling rack, which increases the airflow around the item. The cooling times will fluctuate depending on the temperature

in your kitchen (I estimated cooling times based on a cool room ranging from 20 to 25°C/68 to 78°F).

If you don't have a cooling rack, you can always improvise by using anything that allows airflow under the pan or baking sheet, such as an extra oven shelf. Whatever you use, be sure that it is stable.

DOUBLE BOILER

A double boiler is a double saucepan with a lower section that holds water and an upper section that holds the food to be heated.

I must confess I do not own a double boiler. For all these years I have always improvised, typically using a 3 litre/5 pint stainless steel or heat-proof glass-ceramic bowl placed over the top of a 3 litre/5 pint saucepan. This set-up accomplishes all you need from a double boiler: the top pan does not come into contact with the water in the pan beneath, the item is heated or melted slowly, and the steam is prevented from coming into contact with the food being heated.

ELECTRIC MIXER

Although a heavy-duty table-top electric mixer is a substantial investment, it is essential for achieving professional results with many of the Desserts To Die For. Various recipes such as the Lemon and Fresh Berry 'Shortcake' (see page 54) require lengthy mixing times, and others like the Buttery Bun Dough (see page 102) necessitate the incorporation of ingredients into a rather rigid mass. These tasks are difficult to do by hand or even by using a hand-held electric mixer. In every recipe using an electric mixer, I also list the proper attachment (balloon whisk, flat beater or dough hook). The success of the recipe depends on using the proper attachment. So, if you want great desserts, bite the bullet and buy a table-top mixer.

FOOD PROCESSOR

As much as I enjoy using a chef's knife to slice, dice and chop, some of these tasks are best accomplished by using a food processor. Whenever noted in the equipment section of a recipe, the food processor will not only save you time but will also yield results superior to those achieved by hand.

Nuts, for instance, can be chopped more finely and uniformly in the food processor than is possible otherwise. The downside to using the processor is the cleaning time; this is quite often the most dangerous time—especially when handling the very sharp metal blade.

ICE CREAM MAKER

The only thing smoother than the delicious ice cream recipes in *Desserts To Die For* is making them in an electronically cooled independent ice cream maker. For testing in this book, we used the same machine I have used since 1987, a workhorse from the Simac Appliance Corporation that produces about 2 litres/3¼ pints of ice cream or sorbet per batch. Whichever manufacturer you select for an ice cream maker, I suggest selecting a machine with a removable bowl, which makes cleaning it easier.

Smaller machines that operate on elbow grease also create fine results (just don't buy any that make less than 1 litre/2 pints). These hand-cranked machines are economical, simple to operate and virtually never break down. All of our ice cream and sorbet recipes can be adjusted to suit whatever size machine you purchase (divide recipes in half or in quarters).

OVENS

While turning on your oven sounds simple enough, getting it to the correct temperature is quite another story. Fairly exact temperatures are essential for successful baking. Almost without exception, I have found ovens in home kitchens to be notoriously out of calibration no matter their vintage. Temperature variances of 10 to 30°C/25 to 75°F are the norm.

Sow how then can you successfully bake? You need an accurate oven thermometer, available at a kitchenware shop. Put it in your oven and use it to set the oven temperature accurately.

How about preheating? Depending on oven capacity, the heat source and the quality of the insulation, it takes from 20 to 45 minutes to preheat an oven to 150°C/300°F (natural gas–powered ovens take less time to preheat than do electric ovens). Be sure the oven temperature reaches the desired setting before the item is placed in the oven. Incorrect oven temperature both affects the baking time and inhibits rising.

All the Desserts to Die For were tested in a conventional oven, not fan-assisted.

PIPING BAG

I have always enjoyed squeezing buttercream out of a piping bag, a process that is called 'piping'. To pipe an exquisite row of buttercream stars or shells is indeed a pleasurable endeavour. Always choose a piping bag suitably sized for the task, and be certain not to overfill the bag or the contents will come oozing out of the top. Filling a piping bag will be easier if you first fold down about one third of the bag, from the inside out, like a cuff. Then carefully fill the bag with buttercream, ganache, mousse, meringue or whatever while holding the bag in one hand directly underneath the cuff. After the bag is filled (but not too full), unfold the cuff and twist it closed. Hold the bag with one hand placed over the twisted top and squeeze the bag firmly while using the other hand to guide the tip of the bag.

Check out your local kitchenware shop for a selection of piping bags. I prefer the plastic-lined cloth bags, and generally find a 45cm/18in bag the most useful.

Baking parchment can be fashioned into a piping cone, especially for use with lighter icings and for fine decorating. First, roll a sheet of parchment into a cone. Clip the narrow end of the cone to make an opening that is the desired width of the piping. Fill and use the parchment cone as described for the piping bag above.

RUBBER SPATULA

Just when you thought it was safe to pour the mixture into the tin, I tell you to 'finish mixing with a rubber spatula'. Why have I spent the big money for a table-top mixer only to have to resort to completing the task by hand? A rubber spatula makes it possible to combine thoroughly and remove all the mixture from the sides of the bowl, as well as from the beater, dough hook or balloon whisk.

WHISK

What comes in a variety of lengths as well as degrees of stiffness? Well, whisks, of course. These utensils are an essential item in any cook's *batterie de cuisine*. Although I did not specify the type of whisk needed in each recipe, a general rule would be to select the stiffer whisks for sauces (the length should be determined by the volume of product in the saucepan) and the more flexible types for whisking meringue and whipping cream.

STAINLESS STEEL BOWL

I have been a strong advocate for stainless steel bowls since I started writing cookery books in 1987. I like these bowls because they are a worthy investment in equipment that will not break; they are non-reactive (which is an important consideration when storing foods, especially those which are acidic); and they are easily cleaned, which helps keep 'Uncle Sal' (salmonella) out of your food.

THERMOMETERS

OVEN THERMOMETER

Do not bake without an oven thermometer in your oven (as mentioned previously, many ovens are not calibrated properly). I suggest the mercury-filled tube thermometer over the spring-style. Remember to remove these thermometers from your oven if you are electronically cleaning since the high heat of the cleaning cycle will ruin the thermometers.

INSTANT-READ THERMOMETER

For accurate temperature readings, select a high-quality thermometer with a range of about -18 to 105°C/0 to 220°F. Keep the packaging that describes how to recalibrate the thermometer. To minimise the need for recalibration, store the thermometer in a safe place (that is, not under all your kitchen spoons and whisks). And remember that this thermometer is not designed for oven use.

SOURCES

CHOCOLATE

The Chocolate Society
Clay Pit Lane
Roecliffe
Boroughbridge
YO5 9LF
Phone: 01423 322230 for mail order catalogue

Roccoco Chocolates
321 King's Road
London SW3 5EP
Phone: 0171 352 5857 for mail order catalogue
Fax: 0171 352 7360

DRIED FRUIT

Julian Graves Limited
Ham Lane
Off Stallings Lane
Kingswinford
West Midlands DY6 7JH
Phone: 01384 277772 for mail order catalogue

KITCHENWARE

Divertimenti (Mail Order) Limited
P.O. Box 323
Yateley
Camberley, Surrey GU17 7ZA
Phone: 01252 861212 for mail order catalogue
Fax: 01252 876770

David Mellor
4 Sloane Square
London SW1W 3EE
Phone: 0171 730 4259 for mail order catalogue
Fax: 0171 730 7240

B. R. Mathews & Son
12 Gipsy Hill
Upper Norwood
London SE19 1NN
Phone: 0181 670 0788 for mail order catalogue

COFFEE

Algerian Coffee Stores
52 Old Compton Street
London W1
Phone: 0171 437 2480 for mail order catalogue

BIBLIOGRAPHY

Amendola, Joseph. *The Bakers Manual for Quantity Baking and Pastry Making.* New York: Aherns Publishing Company, Inc., 1960.

Baggett, Nancy. *The International Chocolate Cookbook.* New York: Stewart, Tabori & Chang, 1991.

Beranbaum, Rose Levy. *The Cake Bible.* New York: William Morrow and Company, Inc., 1988.

Braker, Flo. *The Simple Art of Perfect Baking.* New York: William Morrow and Company, Inc., 1985.

Brody, Lora. *Chocolate.* New York: Time-Life Books, 1993.

Chalmers, Irena. *The Great Food Almanac.* San Francisco: Collins Publishers, 1994.

Choate, Judith. *The Great American Pie Book.* New York: Simon & Schuster, 1992.

Desaulniers, Marcel. *Death by Chocolate.* New York: Rizzoli, 1992.

Etlinger, Steven, and Irena Chalmers. *The Kitchenware Book.* New York: Macmillan Publishing Company, 1993.

Glenn, Camille. *The Heritage of Southern Cooking.* New York: Workman Publishing, 1986.

Heatter, Maida. *Maida Heatter's Book of Great Desserts.* New York: Alfred A. Knopf, 1974.

Lipinski, Robert A., and Kathleen A. *The Complete Beverage Dictionary.* New York: Van Nostrand Reinhold, 1992.

Mariani, John F. *The Dictionary of American Food & Drink.* New Haven and New York: Ticknor & Fields, 1983.

McGee, Harold. *On Food and Cooking.* New York: Charles Scribner's Sons, 1984.

Medrich, Alice. *Cocolat—Extraordinary Chocolate Desserts.* New York: Warner Books, 1990.

Scicolone, Michele. *La Dolce Vita.* New York: William Morrow and Company, Inc., 1993.

Stewart, Martha. *Pies & Tarts.* New York: Clarkson N. Potter, Inc., 1985.

Tyler-Herbst, Sharon. *Food Lover's Companion.* New York: Barron's, 1990.

Walters, Carol. *Great Cakes.* New York: Ballantine Books, 1991.

INDEX

METRIC CONVERSIONS

MEASURING SPOONS

U.S.	Metric	U.S.	Metric
¼ tsp	1 mL	¼ tbsp	5 mL
½ tsp	2 mL	½ tbsp	10 mL
¾ tsp	4 mL	¾ tbsp	15 mL
1 tsp	5 mL	1 tbsp	20 mL
1¼ tsp	6 mL	1¼ tbsp	25 mL
1½ tsp	7 mL	1½ tbsp	30 mL
1¾ tsp	9 mL	1¾ tbsp	35 mL
2 tsp	10 mL	2 tbsp	40 mL
2¼ tsp	11 mL	2¼ tbsp	45 mL
2½ tsp	12 mL	2½ tbsp	50 mL
2¾ tsp	14 mL	2¾ tbsp	55 mL
3 tsp	15 mL	3 tbsp	60 mL

MEASURING CUPS

U.S.	Metric
¼ cup	50 mL
⅓ cup	75 mL
½ cup	125 mL
1 cup	250 mL
1¼ cups	300 mL
1⅓ cups	325 mL
1½ cups	375 mL
2 cups	500 mL
2¼ cups	550 mL
2⅓ cups	575 mL
2½ cups	625 mL
3 cups	750 mL
3¼ cups	800 mL
3⅓ cups	825 mL
3½ cups	875 mL
4 cups	1 L
8 cups	2 L
16 cups	4 L
20 cups	8 L

MEASURING LIQUIDS

U.S.	Metric
½ oz	15 mL
1 oz	30 mL
1½ oz	45 mL
2 oz	60 mL
2½ oz	75 mL
3 oz	90 mL
3½ oz	105 mL
4 oz	125 mL
4½ oz	140 mL
5 oz	155 mL
5½ oz	170 mL
6 oz	185 mL
6½ oz	200 mL
7 oz	220 mL
7½ oz	235 mL
8 oz	250 mL
16 oz	500 mL

MEASURING DRY INGREDIENTS

U.S.	Metric
½ oz	15 g
1 oz	30 g
1½ oz	45 g
2 oz	60 g
2½ oz	75 g
3 oz	90 g
3½ oz	105 g
4 oz	125 g
4½ oz	140 g
5 oz	155 g
5½ oz	170 g
6 oz	185 g
6½ oz	200 g
7 oz	220 g
7½ oz	235 g
8 oz	250 g
8½ oz	265 g
9 oz	280 g
9½ oz	295 g
10 oz	315 g
10½ oz	330 g
11 oz	350 g
11½ oz	365 g
12 oz	375 g
12½ oz	390 g
13 oz	410 g
13½ oz	425 g
14 oz	440 g
14½ oz	455 g
15 oz	470 g
15½ oz	485 g
1 lb (16 oz)	500 g
1 lb 8 oz	750 g
2 lb	1 kg
3 lb	1.5 kg
4 lb	2 kg
5 lb	2.5 kg